Libby's "riches to rags to reality" story affir[?] ering love can instill in her child the strengt[?] [?]g reality, to work through her grief, and create a life-fulfilling future. She shares her story with humor, pathos, and empathy.

Pickens Halt, MFC
Author of *How We Grieve: Regression and Regrowth*

I recently journeyed through Libby's challenging formative years by reading her memoir, *What Lies Within*. The author skillfully creates a sense of anticipation along the way that won't let you quit reading until the last triumphant page.

Deb Moore, Personal Historian
Author of *I'll Be Seeing You*

Libby Atwater's remarkably honest and compelling memoir, *What Lies Within*, will inspire any reader who continues to struggle with forgiveness of the past. Libby shows with her amazing skill as a storyteller how she learned from heart-breaking losses and disappointments without rancor and remorse to become who she is today—a successful author and personal historian, wife, mother, and grandmother. Libby's memoir of her growing up years in the turbulent fifties, sixties, and seventies is one of the most engaging and heartwarming stories of hope and healing I've ever read.

Pamela H. Daugavietis
Author of *Through the Eyes of a Child:
The Story of Helen DeVos Children's Hospital*

Libby's story is the amazing journey of a young girl who could have been bitter at what the world had given her. Rather than feel sorry about her lot in life, she set goals and achieved so much. She is truly an amazing person.

Juliane Bustillos

WHAT LIES WITHIN

A Memoir

By

Libby J. Atwater

Published in the United States by Choose Your Words,
http://www.chooseyourwords.net.

Book design by Catherine Baker, Ventura, California.
Cover design by Amy Schneider and David Reeser, Ojai Digital,
http://www.ojaidigital.com.

With love and gratitude
to
Ruth, who nurtured me;
Unc, who expanded my horizons;
and
Don, who encouraged me to follow my dreams.

Hillside, New Jersey; Spring 1961

I stopped on the stairs, halfway down from my second-floor bedroom, on a spring morning in 1961. My mother was talking on the telephone, and I was headed to breakfast. Her words stopped me in mid-flight.

"I think Libby may need to see a psychiatrist," she said. "She's not handling things very well."

Tears welled in my eyes, and I fought them back. I cried easily, but I did not want my mother to know I'd heard her. I sat down, trying to catch my breath and hear the rest of her conversation.

"She doesn't understand so many things. Maybe it would help if she talked to someone," Mommy continued. "What do you think?" she asked the caller.

I could not hear the reply, but I was no longer hungry. "My mother thinks I'm crazy. She wants me to see a psychiatrist." I kept repeating. Why would she think that?

I pulled myself together, and after I heard her hang up, I calmly went downstairs. Mommy did not know I'd been listening.

* * *

Sixteen months earlier, in mid-December 1959, I first met my mother's brother, whom she had not seen in thirty years. At the time I lived in a middle-class suburb of Newark, New Jersey, with my mother, father, sister, and dog. At this first meeting I never suspected that in four years' time, my unknown uncle would become my "parents."

After that December day, the life I'd known as a child slowly began to dissolve. Change was afoot, but I had no idea of its magnitude.

Each day brought new revelations and uncertainty. Something was terribly wrong in my home, and I felt sad being there. To escape, I spent most of my time after school and on weekends at friends' homes. Perhaps that's why my mother wanted to get me help.

After hearing her words that morning, I grew determined to show her just how strong I could be.

What lies behind us and what lies before us
are tiny matters compared to what lies within us.
And when we bring what lies within us
out into the world, miracles happen.

—Ralph Waldo Emerson

Contents

PART I

Family Secrets

Things fall apart; the center cannot hold.

—William Butler Yeats

1

An Unknown Uncle

*T*he snow-laden sky unleashed its heavy burden, and flakes descended, slowly at first, and then with greater intensity. I watched from our living room window as the crystals swirled in random patterns, blown by the wind. Eventually they began to stick to the ground, and within an hour, Hillside wore a new white coat that brightened the grayness of the New Jersey winter day. I loved snow but realized it would delay the arrival of our special guest. "Mommy, when will he get here?" I asked anxiously.

"I don't know," she answered. "The snowfall is growing heavier, and he may not be able to land. We'll just have to wait."

Waiting was not something I did well. At eleven, I was a typical child, impatient and filled with anticipation. I viewed life as a time of endless waiting—for school vacations, trips to New York City and Coney Island, going down the shore (a term easterners use for going to the beach), and countless other childhood delights. I also waited for something to happen that would upset the sameness of our daily existence in a small suburb, where it seemed that nothing much happened.

The wait seemed endless that December afternoon, as I peered out the window trying to catch a glimpse of the man who had assumed mythical status in our household—my mother's long-lost brother. His presence had been a secret until only six months earlier.

I grew up in the 1950s—a time of secrets. If a neighbor had an illness, a friend had marital or financial problems, or a relative disappeared from one's life, adults kept the information to themselves and whispered about it when the children were out of earshot. If my Orthodox Jewish parents needed to discuss something secret in front of my sister and me, they spoke Yiddish, until the day they figured out that I understood what they were saying. After that, my parents were closemouthed in my sister's and my presence.

The biggest secret in our house was that my sister and I were adopted. Perhaps it wasn't a secret as much as a subject that never came up in daily conversation.

My earliest childhood memory is the day our parents told us we were adopted. I was about two years old, and I sat on one of the twin beds in the room Blanche and I shared asking, "Adopted? What does that mean?"

"It means we're not really theirs," Blanche replied. "Someone gave us away, and our parents took us home, but we don't really belong to them."

"Oh," I said and continued as if nothing had changed. I was too young to understand what my sister meant.

Sometime during my childhood, I forgot that I was adopted. Blanche never did. As far as I was concerned, I was Ruth and Harry Berger's younger daughter. They were my mommy and daddy. Blanche was my older sister by four years. Poppy was our grandpa, and we were a family. Today we'd be called dysfunctional, but in the 1950s we functioned about as well as other families who lived nearby. The subject of adoption didn't come up again for many years.

Our adoption was just one of the secrets my parents harbored. A second secret followed the death of my father's brother, Joe, when I was four years old. I remembered visiting Uncle Joe as he grew weaker from the cancer that claimed his life at age fifty-two. He lay on a *chaise longue* in the living room of his home, looking pale and weak as Aunt Rose gave him a shot for pain. Watching her plunge the needle into his emaciated arm frightened me, and I turned away. I hated shots, which were used to treat everything in the early 1950s. Aunt Rose had no trouble giving shots, so I kept my distance.

I vaguely remembered my cousins Martin and Neal, Aunt Rose and Uncle Joe's sons, whom we saw often before their father died. Those were the days when I thought we were one big happy family. Aunt Rose's sister and her husband, Aunt Pearl and Uncle Moe, lived next door. In fact, my parents bought the house near Pearl and Moe because they were best friends. Since Uncle Joe's death seven years earlier, we had not seen Aunt Rose's family again. I wondered why.

Martin Berger holds his brother Neal.

Years later I learned about the fight between my father and Aunt Rose near the end of Uncle Joe's life. It was over a window shade. Aunt Rose and my father were inconsolable as they watched the man they loved slipping away. Aunt Rose insisted on drawing the shade; my father wanted his brother to die in the light. She pulled the shade down; he drew it up. Their antics grew more intense, and I was told that my father struck his sister-in-law, thereby ending our ties to their family for thirty years.

Our immediate family was small and consisted of my father, mother, sister, and me. That December my sister, who was four years older than I, had been away for several months, and I was an only child.

Our remaining relatives consisted of my mother's aunt and first cousins in upstate New York and my father's aunt, uncle, and cousins in Philadelphia. My father's father, our Zayde, was the only remaining grandparent, and he lived in Philadelphia.

The third big family secret was revealed when a letter arrived from my mother's aunt Florrie in upstate New York only six months earlier, stating that my mother's brother was alive and wanted to contact her. I was excited. I had an uncle—a new family member at last.

"Why didn't you tell me you had a brother?" I asked as she read his letter. "What's his name?"

"It used to be Abraham, Abraham Dickstein, but now he's changed it to Richard Stein," she answered.

"Why would he change his name?"

"I don't know, but that explains why I had such trouble finding him when my father died. I placed ads in newspapers all over the country trying to locate him but never succeeded. I wasn't sure he was still alive."

"Do you think he'll come visit us? I'd love to meet my uncle. He can stay in my room, and I'll sleep in Blanche's room."

My mother smiled. For me to give up my room and sleep in my sister's room was the ultimate sacrifice. She finished reading and began writing a response. For a few weeks the letters went back and forth from our home in Hillside, New Jersey, to my uncle's in Alhambra, California.

Then one day in the fall, Uncle Richard telephoned and said he'd like to visit for the holidays. He would arrive the second week in December and stay through the beginning of the new year.

As December approached, I could not contain myself. I cleaned my room thoroughly and moved my clothes and books into my sister's room, where I carved out a corner.

Blanche was living at Roosevelt State Hospital in Menlo Park in December 1959. She had been committed after her failed suicide attempt the previous summer. My Saturdays that fall were filled with trips to the hospital near Princeton to see her while my friends played and went to movies. My uncle's visit would be a welcome diversion.

Today I'd awakened filled with excitement. School was still in session, and I could barely get through my classes. Uncle Richard would arrive that evening. With the snowfall growing heavier, I worried that he would not get to our house. As darkness approached, I took up my post at the living room window, watching and waiting—my childhood pastime.

When the doorbell finally rang, I ran to answer it. There stood the most unusual looking man I had ever seen. His dark hair was streaked with auburn and gray, like my mother's, and his hairline receded slightly. His warm smile lit up his face, which was framed by long, bushy eyebrows that extended at least two inches from his forehead, set above clear hazel eyes. A mustache nearly equal to his eyebrows grew beneath his long, aquiline nose. With his rugged good looks he resembled the actor Adolph Menjou.

My mother was right behind me as I opened the door. She hugged her brother for the first time in thirty years, as I watched, wide-eyed, wondering what had caused such a long absence. It would be a few years before I'd learn the reasons, as with Aunt Rose's family.

As I stood there watching them embrace, I saw their strong resemblance to each other. Both had hazel-green eyes and auburn hair now streaked with gray. My uncle stood several inches taller than my five-foot, two-inch mother and looked slim compared to her. My mother had gained at least fifty pounds since my uncle last saw her, and he tried to hide his surprise as he looked into her face and smiled. My mother's nose was short and pert, her features even, and she looked pretty when she smiled.

Mommy looked beautiful all dressed up.

I once asked, "Mommy, how did you get such a cute little nose?"

"When I was about four, I stood near the stove when my mother was cooking. I reached for something and burned the tip of my nose on the stove. It's been this way ever since," she answered.

Soon my father returned from work. Daddy was nearly six feet tall and wore his straight white hair slicked back. He had a pleasant face with large brown eyes. He gave me a big hug and kiss when he came in the door, then turned to the brother-in-law he had only met one or two times. "Richard, how are you?" he asked as the two shook hands. "It's been years. Are you ready for a great meal and a good visit?"

My uncle nodded, and the four of us sat down to dinner. My mother loved to cook and bake, and she had prepared a special meal for her brother's arrival: oven "fried" chicken, mashed potatoes, green beans, and Hershey syrup cake (my favorite) for dessert.

As we ate, Uncle Richard dabbed at his mustache with his napkin and said, "Ruth, you can really cook. Living alone, I don't get meals like this too often." Between mouthfuls, he told us all the things he wanted to do during his visit. "I'd like to take you to some Broadway shows, go to Radio City Music Hall, and see the sights of New York. It's been so long since I was in New York."

My mother demurred. "I'd love to go with you, but we'll have to plan our trips around my other commitments. I don't have that much freedom, but Libby will be on vacation in a few days. Why don't you take her to New York with you? I'll join you on days that I can."

My uncle agreed, and I realized I had been chosen. Instead of my older sister always being the one to go on special outings, I would be. "Oh, Mommy," I said, "I'll be happy to show Uncle Richard around."

I loved New York. It was only about twelve miles away, and I spent much of my childhood in the museums there with my mother and sister or on school field trips. We especially enjoyed going to the city to see our cousin Davida, Aunt Florrie's daughter. Together we'd tour the Museum of Natural History, the Hayden Planetarium, the Metropolitan Museum of Art, Chinatown, Times Square, Greenwich Village, the ballet, and Central Park. At Christmas and Easter holidays we'd go to Radio City Music Hall to see the latest holiday film and watch the Rockettes perform. Each time we'd have to wait in a blocks-long line to buy tickets, often in freezing weather, but that was part of the experience.

The previous holiday season my mother, Davida, and I had gone to see the New York City Ballet perform *The Nutcracker*. The Sugar Plum Fairy was played by Maria Tallchief, a long, lean beauty who was a real Indian, or Native American. Her movements mesmerized me, and I dreamed of dancing, although I was a clumsy, awkward child. On my eleventh birthday, my mother bought me a recording of *The Nutcracker Suite* that I played endlessly on the Victrola in our living room.

This holiday season with my newfound uncle would be magical. He had such plans, and they all included me. I was no longer "the baby," too young to go along, as I'd been every time Blanche received an invitation to New York. There were many times she went off with friends' families, and I'd stayed home and cried. My uncle's first outing to the city would be just with me. I felt so special.

After school let out for vacation, my uncle and I made our first foray into New York. We went into the city midday on the bus and made the Museum of Natural History our first stop. I always loved the entry hall where the huge brontosaurus skeleton stood. I stared at it for a very long time. Afterwards we went next door and stargazed at the Hayden Planetarium, then walked across to Central Park. Although I'd been in Central Park many times before, I'd never ridden in a hansom cab. Today would be different. Uncle Richard hailed a cab, we climbed aboard, the driver covered us with a blanket, and off we went, trotting through Central Park. The weather had grown colder, and I was thankful for the blanket, yet delighted by the ride. I loved sitting in the cab as the horse clip-clopped down the street.

When the cab ride ended, Uncle Richard said, "Let's go to Lindy's for dinner. It's near the theater, and we can have cheesecake for dessert."

Lindy's was a diner on Seventh Avenue, famous for its cheesecake—and its celebrities. Their autographed pictures papered the walls, and anyone who wanted to be seen or eat good food went to

Uncle Richard and I made our first trip to New York City.

Lindy's. I'd never been there, but I had heard about all its special cheesecake varieties: strawberry, cherry, and blueberry. I nodded and off we went.

As we sat in the booth, I looked at the walls, covered with eight-by-ten photos of stars of the stage and screen. I recognized the faces and some of the names.

After dinner we browsed the stores in the theater district. My uncle discovered a record store and said, "I love to read and listen to my records in my spare time. I have about 1,000 albums back in California. I love the tenors, especially Caruso. When I play his recordings, I turn the volume up on my hi-fi until my trailer shakes." We found no Caruso, but I spotted a recording of the Grieg *Piano Concerto in C# Minor* played by Eugene Ormandy and the Philadelphia Philharmonic Orchestra. This was one of my favorite pieces, and I'd mastered the theme on the piano. The flip side contained Rachmaninoff's *Rhapsody on a Theme of Paganini*. Uncle Richard bought it for me, and whenever I hear these works I think of him. He enhanced my love of classical music, which my mother introduced to me at an early age.

That evening I saw my first Broadway show, *My Fair Lady*, with the inimitable Rex Harrison starring as Professor Henry Higgins. We sat in the center orchestra section, right near the actors. The costumes were elaborate, the scenery revolved, and the music delighted. I was already familiar with it, because the show had been on Broadway for nearly five years. I watched in awe. It was all so wonderful.

Two and a half hours later, we made our way to the Port Authority and the bus that would take us back to Hillside. It was nearly eleven, and snow had begun to fall once more. The bus dropped us in Hillside, but it wasn't the stop where my mother had arranged to meet us. We stood outside and waited, but she did not come. There were no phone booths nearby, and my mother would not have been home if we'd tried to call. She was sitting in her car waiting at a different bus stop. We saw the headlights of an approaching car through the storm, but when it got closer, we realized it was not my mother's car. The driver stopped and asked, "Do you need help?"

"We've been waiting for my sister to pick us up, but we must have gotten our signals crossed. Could you give us a lift?" my uncle asked.

I was frightened. My mother had always taught me not to speak to strangers and never, ever hitchhike. Now her younger brother was doing both, and I was along for the ride.

"Get in, Libby," my uncle said, and off we went. I sat silently beside him, too afraid to speak. The kind stranger deposited us at our front door, and my uncle thanked him profusely. Mommy stood at the open door as we approached, and the fear on her face turned to relief when she realized we were all right. "I was so worried when you didn't get off at the bus stop," she said. "Next trip I'm coming with you."

On our next outing, the three of us took the train from Penn Station in Newark to New York's Penn Station. From there we walked all the way to Rockefeller Plaza, a distance of twenty city blocks, in freezing temperatures. My mother, a smoker, huffed and puffed a bit, but she did not complain. We ate dinner at Manny Wolfe's Steak House, where I tasted my first chateaubriand. My uncle agreed to share this prime beef cut surrounded by a bouquet of vegetables, as it was only prepared for two. I had never eaten food that was presented so beautifully, and I felt like a princess that night.

Afterwards we attended the play, *A Majority of One*, starring Sir Cedric Hardwicke and Gertrude Berg, famous actors of that period. Sir Cedric was made up to be a Japanese man, and I believe this was a love story marred by prejudice, although I did not fully understand the plot. I sat a mere fifteen feet from the stage, engrossed in the action. I knew Gertrude Berg from her television series, *The Goldbergs*, and Sir Cedric Hardwicke as Pharaoh in the film *The Ten Commandments*. I had never been so close to famous actors before.

On our final New York outing, we began with dinner at Mama Leone's, a well-known Italian restaurant with the ambience of a Roman garden. Our most memorable excursion took place on New Year's Eve, when my mother, uncle, and I saw The Music Man, starring Robert Preston in his award-winning role. Toward the end of the performance, we could hear horns blowing outside on Times Square, their sounds overtaking the music inside.

Afterwards we joined the New Year's Eve revelers, and my uncle bought me a horn. It was bitterly cold that night, and I was tired after the show ended. To keep busy, I stood between my mother and uncle and blew my horn at everyone that passed—especially the sailors—and there were a lot of them. They stopped and blew their horns back at me, smiling at this silly, awkward girl in a charcoal-gray wool coat and red beret. I loved it.

When the crystal ball dropped, signaling the start of the new decade—1960—everyone began kissing and hugging. The sailors grabbed nearby women in strong embraces. My mother put her arm around me and held me close. Uncle Richard hugged his sister for the first New Year's Eve in thirty years. What a wonderful reunion they shared!

People were stacked ten deep and tightly packed. A few minutes after midnight, this mass of humanity assumed a life of its own as it moved away from Times Square. We became trapped in the crowd and could only walk in the direction it went. The crowd moved down Broadway, and we were shocked by the number of women's shoes left lying on the ground this bitter cold night. Many had been literally swept off their owners' feet.

Eventually we made our way to Penn Station to board a Hudson Tube train to New Jersey. As we descended the stairs to the platform, a drunken man behind us fell and his legs slid under me, scraping my legs and running my nylon stockings with the heels of his leather oxfords. He mumbled an apology, and I clung to my mother and uncle, frightened by this drunken stranger's intrusion. Then I dozed off between them until the train arrived in Newark.

Uncle Richard returned to California a few days later. Before he left, he gave me a special present, one that he and my mother had created during his visit. When I was eight, she'd started a cultured pearl necklace for me with six pearls. The tradition was to add pearls each year on birthdays and special occasions, but my mother had not been able to add any for the past few years. Uncle

Richard purchased the pearls to complete the necklace, which has become a treasured heirloom.

The reunion of my mother and her brother was the end of the first family thirty-year absence and the beginning of a new relationship that would become prominent in my life. The second thirty-year absence, between Aunt Rose, her sons, and me, would not be resolved until I became an adult—two decades after my father, who was said to be its cause, had died. The third long absence—that of my sister Blanche—has continued for more than thirty-three years.

I don't know why my long-lost uncle chose that year to connect with his sister or where he earned all the money he spent that holiday season. I do know that he was determined to reunite with his sister in style. We ate at world famous restaurants, visited New York landmarks, wandered the city's streets, and just had fun. I found it to be such a welcome break from my life in Hillside.

The holiday season of 1959 was definitely my most memorable, and it changed the course of my life. I saw my mother enjoy herself for the first time in many years, and I met my uncle, a man unlike anyone I'd ever known. Little did I realize how great a role he would play in my life for the next decade.

2

The Landscape of My Childhood

The landscape of my childhood was filled with oaks and maples that swayed beside two-story, wood-sided homes with front stoops where parents sat smoking cigarettes on summer evenings while children chased fireflies. Hillside was a town where neighbors spent time together, chatting while raking leaves and watching them burn in the fall, visiting over coffee and cigarettes on winter mornings, taking storm windows down and putting up screens in the spring, and talking on front stoops during sultry summer evenings when sitting inside became unbearable. Doors remained open, yards unfenced, and we each knew which door to enter when dropping by a neighbor's house.

Children floated freely between households and felt welcome in all. We walked to school together, sledded down the hills for which the town was named, jumped into puddles on rainy days, and traveled on foot to the places we frequented—the corner grocery, candy store, library, synagogue, and Jewish center—unaccompanied by adults.

In the 1950s and '60s, Hillside, a suburb of Newark, was approximately one-half Jewish. I grew up thinking that most of the world was Jewish. The few Catholic families who lived among us attended Christ the King Church; some sent their children to its parish school, while others' children attended Hillside Avenue School with the rest of the neighborhood kids. The Batchelors, Fitzsimmonses, Pavlaks, and Yugoslawskis dwelled happily among their Jewish neighbors, and we all got along well. I did not know there were Protestant religions until I became a teenager.

While my neighborhood on Highland Avenue was warm and welcoming and my parents loving, my world was filled with fear. I hated loud noises and cringed when the monthly air raid sirens wailed at ten on Friday mornings. Most times I hid under the kitchen table, as instructed by my mother. Once I crouched on a neighbor's front steps, unable to move, thinking the unceasing wail came from the dreaded garbage truck.

I feared the garbage truck with its loud gears, horrible smell, and huge compartment where trash was compacted. I'm not sure if it was the noise or the worry that one day I would get thrown in the back of the truck and be ground to bits. Being chased by the garbage truck was a recurring childhood nightmare, and I would wake up screaming. Sadly, the fate I feared is exactly what happened to two sanitation workers in Memphis, Tennessee, just before Dr. Martin Luther King Jr. was assassinated in 1968.

Many of my fears were instilled by my older sister, Blanche. Born in 1944 while World War II raged, she was adopted shortly after her birth. Her baby picture shows a smiling cherub, impeccably dressed in a short-sleeved white cotton blouse with a Peter Pan collar and an embroidered front placket edged in lace. The blouse is neatly tucked into a pleated plaid wool skirt. White leather high-top shoes, white anklet socks, and a white bow attached to wisps of blond hair that surround her smiling face complete the outfit. In this photograph, Blanche is the picture of childhood innocence, her left hand outstretched as if to wave hello. But there is a hint of mischief in her smile, perhaps a portent of things to come.

My parents had been married nearly eighteen years when they adopted Blanche, and both had plenty of love to share, although they lacked parenting skills. I'm told that before I was born she swatted at the crystal chandelier in the dining room with a broom and broke new toys with abandon. My parents did not know what to do with her.

When I was adopted four years later, the situation had not changed. Perhaps they believed I would be different—and I was. We were named for deceased relatives, the Jewish custom. Blanche was named for the two grandmothers we never met. I was named after my great-grandmother and great-uncle. Libby means "an oath of God" in Hebrew.

In childhood Blanche was always physically larger, and her size and strength intimidated me. We did not look at all alike. Her blond hair turned light brown as she grew older and was cut short in a Buster Brown style because it was so straight. My mother often gave it

Grandma and Mommy were best friends.

a permanent wave to give her some curls. My eyes were blue, my hair light blond and curly, and I was called "the baby." My mother would style my curls in ringlets and dress me like Shirley Temple, the child screen star everyone adored. It's no wonder my sister resented me.

Her torture began when I was quite young. She knew I found areas of our house forbidding, and she delighted in teasing me. The bedrooms were upstairs, and I went up first every night, since my bedtime was earlier. Just before I climbed the stairs Blanche would taunt, "The bogeyman is going to get you," and I would freeze. Although I did not really think the bogeyman existed, I hesitated. The upstairs light switch was located halfway down the hall, which meant I was in total darkness when I reached the upstairs landing. Each night I began to sweat as I climbed the thirteen stairs, begging someone to come with me. I could feel my heart flutter as I flailed my arms in front of me, shooing away imaginary villains in the dark. When my hands finally reached the switch and I flicked it on, I'd breathe a sigh of relief and run into the room I shared with my sister. Then I'd jump into bed and hide under the covers, leaving only enough opening to breathe.

Blanche and I shared a room when we were young, so that our live-in maid, Mary, could have the small, L-shaped room next to ours. Poppy, our mother's stepfather, lived in the downstairs bedroom because he needed a cane to walk and climbing stairs was difficult.

The small upstairs bedroom next to ours became empty the day Mommy awoke to find Mary shoving my mother's jewelry into her pockets while she thought my parents were asleep. Afraid she would harm them, my parents waited until later that morning to confront Mary, recover the jewelry, and ask her to leave our house. After that, my parents only hired day help, and I recall an assortment of housekeepers who came and went.

When I look back on my childhood, I realize that beneath our lovely suburban lifestyle ran an undercurrent of violence. My fears were not unfounded, I later learned.

Most of the time I was a happy child, and I liked sharing a room with my sister. I naively believed she would save me from the things I feared. I wanted to look up to her and have her protect me, but it rarely happened. She delighted in telling me scary stories, making me feel more insecure.

Occasionally, she would come through and be the sister I hoped for. One of those times was when I was five and still had training wheels on my bike.

"Libby, don't you think it's time we took those off?" my mother asked one summer day.

"Mommy, I still can't balance," I answered.

"You don't know what you can do until you try," she said. That night my father removed the training wheels.

The next morning Blanche said, "C'mon, Lib. Let's ride your bike." I got on my bike and Blanche stood beside me, holding me up as I pedaled. Back and forth we went on Clark Street that warm summer morning, Blanche holding and me pedaling. And then I looked back. Blanche was standing twenty feet behind, and I was riding on my own.

"I did it, I did it," I squealed in delight.

Blanche stood there with a huge grin on her face. "See, Lib, I told you you could ride your bike." That memory is one of my happiest of my older sister.

But as we grew, our differences became more pronounced. Blanche was messy; I was neat. Nature seemed to win out over nurture. We had different personalities, although we were raised together. I made my bed every day and put everything in my room in its place. Blanche refused to make her bed and scattered dirty laundry across the dresser, the floor, and my neatly made bed. When she ran out of clean clothes to wear, she took mine. Too often she ruined my summer outfits when she "borrowed" my shorts, which were much too small for her, and the seams or zippers burst. I began to resent having to share my space with someone so inconsiderate.

She played music late at night and early in the morning when I was trying to sleep, and sometimes she'd take the screen off the bedroom window and sneak onto the roof to talk with friends.

I was finally given my own room after a weekend in which Blanche decided to play the ultimate prank on my parents, and she made me her unwilling accomplice. "Lib, let's pretend that someone broke into the house last night and made a mess," she whispered early one Sunday morning while our parents were still asleep.

"That doesn't sound like a good idea," I responded.

"It will be exciting. I can't wait to see the looks on Mommy and Daddy's faces when they come downstairs," she replied. "Don't you say a word, or I'll kill you. Do you understand?"

I nodded, believing she would.

Blanche then began grabbing eggs and milk from the fridge and pouring them on the kitchen floor. She took flour and sprinkled it on the counter, opened cabinet doors and kitchen drawers, threw cooking implements on the floor, and then left the front door ajar.

After she finished her mischief, she went upstairs and yelled, "Mommy, Daddy, wake up. Someone broke into the house." I stood silently behind her, afraid to say a word.

When our parents came downstairs, they were upset by the mess but not convinced that it wasn't homemade. "Blanche, did you and Libby do this?" my father asked.

"Oh, no, Daddy," she replied. "Someone broke in. You need to call the police."

The detectives arrived within minutes, since the police department was down the street. Blanche and I were questioned for what seemed like hours. I felt uncomfortable. My mother had taught me that lying was a sin. Casting my eyes toward the floor, I answered each question in a monosyllable. I knew the policemen could tell I was lying, and I was scared.

After that morning, the empty L-shaped bedroom across from my parents became mine. They filled it with a desk, bookshelves, and a chest of drawers hand-crafted by our neighbor, Joe Goodman, a master craftsman and high school shop teacher. He designed a built-in desk to go under my bedroom window and huge bookshelves that surrounded the window and rose to the ceiling from the desktop. Over time, the bookshelves became filled with books I acquired through book clubs or as gifts. There was also a chest of drawers, and one drawer contained a hiding place covered by a panel, where I placed precious things. I'd already learned that Blanche stole money from my piggy bank, and I'd given up trying to save as long as she had access to my room.

Blanche Berger, age eight or nine.

Naively, I believed that Blanche did not know about the hiding place—until one day I removed the cover and discovered it was empty. "Blanche!" I screamed. "Where is my money? I know you took it. Mommy, why does she always do this to me?" I wailed. "Please do something."

On days when life with Blanche became overwhelming and I needed to get away, I would pack my small camp bag with personal items and announce, "I'm going to Honolulu." I had no idea where Honolulu was and would take a walk around the block, eventually to return home.

My parents finally purchased a lock for my bedroom door shortly after that, and no one was allowed in my inner sanctum unless I was there. My room became my refuge, a place where I could shut my sister out and spend time in my own world. I read for hours, wrote letters to Aunt Florrie, Zayde Berger, or Aunt Bessie and Uncle Charlie. I drew pictures, played with dolls, and sometimes sat staring at the huge maple that stood outside my window on the Gelfonds' property next door.

The lock did not protect me from my own naiveté. One night Blanche arrived home with a rubber rattlesnake that looked very real. She knocked on my door and showed it to me. "Yuck," I shrieked and slammed the door in her face. I hated snakes and could not even look at them in movies or on television shows. My heart raced, and I jumped into bed and hid under the covers.

After a while, it grew quiet in the hallway. I heard water running in the bathroom sink and assumed Blanche was washing her face. Because the night was warm, I opened the door. The large rubber snake flew into my face, and I screamed in horror.

"Gotcha!" yelled Blanche.

Five minutes later my mother came running into the house and up the stairs. "What on earth is going on here?" she screamed. "I was playing cards at the Goodmans' house, heard the screams, and thought someone was being murdered."

Sometimes my parents entered my room to put things in the safe hidden inside my closet wall. I always wondered what they kept in the safe and worried that if someone broke into the house, he'd head for my bedroom, where the safe was hidden. Then I'd tell myself that no one knew about the safe except our family.

Some summer mornings I awakened to hot, humid days and couldn't wait to go downstairs to escape the heat. By afternoon, the clouds would grow dark and large, and the wind began to rustle the maple leaves next door until streaks of lightning appeared in the sky. Loud claps of thunder followed, and I shut myself in my room, frightened by the noise and the growing storm. I'd lie on my bed and read as the wind-whipped leaves were pelted by large raindrops. After a while the thunder ended, the rain ceased, and my world would be calm once more. I weathered many storms safely in my abode.

My second favorite room in our house was the kitchen, which was filled with the tastes and smells of my mother's cooking and baking. It was on the main floor with the living room, dining room, Poppy's bedroom and bath, and the breakfast room, which our parents added when they remodeled the kitchen. My mother chose modern colors, cocoa brown and powder blue, for the new metal kitchen cabinets, and the kitchen would have an electric stove and two ovens. It would even have a dishwasher. The refrigerator would be painted powder blue to match the cabinets. My mother was delighted.

I must have been about four when the remodel began. The workmen dug a three-foot ditch in the backyard for the foundation's footing. Blanche, the ultimate tomboy, enjoyed in jumping in the ditch when our parents weren't watching. One day my mother saw her through the window and came running out, admonishing, "Girls, stay out of the ditch. You can get hurt."

Mommy's warning was enough for me, the cautious child who listened. I did not want to make her angry and worried that she would no longer love me if I misbehaved.

After Mommy went back inside, Blanche urged, "Come on, Lib, jump in the ditch. I won't tell Mommy."

I eyed the ditch nervously, not wanting to get hurt or displease our mother. I also desperately sought my sister's approval and wanted to do what she asked.

"Come on, Lib. It's easy. You'll be in and out before she knows it. Don't be afraid. You can't get hurt."

Trusting her, I jumped—and then I realized how deep the ditch was. I couldn't climb out. I reached my hand up for Blanche's help. She had already run into the house yelling, "Mommy, Libby's in the ditch." My mother pulled me from the ditch and sent me to my room. Blanche went off to play with a friend.

I vowed not to listen to my sister after that, but my need for approval won out over common sense. I wanted to be her friend.

One time the two of us decided to go up to the attic to find some books my parents stored there. I loved to leaf through the leather-bound editions of Dickens, Poe, and Shakespeare. Getting to the attic was not an easy task. We had to ascend a set of wooden stairs that unfolded from a trapdoor in the ceiling outside my bedroom. Blanche assured me it would be no problem, pulled the chain on the trapdoor, and let the stairs fold out. "Follow me," she said.

In the light-filled attic I became so entranced by the books that I didn't notice Blanche was gone—until I heard the trap door close.

While our attic was warm and light, our basement was dark, damp, and full of hidden corners where the bogeyman could hide. I hated going down there alone. The main area was covered by a concrete floor upon which sat a monstrous oil burner that emitted loud sounds as it produced heat. There were also a washer and a dryer, which contributed their share to the cacophony. Near the washer and dryer stood an industrial-sized ironing machine that my mother used to iron sheets, underwear, and socks. I was told that when Blanche was a toddler, my mother sat her in front of the washer to keep her entertained. Perhaps sitting and staring at all those loads of laundry took its toll.

The basement contained three smaller rooms off the main room: a primitive half bath, a cold-storage room, and a small playroom. Mommy kept seasonal clothes, such as woolen jackets and furs, in the cold-storage room, which smelled like cedar and mothballs. When Blanche and I grew older, we would help her take one season's clothes downstairs and bring the next season's up. Our playroom was painted dark brown, housed our Amana freezer, and had built-in toy benches. One day Blanche and I decided to make pancakes with plaster of Paris and pour them on the benches, where they solidified. We did not use the playroom often because there were no toys in it, and the damp, dark space was not invit-

I loved to pretend I was a bride and wore a headpiece and skirt I made from crepe paper.

ing. Sometimes we'd play hide-and-seek with friends in the basement when the weather was bad and we were really bored. Most days we avoided it.

Occasionally, my mother asked me to go down to the basement and get something out of the freezer or grab a bottle of seltzer at the base of the stairs. I'd hurry down, leaving the door to the kitchen ajar, grab the item, and run back up the curved stairs as fast as I could, my heart racing. The only times I felt comfortable in the basement were when my mother was with me, hanging the laundry on lines stretched across the large open area or using her industrial-sized ironing machine to press sheets and underwear.

Most winter evenings my mother, sister, and I sat in the living room watching television while Poppy and my father worked at the bar Poppy owned in Newark, the other landscape of my childhood. Newark was where our aunt and cousins lived, my father worked, and my mother shopped. It was "the big city" compared to our small township.

Poppy was my mother's stepfather. My grandmother, Blanche Owsow-itz Goldstone, was a divorcée with two small children when she met this tall, handsome man with dark, wavy hair and huge brown eyes. He was kind and

My grandmother, Blanche Goldstone, hugs her children Ruth and Abraham.

charming, and after they married, he adopted her two children. My mother and her mother were close, more like sisters than mother and daughter. After my grandmother died, my mother took good care of Poppy, who was her father for all intents and purposes. He lived with us and suffered from Buerger's (ironically pronounced like our last name) disease, a circulatory disorder that affected his legs and caused him to use a cane.

Poppy's bar was on the corner of Avon and Ridgewood avenues in Newark. He and my grandmother had lived nearby and raised their family there. Poppy purchased the tavern after Prohibition ended. His place of business was a dark, beer-scented, clapboard tavern where locals came for a drink after a hard day's work. His patrons were all regulars who had known him for years, and they were mostly Negroes, as black people were called at that time.

Before he purchased the bar, Poppy had allowed bootleggers to set up stills in his factory in Harrison during Prohibition. Just before they planned to activate the stills, he received a call: "Morris, there's going to be a raid. We need to shut down." So he did. He never made a second attempt.

When Prohibition ended, he and my grandmother opened the Worthington Bar and Grill in Harrison. This business thrived well into the 1940s, before Poppy bought the tavern in Newark, which also produced a good living. My grandmother enjoyed both venues and often sat around the bar with the customers talking and laughing like one of the "boys." After my grandmother died, as Poppy grew older and more infirm, my father became the main man at the Newark tavern. Occasionally, he stopped by with me and stood me on the bar. His patrons would ooh and aah at me, a pale-skinned, towheaded little girl with chubby cheeks, curly hair, and blue eyes. I smiled at these strangers, working-class men and women who came for their nightly drink and companionship.

Poppy and Daddy had good rapport with their employees and customers; many of them did odd jobs for my parents at our home. Sometimes their relatives helped Mommy with the housework. Because I had met these individuals at my father's bar, I felt comfortable with them. I especially liked Earl, his kind bartender, who always had a smile for me.

When I was born, my parents lived on Keer Avenue in the Weequahic section of Newark, a predominantly Jewish area. The Weequahic section housed my Aunt Rose and Uncle Joe and their sons, Martin and Neal, on Wynd-

Daddy, Poppy, and Uncle Joe
got along well.

moor Avenue only blocks away. The area, high school, and nearby park were named for the band of Native Americans who originally settled in the vicinity.

My family moved to Highland Avenue in Hillside when I was six months old, but we spent a great deal of time in Newark. Hillside was my home, but Newark was my haunt. Chancellor Avenue held some of my favorite eating places, including Sid's Hot Dogs and the pizzeria, where I could buy a slice for fifteen cents. Across the street stood Weequahic High School and farther down the block was the Jewish center, where I took folk dancing, drama, and cooking classes after school. I was born on Chancellor Avenue in the city of Irvington, only a mile or so away from where I spent much time during my youth.

We went to Weequahic and Branchbrook Parks in Newark to ice-skate in the winter, ate at the Tavern on North Broad Street, or visited doctors and our dentist in the Newark Medical Towers.

The day I broke both bones in my right forearm and needed surgery, I stayed overnight alone in a Newark hospital, and the experience made me never want to go back. That cold January day had begun with a trip to the Saturday matinee at the Mayfair Theater in Hillside with a friend. While walking home, we encountered some boys from our third-grade class. They started throwing snowballs at us, made from remnants of a snowfall a week earlier. Of course, we picked up handfuls of snow and returned their fire. As I ran after one of the boys with a snowball clutched in my hand, he suddenly got down on all fours and I flew over him, landing directly on the cold, hard ground on my right arm. I heard a noise that sounded like a spring popping as I hit the frozen earth. When I stood up, my arm felt heavy and hurt badly. I supported it with my other arm for several blocks until I reached home.

Our family doctor came right to the house, examined my arm, made a temporary splint using two magazines and a pair of shoelaces, and sent me off to the hospital's emergency room.

After waiting for a very long time, I was examined and x-rayed. The film showed that I had broken my radius and ulna, and the bones that had once been straight now looked diamond shaped inside my arm. The orthopedic surgeon determined I would have to be anesthetized to set them back in place. "Her arm may never be straight again," he warned Mommy, "but I'll do my best."

After I returned from the operating room, I was placed in a large ward with one other child, a black infant in a crib on the other side of the room. Mommy came to see me with her friend, who urged me to let Mommy go home and get some rest. I reluctantly said, "okay," wanting to please Mommy.

I spent the night screaming in pain, but no one answered my calls. The nurse came in before Mommy left and put an ice bag on my arm, but the ice bag leaked all over me and the bed. My cries for help went unheeded. When the morning shift arrived, the nurse discovered me soaking wet and exhausted. I was relieved when Mommy and Daddy arrived to take me home. Daddy even bought me a coveted Revlon doll to ease the pain. Mommy thought he was spoiling me.

That experience made me never want to go to the hospital again.

I preferred downtown Newark where my mother and I went shopping for school clothes and holiday outfits. We would lunch in Bamberger's tearoom and make the rounds of Kresge's, Klein's, and Ohrbach's.

Sometimes my best friend Neil and I went to the movies in downtown Newark. The summer we were ten, we walked a few blocks to the bus stop on Maple Avenue and paid fifteen cents to ride the bus all the way downtown. Then we found the movie theater, watched a double feature, hopped back on the bus, and walked home. Our parents thought nothing of it, and we felt so grown-up to go downtown by ourselves.

I did not realize until many years later that the two landscapes of my childhood defined two different worlds. My privileged existence in a predominantly white suburban township with excellent schools and community services directly contrasted with the realities of the large, multiracial, multiethnic city of Newark. I felt free to come and go between both places and was comfortable in each.

My greatest fears came from the world inside my home.

3

My First Marriage

I married Neil Goodman when I was three years old. He was four. We were inseparable and played together from the time we could walk. Throughout our toddler years, we became best friends. One day while we were playing, Neil turned to me and asked, "Bibby [he couldn't say the letter *L*], will you marry me?"

"Yes," I replied. It seemed the right thing to say. Then we went inside and announced to our mothers—Ruth Goodman and Ruth Berger, who were having their morning coffee and cigarette break—that we were married. They both smiled.

Neil and I decided to inform the entire neighborhood. We went next door to Aunt Pearl and Uncle Moe's house and said, "We just got married."

Aunt Pearl and Uncle Moe replied, "How nice! You certainly make a beautiful couple. Would you like a piece of candy to celebrate?"

Aunt Pearl and Uncle Moe lived in the house between Neil's and mine. Aunt Pearl was not really my aunt, but her sister, Rose, was married to my father's brother, Joe. The families became best friends and bought homes next door to each other. The three families saw each other often, although my parents seemed closer to Pearl and Moe.

Word spread quickly throughout the neighborhood about our marriage, and our parents' friends would tease us whenever Neil and I were together, which was most of our waking hours. Our mothers spent lots of time together for coffee breaks, shopping, visiting friends, card games, and errands.

The marriage didn't change our relationship; Neil and I continued to be best friends. As children in the 1950s, we spent a lot of time with our parents, but we had little supervision when on our own. We freely roamed the neighborhood between our houses, going from yard to yard, since few families had fences. Often we played in large groups with the other neighborhood kids, Sandy and Bobby Bloom, Joanie Milch, and Tommy Pavlak. Sometimes other friends joined us, and occasionally, Neil's older sister, Ellen, or Blanche, would watch us.

Mrs. Goodman took my mother to run her errands because my mother did not drive. She'd had a bad car accident on a winding mountain road as a young bride. Her mother and mother-in-law were passengers in the car, when my mother, who was at the wheel, lost control. Her choices were limited: run into the mountainside or go off the cliff. She chose the former and had a two-inch scar on her chin as a result.

"Ruth, were you trying to kill us?" both mothers asked when the car hit the mountain. They were clearly shaken, and dear Mommy did not drive again until I was in the fourth grade, several decades after the accident and long after her mother and mother-in-law were dead.

It was fun to go everywhere with the Goodmans, and Neil and I managed to behave as best we could. People thought we were a cute couple. Neil's looks directly contrasted with mine. He had dark straight hair, big brown eyes, and olive skin that tanned easily. His handsome features always drew comments from strangers.

Neil was definitely more mischievous than I was. One day, shortly after we were married, Neil had to relieve himself as we waited on Lyons Avenue in Newark while our mothers were inside a store shopping. Neil unzipped his fly and peed on the tire of a nearby car. Ruth Goodman had a sixth sense.

She turned around and saw him, flew out of the store, and quickly zipped him up. "Neil, I've told you a hundred times not to do that. You're not a dog! No ice cream for you today." Then we all got in the car and left.

When we weren't with our mothers, Neil and I would often go down to his basement and watch his father working with wood. Joe Goodman was a high school shop teacher and an excellent craftsman. He'd created all of the built-in cabinets, furniture, and baseboards in the Goodman home, using unusual fruitwoods and applying beautiful finishes. Their house always smelled like freshly cut wood, especially the basement, where Mr. Goodman's shop was set up.

Neil's home and friendship were great respites from my older sister, who spent most of her waking hours thinking of ways to torture me. But sometimes Neil and I were together too much. Occasionally we fought. Because Neil was stronger, I was a dirty fighter. I'd scratch him with my fingernails, and he'd go home dripping with blood and crying. When Mrs. Goodman came over for coffee later that day, she'd say, "Libby, what did you do to Neil?" I would look sheepish and feel bad, especially when the punishment was imposed—no playing with Neil.

A few days after these fights, Neil and I would beg our mothers to let us play together again. Eventually they'd relent, but first they'd say, "Now remember, no fighting." And everything was all right for a while.

One of our favorite places to play was on Aunt Pearl and Uncle Moe's back stoop. We'd sit up there and pretend for hours. We'd play cops and robbers, cowboys and Indians, hide-and-seek, and whatever other games we could conjure up.

While we were sitting on the stoop one summer morning, Neil leaned over and said, "Mahoy, Bibby, mahoy." I just looked at him, not knowing what language he spoke. "Mahoy, Bibby, mahoy," he repeated. When I didn't move, he gave me a gentle shove, just enough to throw me off balance and send me tumbling down the stairs. I landed on the asphalt driveway with a thud and began to cry. Aunt Pearl came running out and took me home.

I could not stop crying, and my mother called the doctor. Off we went to Dr. Oris in Ruth Goodman's car. He examined me and sent us off to Dr. Fortel, who took some x-rays. My arm was broken and had to be put in a cast. I sat in Dr. Fortel's examining room as he immobilized my arm by applying layers of plaster. My mother sat beside me, tears streaming down her face.

Neil loved to hug me.

When we got home, Daddy made a fuss and brought me presents and ice cream. Blanche, Ellen, and all the kids in the neighborhood signed my cast. And Ruth Goodman interpreted what Neil had said earlier in the day. "Mahoy" meant "move over." Thus, the gentle shove and ensuing fall. No matter. Neil came and gave me hugs and kisses. We were still best friends and still married, despite his speech impediment.

The year Neil started kindergarten, I was upset because I was too young to go with him. When I started kindergarten the following year, Neil and I walked to Hillside Avenue School together, right behind one of our sisters or an older neighborhood child. We would often stop to play on the way home, especially on rainy days when we took turns jumping in the puddles that formed in the storm drains we passed on the way. Sometimes my feet were soaked when I walked in the door, despite my rubber boots, and my mother would ask, "Libby, where did you and Neil go?"

"Oh, we just jumped in the sewer," I replied, smiling.

When it snowed, it took us longer to get to school. We'd slip and slide downhill all the way, and some days we barely made it home, walking uphill on icy cobblestone streets. After a few minutes at home, we'd change our clothes and go out to play in the snow once more. We made snowballs, snow angels, and snowmen while outside in the cold. Occasionally, our snowmen contained an unexpected brown lump or yellow stain from one of the neighborhood dogs.

As Neil and I advanced through grammar school, we remained best friends, but we finally decided to divorce when we were about seven or eight. Marriage was too confining.

Our friendship endured, and we still spent lots of time together—walking to school, riding our bikes, going to Saturday afternoon movies, playing a board game or cards, or going to the swim club in the summer. Once in the pool, we swam like fish across the Olympic-sized pool and only came out when our lips and fingernails turned blue from the cold.

One of our favorite activities was exploring. We'd pretend we were adventurers and try to discover new places. The township of Hillside afforded us a great opportunity to do this when it built a new city hall that contained a public library and a police station only four blocks from our homes. We walked in the front door and then entered the stairwell that led to the different floors, where we looked around. This game was great fun on days when we were bored and could think of nothing else to do.

One day an adult spotted us in the stairwell and yelled, "What are you kids up to?" Neil and I ran and never looked back. We heard a man's footsteps behind us, but whoever yelled at us gave up the chase. For days afterwards we were certain that the police were going to show up at our homes and question us. They never did.

We gave up exploring city hall and broadened our vistas by exploring the parks where Neil played his Little League baseball games. Our favorite was Conant Park, where our mothers would sometimes take us for picnics before the games. We loved the plush green lawns that stretched across the picnic area, bordered by the Elizabeth River and an expanse of woods. At Conant Park we felt like we were in the country, although we were only a few minutes from the streets and stores of Hillside.

I would go to Neil's ball games and cheer him on. He was an outstanding athlete but not much of a scholar. To help him practice we'd play stickball on Highland Avenue, being careful to dodge the cars that frequently drove up and down our hill.

As we matured, Neil grew even more handsome, and we still spent a lot of time together. Sometimes we hopped on the bus and headed to downtown Newark to see a movie, something we'd been doing since we were ten. The year Neil was twelve and I was eleven, we ventured downtown to see the new Alfred Hitchcock movie, *Psycho*. We'd heard it was scary, but I felt safe as long as I had Neil beside me. When actress Janet Leigh screamed as she was being stabbed in the shower, Neil screamed and hid his eyes, too. Each time a murder took place, we cringed and hugged each other. When the movie ended, we were both quite shaken. We both preferred taking baths for a long time afterwards.

When I was in seventh grade, several classmates realized that I was Neil's best friend and asked for introductions. I fixed him up with my friend Ronnie. They hit it off, and I was happy. Neil and Ronnie went together for a few years. I had a future as a matchmaker.

My first marriage may have been short, but it taught me the value of love and friendship. Sometimes I wonder where Neil is and how he's doing. It would be fun to catch up and discover how the years treated us. I know I could find room for my old best friend in my life.

4

The City of Brotherly Love

Philadelphia, the City of Brotherly Love, beckoned each month when we went to visit Zayde Berger, my father's father. Daddy, Blanche, and I made the two-hour drive from Hillside on the New Jersey Turnpike, with Daddy and Blanche in the front seat and me in the back. Sometimes Mommy joined us, especially if the entire family circle was meeting, but Daddy often took Blanche and me on his own. My father's driving made Mommy too nervous.

Blanche and I liked our outings with Daddy. He often took us down the shore on Sunday afternoons when the weather was warm, and we'd enjoy the boardwalk amusements in Asbury Park. Daddy indulged us with hot dogs, candy apples, caramel corn, and cotton candy as we made our way from ride to ride. These Sundays always culminated in lobster dinners at one of the board-walk restaurants. I found wearing a bib fun and enjoyed cleaning my hands afterwards in the finger bowl filled with warm water and lemon.

Trips to Philly were fun because we stopped at Howard Johnson's restaurant for lunch along the way. I loved the fried clams with tartar sauce. Blanche usually ate a hot dog. On one our of our stops, Blanche asked to go to the bathroom alone. When she returned to the table a few minutes later, she declared, "Daddy, there are strange toilets here. I walked in but couldn't find a place to go."

"Let's see what the problem is," Daddy replied.

They walked to the restroom where Blanche had been and he said, "Honey, that's the men's room. The other one is for you." We laughed about Blanche's mistake for a long time.

While he drove down the New Jersey Turnpike towards Philly, Daddy puffed on his cigar. In the winter he kept the windows closed. Even in warmer weather, the windows were nearly closed, filling the car with noxious fumes. By the time we arrived at Zayde's, I was often nauseated.

Cars had no seat belts or air conditioning in the 1950s, and sometimes we didn't make it to Philly. "Daddy, I don't feel so well," I called from the back-seat one summer morning when I was six. He pulled over so that we could get some fresh air.

"Hold on," he said, but it was too late. Before he could stop the car, my breakfast came up all over the seat and the summer outfit I'd chosen to wear to Zayde's house. Daddy stopped at the closest Howard Johnson's, and Blanche took me to the ladies' room to clean up. At times she could be the caring, doting sister I longed for. When she washed my face and brushed my hair, I realized this was one of them.

"It's okay, Libby, you'll be fine," Daddy assured me when we got back to the car. He hated to see his "baby girl" feeling ill and gave me a big hug and kiss, despite my sour smell.

When we arrived in Philadelphia, Daddy headed straight to Broad Street in downtown Philly to buy me a new outfit. He knew the neighborhood well, having owned a clothing store on South Street before he married my mother and went into the tavern business with her stepfather.

"Oh, Harry, what cute daughters you have," his former neighbor said. "Here, let's find something for the younger one to wear." She kindly found replacements for my sour-smelling clothes: a pair of light-blue shorts, a sleeveless white cotton blouse with a goldfish embroidered on the front, and some white anklets. The blouse became a favorite, and I wore it until it no longer fit. Later that summer I wore that blouse to sit for a pastel portrait on Collins Avenue in Miami Beach, Florida. The picture still hangs on the wall in our home.

Zayde looked forward to our visits and greeted us with hugs and kisses. A longtime widower who'd lost his older son, Joe, when I was four years old, he spent his life praying and awaiting family visits. He was a round, swaybacked man with thinning white hair, a petite white mustache, a small goatee, and a big smile.

Zayde Berger prayed every morning before breakfast.

I was told he was a house painter when he was younger, but by the time I was born my father was nearly fifty and Zayde was an old man. He had become a cantor at synagogue, and the family revered him in his new role.

As an Orthodox Jew, Zayde always kept his head covered, either with a *yarmulke* (skull cap) or a hat. Each morning he arose early, washed and dressed, and then put on his *yarmulke*, *tallis* (shawl), and *tefillin* (small boxes containing biblical passages) to begin his daily prayers. He spent an hour at his devotions, and we knew never to disturb him when he visited us in New Jersey. I usually watched in awe from the stairs leading down from our bedrooms, wondering about this daily ritual that was a mystery to me.

Zayde lived in a two-story row house on cobblestoned 1936 South Galloway Street in Philadelphia, a neighborhood so different from my own in Hillside. Located in South Philly, his street lacked trees and always appeared a dingy brown, even in spring. Most of the other neighborhood residents were Negroes, but our family had always lived and worked among people of color, so we felt comfortable here. The neighbors treated Zayde well.

Daddy holds my hand as we walk
down the street.

We would walk down South Galloway to the corner candy store and buy twelve-inch pretzels as snacks. Most of the locals covered their pretzels in mustard, but Blanche and I preferred ours plain. We watched the neighbors relish theirs and wondered what difference the mustard made.

Zayde's home was not far from Carpenter's Hall, where the Declaration of Independence was signed. During most visits, Daddy would take Blanche and me there to show us the Liberty Bell, and I would always put my finger in the crack. "You broke it," Daddy joked, and we all laughed.

Our day trips often included visits to Zayde's sister, Aunt Bessie Fingerhut, and her husband, Uncle Charlie, who lived on the first floor of a two-family home in Strawberry Mansion. Aunt Bessie must have been all of four-feet, eight-inches tall, because she had rickets as a child. She wore her long gray hair in a bun and thick glasses. She was not a pretty woman, but she was kind and proud. One time, Aunt Bea took Aunt Bessie to the doctor, and he asked Aunt Bessie's age. Bessie leaned over to Bea and asked, "Bea, do I have to tell him the truth?"

Uncle Charlie was a tall, bald man with a big paunch and bad dentures. Half the time we spent with him, he made gyrations with his mouth that resembled "monkey faces." Blanche imitated him very well, partly because of her prominent underbite. All the way home in the car she would do Uncle Charlie imitations while I giggled away beside her in the backseat.

Aunt Bessie and Uncle Charlie had no children and were always very kind to Blanche and me. At the dinner table, Uncle Charlie would sit beside me and whisper, "Libby, do you want some of this? Eat, eat, it's good for you." Before I could reply, he'd put more food on my plate.

Aunt Bessie was an excellent seamstress and earned extra income with her skills. Occasionally, she had fabric left over from a client's job and made me a skirt from it. I loved these handmade fashions, although some were made from drapery materials. Blanche looked at me and laughed, "So Aunt Bessie made you a skirt out of a drape again." I had not yet read *Gone With the Wind*, so I proudly wore her creations to school, because she made them, and I loved Aunt Bessie.

The summer I was eight, Aunt Bessie and Uncle Charlie invited me to stay with them for a few days. I was delighted. "Are you sure?" my father asked before leaving me there.

"Yes, Daddy, I promise to be good."

Before we went to bed that night, Aunt Bessie brushed my long, blond hair and plaited it. Then she placed me in between her and Uncle Charlie in their double bed, which was in what would have been the dining room. (Many two-family houses had once been grand mansions, and after they were divided and the floors rented, residents improvised how the rooms were used.)

I was terrified. I had not expected to sleep between these two old people. Uncle Charlie went to sleep immediately and began snoring loudly. The room was warm, and we were all too close. I could not go to sleep and began to cry softly.

"Libbala [Yiddish endearment of my name], what's wrong?" Aunt Bessie asked.

"I want to go home. I miss Mommy and Daddy."

"It'll be all right," she said. "Tomorrow I'll take you to the Philadelphia Zoo. We'll have fun."

"Okay," I whimpered before finally falling asleep.

The next morning Aunt Bessie awoke and made six meatball sandwiches to take with us to the zoo. Then we took off on the streetcar.

I don't remember much about the zoo, except that when we got there I wanted a hot dog. "But Libby, I made all this good food. You have to eat some," Aunt Bessie urged. She bought me a hot dog, and then I ate a meatball sandwich, too, so that she wouldn't be too upset. No wonder I was a chubby child.

My visit lasted only three days, but they seemed the longest of my life. Aunt Bessie and Uncle Charlie were disappointed. I was homesick and so relieved when Daddy came to pick me up. While I dearly loved this elderly aunt and uncle, I realized that day visits suited me better.

Our day trips to Philly were exciting outings, but they were not nearly as exciting as the journeys we made at Passover. This was a major holiday for our family, and we began our Passover ritual by buying new clothes for the celebration. Mommy would take Blanche and me shopping in downtown Newark to purchase our spring finery at stores like Bamberger's, Ohrbach's, Kresge's, and Klein's. The department stores offered the variety we needed—new spring coats, dress shoes, anklets, gloves, and two dresses or outfits each—one for each night of Seder. I especially remember the beige wool topper coat and the navy-blue serge suit with the white Peter Pan collar. To complete the outfits, we visited the millinery store owned by my mother's cousin. I loved hats and was delighted for this annual opportunity to try on so many and purchase one or two. My red wool beret and navy straw sailor hat were my favorites.

After buying us new clothes, my parents would make reservations at the Benjamin Franklin Hotel in Philadelphia, for our overnight visit because Zayde's house was too small to accommodate the four of us. They booked two adjoining rooms, and I roomed with Blanche.

I thought the Benjamin Franklin was a beautiful hotel, with its luxurious lobby that had off-white marble floors and large picture windows that overlooked downtown Philadelphia. The lobby was quiet, a place where guests sat and read or waited for a ride or a room. A gentleman dressed as the hotel's namesake walked about greeting everyone. "Look, Daddy, that's Benjamin Franklin," I uttered the first time I saw this man. Daddy smiled and patted me on the head. I was always naive and had no idea that the man was an actor, or I loved history enough to pretend that he was actually Benjamin Franklin.

Zayde hosted the first night's Seder at his home, and only our immediate family attended. We ate the traditional foods—matzo (unleavened bread), gefilte fish, matzo ball soup, *charoseth* (chopped apples, raisins, and nuts in red wine), matzo kugel (pudding), and roast chicken—that Zayde purchased at a kosher restaurant. We also held an abbreviated version of the Passover service, telling the story of how the Jews were delivered out of Egypt. As the youngest, I was most engaged in one aspect of the service—asking the four questions (in English) about what makes this night different from all other nights:

1. On all nights we need not dip even once, why on this night do we dip twice?

2. On all nights we eat *chametz* (leavened foods) or matzo, why on this night do we only eat matzo?

3. On all nights we eat any kind of vegetables, why on this night do we only eat *maror* (bitter herbs)?

The Kaplan Family Circle held its Seder at the Wynn in Philadelphia. Around
table from left, Uncle Charlie; Daddy; Zayde; me; Uncle Jack and Aunt
Sadie; Uncle Ben, Cousin Lucille, and Aunt Sarah; Aunt Fanny
and Uncle Max; Aunt Bea and Uncle Joe; Aunt Bessie

4. On all nights we eat sitting upright or reclining, why on this night
   do we all recline?

I then had to recite the answers.

Daddy prepared me by repeating the questions over and over until I
memorized them. He and Mommy helped if I forgot some words, but I never
did. Zayde smiled proudly when I finished my recitation.

Blanche and I participated in finding the matzo, called the *afikomen*,
that our parents and Zayde placed on a plate, covered with a napkin, and hid as
part of the holiday ritual. Whoever found it received five dollars and hugs from
Zayde.

The second night's Seder was held at a reception hall called the Wynn,
located outside the city. The entire Berger/Kaplan Family Circle attended this
Seder, and some years we numbered nearly one hundred. I remember one year
when the matzo balls in the soup felt like rocks, instead of being spongy. Several of Daddy's cousins fished them out and asked their waiters, "Son, would
you like to play golf tomorrow?" I did not understand the laughter that followed,
but I remember that question so many years later.

Most of our Philadelphia family had the surname Kaplan. In Russia the entire family had gone by the surname Berger until shortly before they left their homeland at the beginning of the twentieth century. Zayde's brother, Solomon, was supposed to be drafted into the Russian army, a twenty-five-year conscription that often led to death from miserable living conditions or anti-Semitism. To avoid being drafted, he changed names with a man named Kaplan, although I do not know the circumstances. The family referred to him as Shlomo Chaim, and he often said the prayers at family gatherings. When this brother arrived in America, he kept the name Kaplan, while Zayde's family remained Berger. For as long as I could remember, we were a family divided by name and the formidable Aunt Rose, dear Uncle Joe's widow. She never attended a family event when our family was present.

Once a month the Kaplan Family Circle gathered for Sunday dinner at a relative's home, usually in Philadelphia. I looked forward to going to Philadelphia and seeing my relatives, some of whom had children a few years older than Blanche and I. My mother dreaded the two-hour drive on the New Jersey Turnpike and Garden State Parkway, sitting in the front seat beside my father. She was always nervous when Daddy drove, because he changed lanes frequently and swayed within his lane. I watched her anxiously from the backseat wondering why she was so frightened, too young to understand. I cowered each time a large truck passed us, fearful it would not see us and we'd be crushed. Years later, when Daddy fell asleep at the wheel while returning from Monmouth Race Track and almost went over the side of the Raritan Bridge, I understood my mother's fear.

Our monthly family gatherings were filled with food, family stories, and lots of hugs. I loved being among so many relatives, as life at home was quiet and often lonely. Sometimes we visited the home of Uncle Joe and Aunt Bea Kaplan, who lived in an elegant house with the living room on the top floor. (Many of my "uncles" and "aunts" were actually my father's first cousins, but we were taught to call them "uncle" and "aunt" in deference to their ages.) Aunt Bea was a classic beauty, reminiscent of the actress Grace Kelly, with her blond hair worn in a bun and soft blue eyes. She often wore a string of pearls and elegant shirtwaist dresses. She possessed impeccable manners and was very kind. At times I felt intimidated by her because she was so proper. Uncle Joe was a well-known ophthalmologist, who sported a balding head of dark hair and a large mustache. They had three sons, Edward (whom we called Dee Dee), Abram, and Stevie. All three were friendly and outgoing like their father, and all three became physicians.

Uncle Joe's brother, Uncle Lou, and his wife, Aunt Shirley, also attended these family gatherings. Aunt Shirley was a petite, pretty lady with long blond hair, twisted into a bun, and an enormous bust. Uncle Lou was a smaller version of his brother, with thinning gray hair and a mustache.

They had two sons, Milton and Stanley. Milton became a cardiologist and moved to Southern California to practice medicine in the late fifties. He was older than Stanley and not as outgoing. Stanley was the family entertainer, who had a beautiful voice and would sing at our monthly family circle gatherings in Philadelphia. I had a crush on this handsome cousin with his blond curls and smooth voice. He was my favorite.

Aunt Fanny and Uncle Max Dunst were always warm and welcoming, and I recall the hugs and kisses this elderly white-haired couple bestowed on me so freely.

Sometimes cousin Earl and his wife from Red Bank, New Jersey, would come and bring their daughter, Marcy. I looked up to my cousin, Marcy, whose age was halfway between Blanche's and mine. We would go off and play and talk while the adults chatted in the other room.

When I was eight, Marcy decided to share some information she'd just learned with me. "Libby, do you know where babies come from?" she asked.

"The stork," I answered quickly.

Marcy just laughed. "Would you like to know the real story?"

I sat there and listened for twenty minutes, disgusted by details that were too horrible to consider. Finally, I said, "Why would people do that?"

"Because it's fun," she replied.

I decided that night that I would find my fun elsewhere for a long, long time. It was all too yucky for me.

Our trips to Philadelphia lasted for most of my childhood, until my parents grew slowly apart. I did not realize this was happening until one weekend when my mother left town suddenly just before Zayde came to visit. I thought this odd, since my mother always did all she could to make Zayde comfortable in our home—taking down the kosher dishes she kept just for him, buying him kosher meals, and tending to all his needs. She did not tell us where she was, and Daddy only said, "Your mother needs to be alone. I'm in charge now." I was devastated.

While Mommy was away, Daddy drove to Philadelphia and brought Zayde to Hillside. In his haste, my father forgot that Zayde would be with us on the Sabbath. Since Zayde was Orthodox and kept kosher, he ate food my parents bought from Moishe's in Newark, using dishes Mommy reserved for him. (She and my Daddy stopped keeping kosher after Blanche arrived.) Daddy did not reach Moishe's before sundown on Friday, and Zayde refused to eat food purchased on the Sabbath. Daddy was beside himself all day Saturday, until sundown came and he convinced his elderly father to take some nourishment. When Mommy returned from her short trip, she was furious with my father for his error. That was the last time Zayde stayed with us in Hillside.

I remember those visits to my grandfather and our extended family in the City of Brotherly Love with affection. They offered a true sense of family, and being together with them was a highlight of my childhood. The relationships established at those gatherings continued for many years but ended abruptly when I was thirteen.

5
Shuffling Off to Buffalo

"All aboard!" shouted the conductor, "All aboard!" In December 1955, I sat snugly in my window seat watching people run along the platform at Newark's Pennsylvania Station, a place I knew well. I'd been here many times to meet relatives and depart for places like New York City and Miami, Florida. More often my mother, sister, and I boarded the tube train that took us under the Hudson River to New York for a Sunday outing. Today we'd be going on a much longer journey—to Buffalo aboard the *Phoebe Snow*, the train that went to upstate New York, where my mother's aunt Florrie lived.

The train slowly began to move, and my excitement grew. I'd never been to Buffalo before, and my mother said there would be snow there. I always wanted snow at Christmas, a certainty in upstate New York, which was much closer to the Canadian border. I also wanted to see the place where my aunt and cousins lived.

Although Aunt Florrie was my mother's aunt, they were about the same age. My great-aunt was a petite, curly haired lady whom my mother's uncle, Morris Owsowitz, met after her family arrived in the United States from England. Uncle Morris, my grandmother's brother, was a large, sturdy man who'd swept this intelligent little lady off her feet. She was only six years older than my mother. I'm told that when they met, my mother asked, "May I call you Florrie?"

"You may call me 'Aunt Florrie,' " the little bride replied. And my mother did for many years. By the time my sister and I arrived, nearly two decades later, the two were on a first-name basis and very close friends.

The train began to pick up speed, and my mother relaxed a bit. She began to point out scenery as the train headed into the countryside. I begged her to tell me stories of the Indian tribes that had inhabited the area—Weequahic, Leni Lenape, Algonquin, and Iroquois. I hoped that these tales would make the forests and mountains we passed through come to life. In school I thrived on the stories of the tribes who had lived here long before the Europeans arrived. So many places in New Jersey and New York still bore tribal names.

Blanche, now eleven years old, stared out the window and listened, too. She didn't like to be confined for long periods of time, and this trip would take several hours, so she was a captive audience.

I was told that Blanche had visited Aunt Florrie in Buffalo when she was three. Mommy said, "The cab stopped in front of Aunt Florrie's house. Your sister and I got out. By the time I paid the cab driver, Blanche was halfway around the block." I laughed when I heard that story. It was such a perfect description of my big sister, someone I admired yet feared.

From an early age, Blanche needed to have her way. She took a broom and swatted the crystal chandelier over the dining room table until Poppy grabbed the broom. She broke all of her dolls and other toys. One day my parents found a rubber doll in the toy store and thought Blanche would like it. Shortly after they gave it to her, they found the doll in the garbage.

"Why did you throw this away?" my mother asked, retrieving the doll.

"I can't break it," Blanche replied.

My mother's goal in life was to try to raise me as best she could, knowing that my sister might undo all her teaching. On this trip, Mommy kept a watchful eye on Blanche. She never knew what kind of trouble her older daughter would find.

For a while, Blanche and I entertained ourselves by walking from car to car, exploring the train. It was fun to see the other passengers, but I hated when we walked between cars. We had to open heavy metal doors that slammed shut loudly behind us, trapping us on a cold platform where we could see the ground fly by beneath our feet.

"Don't look down, Lib," Blanche said protectively.

But I did and felt dizzy seeing the earth moving below the train at such a fast rate.

At noon, Mommy walked us to the dining car for lunch. She had prepared us for this occasion by saying, "The dining car is a very nice restaurant, and I expect you to be on your best behavior."

We promised we would, and when we entered, I thought it was beautiful. Small tables set for two or four persons were covered in white tablecloths. Silver utensils gleamed beside porcelain place settings and glass goblets. A smiling waiter in a white jacket escorted us to our table and handed us menus.

Mommy began to read the menu to us. "Consommé with noodles, fried scallops," she said.

"What are those?" I asked. The food names sounded foreign to me.

"Consommé is broth, and here they put noodles in it. You like noodles," Mommy replied. "Scallops are seafood. I think you'll like them. We eat them when we're down the shore."

The *Phoebe Snow* was a long way from the water, but Mommy said the seafood would be good, so I tried it. I could always trust her to order something I liked when we went out to eat. Most of the time I chose hot turkey sandwiches, smothered in gravy. These weren't even on the menu.

The waiter brought our food, and the broth with noodles warmed me on this cool December day. The scallops looked like crisp brown balls, but they were white and moist inside. They tasted especially good when I dipped them in catsup, my favorite condiment.

Blanche and I ate slowly, mindful of our table manners. We had certain rules at our dinner table. Take small bites, chew with your mouths closed, don't talk with food in your mouth, ask others to pass things, and always say "please" and "thank you." We were Mommy's young ladies, after all. One thing we were never to do after a meal was use a toothpick. "Ladies don't clean their teeth in public," Mommy warned.

After lunch we settled back into our coach seats and fell asleep. I must have slept for several hours because shortly after we awoke, the train arrived in Buffalo. Sleepily I stood up and helped Mommy and Blanche gather our things.

I froze at the train's door, looking down the steps that led to the station's concourse. The ground seemed so far away, and I stood there, unable to move. Suddenly this large, broad-shouldered man reached up and lifted me to the ground. I didn't know who he was, but Mommy smiled as she recognized Aunt Florrie's son, Tim. No longer the tow-headed toddler she'd held in her arms, Tim was a strapping young man, just like his father. He picked up our suitcases and led us to the car.

"Sue's preparing dinner, so we'll stop by and pick up my mother on our way home," he said. "That will give you a chance to say hello and drop off your suitcases."

I looked out the window as we rode. Snow, lots of snow, covered the ground, just as Mommy had promised. Tomorrow I'll make a snowman, I thought.

Aunt Florrie lived on the top floor of a two-family house in Buffalo with her daughters Davida (Davey) and Miriam (Mimi). Davey was in her mid-twenties, and Mimi was two years younger. Both had heads full of dark curls, like their mother. Davey was tall and slender, while Mimi was petite like Aunt Florrie.

Aunt Florrie hugged us warmly and said, "I'm so happy you're here." This was her first holiday season without Uncle Morris, who had died earlier that year. I remember that summer morning well. The phone rang quite early. My mother answered it and began to cry.

"Mommy, what's wrong?" I asked. I adored my mother, and she rarely showed emotion in front of me. Stoic, soft-spoken, and loving, she was the center of my world.

"My Uncle Morris died," she answered. "He had a heart attack in his sleep."

I hated to see my mother so upset, and I was much too young to know what a "heart attack" was. I had only met Uncle Morris once, but I felt sad that he had died. My mother said that he owned a slaughterhouse, and Tim worked with him. She thought Tim would take over the business now that his father was dead.

And so we came to Buffalo to spend the first holidays without Uncle Morris with Aunt Florrie and her family. "I'll only take a minute to freshen up," my mother said. "I can't wait to see Sue and meet the babies."

Tim and Sue had two babies—Mike and Judy. Mike was adopted, like Blanche and me. Judy was born nine months later. Now a one-year-old toddler, Mike came to the door with his mother. Judy lay on a blanket in the living room, staring at us with huge brown eyes that seemed too large for her face. She smiled and squirmed, trying to put her tiny feet in her mouth. I found her amusing.

Clockwise from bottom left, Mimi, Davida, Aunt Florrie, and Uncle Morris Owsowitz with their dog

I don't remember what we ate for dinner, but Sue made chocolate cream pie for dessert. It was a favorite and different from the delicious fruit pies my mother baked.

We visited for a while after dinner and

From left, Tim, Mimi, and Davida Owsowitz

then returned to Aunt Florrie's. My mother shared a room with her, Davida and Mimi bunked together, and Blanche and I were assigned to a room with twin beds.

We were tired after our long journey, but Blanche wasn't ready for sleep. Just as I began to doze off, she said, "Libby, did you know that Uncle Morris died in that bed?"

"He did not," I shot back.

"Oh, yes, he did," Blanche answered. "If you go to sleep, you might die, too."

I was instantly awake and very upset. "Stop saying that," I shouted. "You're always trying to scare me. At home you tell me the bogeyman is waiting to get me in the dark upstairs. Why can't you just leave me alone?" I wailed. "I want Mommy."

Mimi must have heard us because she came into our room. "Girls, keep your voices down. Our mothers are asleep."

Tears stung my eyes. I'd upset my cousin, and I was afraid of my sister. I burrowed under the covers, leaving the tip of my nose out so that I could breathe, like I did every night. Perhaps if I hid, evil spirits would not find me. At home it was the bogeyman; in Buffalo it was the ghost of Uncle Morris.

The early morning sky was white when we awoke, indicating that more snow would fall that day. After breakfast Blanche and I went outside to make snowballs. I liked to catch flakes of falling snow on my tongue before they hit the ground. The rest of the snow would be fun to play in. After throwing a few snowballs at each other, Blanche and I rolled one into a larger sphere to form the base of our snowman. The crisp air felt fresh, unlike the concrete gray sky that hovered over New Jersey this December.

Catching snowflakes on my tongue in Buffalo seemed far safer than what I once did in New Jersey. I was about four years old, and I recall sitting on our brick stoop after a snowfall, picking up handfuls of snow and eating it from the steps. When my mother discovered me, she rushed me inside and said, "Libby, that's not ice cream. Don't sit out in the cold and eat snow; you could get sick."

Shortly afterwards I came down with a bad case of the croup. No more snow for me!

I liked being in Buffalo, where we could play in the snow and then go in for lunch. During lunch Davida suggested we go ice-skating that afternoon.

"I don't know how to skate," I whined.

"I'll teach you," she responded.

"Don't be afraid, Lib, it's easy," Blanche chimed in.

"Maybe for you it is. You're like one of the boys. You can climb trees, ride bikes, and play stickball as well as any of the neighborhood boys. I'm a klutz," I added. "Remember, my bones break easily."

"Don't be such a chicken," Blanche taunted.

That was all she needed to say. Off we went to the skating rink. The oval-shaped, man-made ice was enclosed with a chain-link fence. Skaters glided around it easily, while neophytes like me quickly headed straight for the fence. I held on to the fence, afraid to fall and break another bone. The single-blade skates challenged my wobbly ankles as I tried to stand. Davey took my hand and led me onto the ice.

While I clung to the sides in fear, I became mesmerized by the skaters. They made it look so easy, and I wanted to join them. After watching Blanche and Davey circle the rink several times, I ventured toward them, dodging more accomplished skaters.

Plop! I hit the ice. It hurt a little, yet I tried to stand up. Each time I'd put weight on one leg, the other would slide out from under me, as if I were a rag doll. Eventually Blanche and Davey skated by. Each grabbed an arm and scooped me up.

I decided that holding their hands was the only way I'd learn to skate. I held on to them tightly. With each turn around the ice, my confidence grew and I began to like skating more. My goal was to make one complete turn without falling. An hour later, I reached it. "Can we come back tomorrow?" I asked. "I'm getting the hang of this now."

"Not tomorrow, but soon," Davey promised as we headed for the exit.

I smiled because I'd finally found a sport I liked, even if I wasn't very good at it. As we skated toward the exit, I noticed that the ice had melted, leaving a huge puddle right where we stepped out of the rink. I headed that way, but both skates slipped out from under me and down I went into the puddle. This time the fall hurt my pride and my rear end. I was wet and cold. Davey and Blanche scooped me up and led me to a nearby bench.

My flannel-lined corduroy pants were sopping wet, and I shivered with cold as Davida hurriedly drove home along the snow-lined streets.

Mommy greeted me with a hug and dry clothes when we returned. She added hot cocoa and two aspirin for insurance, knowing how easily I got sick.

While my first attempt at ice-skating left me with a bruised bottom and wet pants, it made me realize that I could attempt new things and learn them. This first ice-skating trip whetted my appetite for future adventures, and I begged Mommy and Daddy to take me ice-skating in New Jersey. At first we went to Branchbrook Park, where they had a small rink and I could rent skates. After I became better at skating, I received ice-skates one Chanukah. After that, whenever cold weather set in, I'd ask, "Mommy, do you think Weequahic Lake is frozen? Can we go ice-skating?"

"Libby, that lake is not the best for skating. Let's ask Daddy to drive you to Irvington Park. But Daddy will have to test the ice first."

Whenever he could, Daddy took me and my friends ice-skating. I loved soaring around the ice, no longer feeling like the klutzy kid from Hillside, and thanked my cousin Davida for introducing me to this wonderful sport.

She became my mentor as a child, and I looked forward to her occasional weekend visits alone and annual Thanksgiving dinners with Aunt Florrie at our home in Hillside. Both women played major roles in our lives when I was young and as I became a young adult. I will always remember their kindness, love, and strong influence on me.

When I was twelve, these visits ended. I did not know why.

A year later, Davida and Aunt Florrie both got married. Davida married a big-hearted man named David when she was thirty-one. We'd all given up hope that she would ever marry, but once we met David, we understood why she waited so long. They were so well suited to each other. Aunt Florrie, who spent winters in Hallandale, Florida, snagged the most eligible widower in the community where she lived. She was always a charmer, and she certainly charmed Sam Serotte, a sweet man who always had a huge smile on his face. We were delighted for them.

Mommy did not attend either wedding because she no longer went to New York. She was too busy working, trying to support us.

After the weddings, Mommy did not mention Aunt Florrie or her family often. I wondered what happened but was too afraid to ask. Later I realized that she could not bear the turn her life had taken and was simply overwhelmed.

6

The Sunshine State

$\mathcal{M}$iami promised palm trees, warm seas, and year-round sunshine. It was the destination of Easterners weary of cold, gray winters and hot, humid summers. My father went there often, seeking the perennial tan, the best poker game, and the fastest ponies. He always traveled alone and stayed at the South Seas Hotel on Collins Avenue in Miami Beach.

My first trip to Florida was during the winter of 1952 with Mommy, Blanche, and Poppy. Daddy stayed in New Jersey to tend to the family business. As I recall, we went south to improve my health. The family doctor had just made a house call. Noting my frequent upper respiratory infections, pallor, and swollen glands, he said, "I think you should take Libby to Florida. It will be good for her health. She needs to be in a warmer climate." No one complained, except Blanche, who was eight and had to be enrolled in school during our three-month stay.

We took the train from Newark's Penn Station to Miami on that no-frills trip. It was either the *Silver Meteor* or *Champion*, both of which went from Newark to Miami. While we frequently took short train rides to New York, this trip would last all night, and we had not reserved sleeping berths. Our beds would be the straight-backed, wool-upholstered coach seats that made it nearly impossible to sleep. Poppy did his best to make us comfortable, and I was thrilled, when my mother announced, "We're in Jacksonville, Florida, girls. It won't be long before we reach Miami." The long train ride felt like torture.

Because we would be in Florida for the winter, Mommy, Poppy, Blanche, and I rented an apartment. My mother frequently spent the winter in Florida, and in 1941 invited my cousin Martin to spend a week with her there. He was only twelve and enjoyed the time with his aunt.

The winter we went to Florida, Blanche attended school on weekdays. Blanche hated school, and having to go to a different school while we were "on vacation" made it even worse. She had no choice. The first day she came home from school and announced, "My teacher's name is Mrs. Gumbo, like the soup. Isn't that a funny name?" We all agreed and began referring to Blanche's teacher as Mrs. Soup.

She would rather have been going to the beach and enjoying the warm sunshine. I can't recall what I did during the day, but Mommy and Poppy befriended the neighbors in our apartment complex, many of whom were Snowbirds like themselves. They'd play cards and talk about how wonderful the sun felt while people back home were dealing with cold weather and snow.

Blanche made friends with two teenage boys in the complex and brought them home to meet us. "Poppy, Mommy, meet Stevie and Rusty, my new friends." Both boys were much older than she, and my mother wondered why they would befriend an eight-year-old girl. Rumor had it that they had been in reform school.

"Blanche, why don't you invite one of your friends from school over?" she suggested.

"I don't know anyone that well," Blanche answered. "Besides, I have these guys next door."

Stevie and Rusty came by often, and sometimes they teased me. Most of their attention focused on my older sister.

On weekends Mommy kept Blanche busy by taking us both on outings. One time we went to Fort Lauderdale, where the Seminole Okalee Indian

Village was located. Since we had so many places named for Native American tribes in New Jersey and New York, Mommy thought she should introduce us to an active tribe in Florida.

Since Mommy did not drive, and she wanted us to experience Florida, we took a boat for the thirty-odd-mile trip. I loved gliding up the Miami River and dropping chunks of white bread into the water to feed the alligators that swam beside our boat. The captain pointed out other wildlife along the shore, but the alligators fascinated me most. "Girls, don't lean too far out of the boat," Mommy warned, as the alligators snapped up the bread.

When we arrived in Fort Lauderdale, we went to the Indian Village. A tall Indian brave stood sentinel over the village as we disembarked, and I grabbed Mommy's leg in fear. I had never seen a real Native American before. His coffee-colored skin was several shades darker than ours, and his hair was long and black, parted in the middle and plaited into braids. He wore a buckskin shirt and matching pants, beaded moccasins, and a beaded headband around his forehead.

"Libby, what's wrong?" Mommy asked.

I could not reply. This large Indian man stood there stone-faced, which frightened me. I was used to people smiling when they saw me, not staring straight ahead. I clung to Mommy's hand during our entire visit and was happy when we boarded the boat to return to Miami.

Another outing took us to the Miami Zoo, where Blanche was fascinated by the gorilla. She stood before his cage, teasing and taunting the poor creature until he reached into a nearby bucket of oranges, grabbed one, and heaved it at my sister, making a direct hit. Orange juice oozed everywhere, and afterwards Blanche was more subdued with the other animals. For once, she'd met her match.

When spring arrived, we returned to Hillside, and Florida became a pleasant memory.

My next trip to the Sunshine State came two years later, in August 1954, the summer I was six years old. This trip only Mommy, Blanche, and I would go. Poppy was not well enough to join us, and Daddy needed him to help run the tavern.

That August my mother, sister, and I went to Newark Airport, boarded an Eastern Airlines four-engine propeller plane, and flew to Florida. I had never been on an airplane and was excited. "Now, Libby, sit down and put your seat belt on," Mommy said. "In a few minutes, we'll start to go really fast down the runway and then the plane will take off into the sky."

The plane backed out of the gate, taxied to the runway, and then began to accelerate. "Yea, this is fun!" I exclaimed. "I've never gone so fast." The swift trip down the runway lasted only moments and then the plane ascended into the sky. I thought the clouds were beautiful as we became airborne. When we encountered some turbulence, I giggled, thinking that the bumps were fun. "This is like being on a roller coaster, Mommy."

"Don't worry," she answered. "We're just hitting air pockets. Keep your seat belt buckled."

Four hours later we arrived in sunny Florida, where we checked into the Marseilles Hotel, right next door to the South Seas, Daddy's usual haunt. Our adjoining rooms were on the fifth floor, and I could see the beach from our window.

The Marseilles was a lovely little hotel with a large swimming pool and the beach just beyond. Each morning we ate breakfast on the patio overlooking the pool, and I ordered the same meal: scrambled eggs, rye toast, and chocolate milk. Afterwards we changed into our bathing suits and headed for the pool.

I did not yet know how to swim, so I used my inner tube in the water until my mother enrolled Blanche and me in swimming lessons. Mommy was a strong swimmer and wanted us to learn to love the water as she did. Blanche could already swim, but she took lessons to improve her style. I was tentative, clinging to the pool's edges in a crab crawl, especially in the deep end, where the water was ten feet deep.

Our swim teacher encouraged me while Blanche stood by and cheered me on. Gradually, I let go of the side and practiced the crawl while swimming parallel to the side. Eventually I reached the deep water and kept on going. Mommy and Blanche applauded.

Blanche and I wanted to swim in the ocean, but Mommy was wary. The Atlantic was rough and unforgiving. Mommy warned us not to wade out too far. I was cautious and spent most days on the beach with my bucket and shovel while I waited for her and Blanche to take a dip. Mommy made me wear a white sailor hat and white tee shirt over my bathing suit to protect my fair skin from the sun. The layer of zinc oxide on my nose was the final insult and the only sun protection available besides the extra clothing. Ten minutes in the Florida sun had transformed me into Libby the Lobster our first day there, so my mother was vigilant.

I did not realize the ocean's other hazards until the morning I saw my mother and sister emerge from the water and rush to the lifeguard station. Mommy's face was contorted with pain. "Mommy, Mommy, what's wrong?" I asked as I ran toward her.

She pointed to her ankle, which was beginning to swell. "I was stung by a man-of-war," she answered, tears in her eyes. She always acted stoic when Blanche and I were around.

"Don't cry, Mommy," I said. "We're here, and you'll be all right."

The lifeguard grabbed his first aid kit and began to work on her wound. He applied warm seawater and heat to the sting. I later learned that heat inactivates the man-of-war's venom and prevents more toxin from being released.

During this treatment, I worried that my mother would faint. All the color had drained from her face. I knew she would not return to the water that day.

A second lifeguard appeared with a large blob of indigo gelatin that he plunked down on the beach. When I saw the man-of-war, I wondered how something so beautiful could cause such pain.

Mommy rested the remainder of that day, and the next day we awoke to an awful storm. Rain poured down while the wind bent nearby palm trees until they were almost horizontal. "Is this a hurricane?" I asked at breakfast, as we huddled under the awning.

"No," laughed our waiter. "It's just a summer storm. You would not want to be here in a hurricane. I don't think you'll go swimming today."

We went to a movie called *Three Coins in a Fountain* instead. I loved movies but did not understand this one, a love story that took place in Italy. The theme song was very popular, and it remained in my head for days.

I enjoyed live performances even better than movies and was thrilled the day Mommy came home and announced, "Look, girls, I bought tickets for a rodeo at the Orange Bowl. Hopalong Cassidy and Gene Autry will be in it along with other cowboys you've seen on television. It takes place in the evening, so we will have a special night out."

"Yea!" Blanche and I said in unison. We were thrilled to go to our first rodeo, especially because we'd get to stay up late.

That summer Mommy decided to have pastel portraits made of Blanche and me as a memento of our trip. I remember sitting in the artist's open studio on Collins Avenue for what felt like hours, as he sketched me. I wore the white shirt with the goldfish on it that Daddy had bought me in Philadelphia. My platinum-blond hair was styled in a page boy, and my green eyes peered straight ahead in the picture that resulted. "Hold still, please," the artist said.

"Mommy, I'm thirsty," I whined.

"When we're finished, I'll take you girls for lunch and an ice cream soda," Mommy promised.

I did my best to hold still, but the time I spent posing in that chair felt like forever that hot, summer morning.

At the hotel, people commented on my fair hair and would ask, "Do you dye her hair?" My mother usually ignored these comments, but one time she responded, "Yes." Later she said, "People ask such silly questions."

Another time, when we were in the elevator, a stranger stared at us and said, "You're mother and daughters? You don't look at all alike."

"That's right," my mother replied as she took our hands to exit.

"We do too look alike," I declared as we walked through the hotel's lobby. "We all have green eyes."

My mother smiled. Little did I know that strangers' remarks hurt her deeply, since she wanted few, if any, people to know that she did not give birth to her two daughters. That was family business, and she did not share it.

We enjoyed ourselves that month at the Marseilles Hotel, swimming, playing in the sand, eating in restaurants, going to movies, and taking excursions. Our vacation was filled with fun, until late one afternoon when the hotel's elevator became stuck between floors.

Mommy and I heard its alarm sound while we were in the lobby waiting for Blanche to come down for dinner. Mommy called our room, but no one answered.

"I shouldn't have sent her back to get a sweater," Mommy fretted, as she realized that my sister might be in the elevator.

Guests milled around the lobby looking for family members, and several came over to talk with us. "Have you seen Blanche?" Mommy asked. No one had.

My new friend Bella, who'd come to Florida with her aunt, was also missing. Her aunt came over to Mommy, and they sat down together, talking softly.

Time dragged that sweltering August afternoon, but we later learned it was much worse for those stuck in the elevator. At least ten people were inside, including my ten-year-old sister and seven-year-old friend.

Two-and-one-half hours later, workmen restored the elevator's power, the car returned to the lobby, and its doors opened. Mommy ran to hug Blanche, and I waited my turn, truly happy to see my big sister.

"It was horrible in that elevator," Blanche said. "First it stopped, then the lights went out, and after that the fan turned off. There were about ten of us, and we could barely breathe it was so hot."

Bella echoed Blanche's tale, and she, too, seemed very happy to be released from the elevator that had become her prison.

We went to dinner at last, but Blanche wanted to take the stairs when we came back to the hotel. Mommy finally convinced her that the elevator was safe once more, but Blanche took a great deal of convincing.

The afternoon before we planned to fly home, we went to one more movie, *The High and the Mighty*, starring John Wayne, Robert Stack, and Barbara Hale. The story told of an airliner whose engine caught fire while flying from Honolulu to San Francisco. The plane lost power, and it was uncertain whether it would make it across the Pacific safely. I felt tense watching the nervous passengers on the plane prepare to die. Blanche elevated my fear when she turned to me and said, "Libby, I just know our plane is going to crash tomorrow."

"Don't say that," I retorted. "You're always trying to scare me."

"You just wait," she replied.

Mommy made us go to bed very early that night because we had to be at Miami Airport by seven o'clock the next morning. I could not get to sleep, Blanche's words resounding in my ears.

We awoke to a sweltering Miami morning and quickly headed to the rustic airport, which was little more than a runway with outdoor waiting areas. We boarded the plane and took off on schedule. Almost immediately, the plane began bumping around. The blue sky was filled with billowy white clouds, and the turquoise ocean below looked picture perfect, but our four-engine airliner was agitating more than anticipated. The captain announced that we were experiencing a little turbulence, but he expected it to end as we headed out over the Atlantic for the flight north.

Blanche sat there looking smug as the bumps became more pronounced, certain that her previous day's prediction would come true. I tried to remain calm and stared out the window until Blanche said, "Look, Lib, the engine is on fire." The plane began bumping even more.

A few minutes later, the captain came on the radio again. "Ladies and gentlemen, we have a slight problem. One of our engines has failed. While we can make it to New Jersey with three, I don't want to take any chances. We're going to return to Miami Airport."

The plane banked steeply, and Blanche stood up in the aisle yelling, "I'm too young to die. I'm too young to die."

"Sit down," my mother screamed as she grabbed my sister's arm. I was mesmerized by the steep angle of the plane and the beautiful water below.

The stewardess prepared us for an emergency landing, and we made it safely back to Miami.

"Will we get on a different plane?" I asked.

"Of course," Mommy replied. But a new plane never came. We sat outside in the heat for four hours, sipping orange juice and waiting for them to repair our airliner. I was frightened when we climbed aboard the same plane, but this trip proved uneventful. Four hours later we landed at Newark Airport. Daddy greeted us with big hugs and many kisses. "I'm so glad my girls are all right," he said, smiling. "I was so worried."

He wasn't the only one. I never realized how much power my sister had over me until that day. Could she indeed predict the future?

I took no chances. I did not set foot on an airliner for the next twelve years.

7
Summer Camp

Sleep-away camp sounded so magical—swimming, archery, art classes, roasting marshmallows around a campfire, sleeping in a bunk with other girls, and spending most of our time outdoors all appealed to me. Being away from the summer heat and humidity in Hillside and my big sister were also bonuses. I could not wait to go.

Blanche went to Camp Harmony when she was ten, and I envied her. "Camp Harmony, Camp Harmony," I said over and over again. The name sounded idyllic. It offered horseback riding, swimming, archery, and a chance to be out in the country for the summer.

"Can I go, too?"

"Not right now," my mother answered. "In a few years, when you're ten, you'll be ready for sleep-away camp."

Mommy, Poppy, and Daddy visit Blanche at Camp Harmony.

That seemed to be the way it always was. Blanche got to go to Coney Island or nearby Olympic Park because she was older, and I had to stay home. There were many times I cried as I watched my sister leave for an outing with neighbors. I was considered "the baby" and too young to go along.

Blanche and I did attend day camp together. I must have been four, and she was eight the summer we went. Three days a week we rode the bus for what seemed like hours to get to Crystal Lake Camp, the two of us sitting in the back row absorbing the diesel fumes if we happened to be last on the bus. The fumes combined with the summer heat often made me woozy, and I struggled not to become carsick. Upon arrival we'd spend the day with children our own age doing arts and crafts, swimming, and playing games. About three in the afternoon, we raced for the bus, hoping to catch a front seat, away from the noxious fumes, on our ride back home.

At Crystal Lake Day Camp we swam in the pool. No one was allowed in the lake, which was too polluted and unsafe for swimming or any other water activities. My parents laughed at the camp's name, but they felt the atmosphere was safe and thought Blanche and I would enjoy ourselves there. So we spent our days playing ball, doing arts and crafts, swimming, and singing.

Day camp was one adventure after another. One morning when we were only halfway to camp, the bus driver abruptly pulled over to the curb and yelled, "Everyone off the bus now," The counselors quickly escorted us out the doors and lined us up along the sidewalk.

"What's wrong?" I asked Blanche, not realizing that smoke and flames were pouring from the bus.

"The bus is on fire, Lib. We have to stay here."

We stood on that sidewalk in the hot sun for a long time. A reporter from

The Newark Star Ledger spotted us and took our picture. The next morning our picture was in the newspaper with a story about the bus that caught fire. We experienced our ten minutes of fame after neighbors began calling to see if Blanche and I were all right.

At camp Blanche never missed a chance to show off by picking on me at lunch, when all the age groups ate together. She intimidated the other campers with her size and her bravado. More than once she'd say, "C'mon everyone, let's gang up on Libby. We don't want to play with her," just as she did in Hillside. Other youngsters followed her lead, and I often wound up in tears.

One afternoon right after lunch, she knocked me down and jumped on me. Her friend decided to add to the pile and jumped on her. I lay on the ground at the bottom screaming. When the counselors pulled Blanche and the other girl off, I was crying, "My shoulder hurts."

"Don't be such a baby, Lib," Blanche taunted.

I was taken to the infirmary, where the nurse applied an ice pack and made me rest. Then she put my right arm in a sling, and at three o'clock I was put on the fume-spewing bus for the long ride home.

"What happened?" my mother asked when I got off the bus.

"Blanche ganged up on me, and my shoulder really hurts," I whined.

"And they made you wait to go home?" she asked, as her face grew pale.

Off we went to see our pediatrician. He examined me and sent us to an orthopedic surgeon. "The x-ray shows that Libby has a fractured right collar-bone," he announced. "It's called a green-twig fracture, which means the bone didn't break all the way. She'll have to wear a cast for the rest of the summer."

My mother sat beside me while the doctor applied layers of gauze and plaster, creating a hot, heavy figure-eight vest on my small frame. "No swimming, and she'll have to take sponge baths until this comes off," he said.

That summer seemed to be the longest and the hottest of my young life. I never attended day camp again. But sleep-away camp was another matter!

By the time I was ten, my parents no longer could afford Camp Harmony, but I still dreamed of sleep-away camp. They found a Girl Scout camp in Blairstown, which was in western New Jersey near the Delaware Water Gap and the Pennsylvania border. It was several hours away by car, and it fit our budget. I could sign up for two-week intervals. "I'd like to go for a month," I declared.

"Are you sure?" my mother asked. "Do you really want to be away that long?"

"I'm ten now, Mommy. I can go swimming every day and have fun."

My parents agreed, and off I went.

What I pictured was far different from the reality that was Camp Kalmia. The bunks, constructed of roughhewn wood, each contained six cots with orange crates beside them to use as nightstands. They had screens and heavy wooden shutters we could close if the weather grew cold or rainy. A large central outhouse, about one hundred yards away, housed three wooden commodes for the ten bunks assigned to our age group. A separate building held metal troughs we used as sinks. One shower served our group of cabins, so we lined up and waited our turn on weekly shower nights. Since only cold water ran in the sinks and shower, we used the latter infrequently, preferring to bathe in the lake.

Camp Kalmia had many rules and a rigid schedule; as Girl Scouts, we were expected to obey. Each morning we got up, made our beds, and headed to the mess hall for breakfast. One person from each bunk served kitchen patrol (KP) duty daily and went ahead of the others to set the table and serve the food. We were all required to wear our rain boots and carry our flashlights whenever we left our bunks.

At each meal we had to eat at least two bites of everything served, even if we hated it. This rule was strictly enforced and was hardest for me on days when they served liver. Even though it was covered in gravy and smothered with onions, liver had a texture that made me gag. I could not chew it—but I had no choice.

During the first part of the morning we had nature study, arts and crafts, or archery. I loved archery and felt proud that I could hit the target, since I was never a good athlete.

Later in the morning, we swam in Lake Louise. I loved swimming and learning new strokes. The days when we held relay races were especially fun.

After our morning swim we went to lunch and then had ten minutes to choose something from the canteen. Our parents deposited money in the canteen so we could purchase candy, gum, flashlight batteries, or calamine lotion. I used a lot of the last item because the mosquitoes were merciless. One night I counted twenty-seven mosquito bites on my body.

An hour-long rest period followed our canteen visit. This was the time we were supposed to nap, read, write letters, or just lie quietly on our beds. Most of the time we just sat and talked. Often we talked about the counselors, who lived in separate bunks. We decided which ones were pretty, which ones were nice, and which had a boyfriend. We tried to guess their first names, since we had to address each as "Miss" followed by their last names. We wondered whether they had toilets, electricity, and hot water and suspected they did. Why else would these young women work at this camp?

Being the girl who did what she was told, I followed the rules most of the time. Sometimes I got in trouble for talking or laughing too loud during rest period, but I was in good company.

Afternoon activities ended rest period, and evenings were spent around the campfire singing or telling stories. Nights were the hardest for me. I was totally unprepared for the great sadness I felt being away from home. I'd waited so long to go to camp, and I thought I'd be fine, since I'd spent the night at friends' houses many times. At Camp Kalmia I was among strangers, and I missed my family terribly. For the first two weeks I cried every night and wrote long letters home each day. All ended with the sentence, "I miss you so much. Please come and take me home."

Daddy came to see me by himself.

I eagerly awaited visiting day—the second Sunday after I arrived. On visiting day, parents and siblings brought picnic lunches and presents. I could not wait to see my mother and hear the news from home.

When my father's car pulled into camp and he stepped out alone, I almost cried. I ran and hugged him, smothering him with kisses and asked, "Daddy, Daddy, where are Mommy and Blanche?"

"Blanche is sick. She had a very bad headache and fever this morning. Mommy is home with her now waiting for the doctor," my father replied. "I wanted to make sure that you weren't alone, so I came and brought us a picnic."

My face fell when I heard the news, but I did not want my father to see my disappointment. He'd driven so far to ensure I would not be alone. We spent a wonderful afternoon together, and I felt much better about staying at camp after his visit. When I returned home, I learned that the doctor suspected Blanche might have had polio. No wonder my mother didn't come.

The next two weeks flew by, and I was no longer sad. By the time I left Camp Kalmia, I'd decided to return the following summer and stay two months.

I entered fifth grade in fall 1958 and waited expectantly for my return to camp. In July 1959, I left home for my two-month stay.

I had a whole new group of friends my second summer. My bunkmates were friendly enough. I was especially close to two, Franny and Renee. Franny was chubby, happy, and outgoing. Her light brown hair was cut in a short pixie, and her skin tanned easily after a few days at camp. She lived in Clifton, near Jersey City. Renee was from Newark. She was sweet but had trouble adjusting to camp. She fretted over making her bed and whined that the food was too spicy—it hurt her throat. Her pale skin burned easily in the sun, and she always seemed uncomfortable, no matter what we were doing. I felt sorry for her and tried to help, remembering how hard my first summer away was.

I saw Camp Kalmia in a different light my second year. I looked forward to going swimming and did so enthusiastically my first few days. One morning as I walked toward the lake I saw some long, thin, black creatures sunning themselves on rocks near the swimming area. As I got closer, the objects slithered into the water, and I began screaming, "Snakes! Snakes! There are snakes in the lake."

"Calm down, Libby," the counselor said. "They're harmless. We wouldn't let you swim here if there were water moccasins in the lake."

I was not convinced. After that I entered the water gingerly, scanning the bottom for any rapid movements. I thought of East Hanover Swim Club and wished I were there swimming in the pool with Neil instead of in a snake-infested lake.

The snakes were not my only nemesis in the lake. One day my friend Claire and I rowed across the lake during boating class. The weather was beautiful when we started, sunny with just a few clouds in the sky. It took us a good fifteen minutes to row across, when suddenly we heard thunder in the distance, and our counselor motioned for us to head back to shore. Claire and I turned the boat around easily enough, but our oars became stuck in dense vegetation, and we could not move. The storm moved in quickly, and we grew scared. We motioned for help, since we were too far from shore to yell.

Miss Polleco and Miss Jones jumped into another boat and rowed toward us. When they reached our rowboat, one of them removed our oars from their holders and lifted them out of the water to free them. The other hitched a tow-line to our boat and began rowing as the rain poured down. Huge streaks of light-ening lit up the ever-darkening sky, and we were relieved when we made it to shore minutes later. "Run for the boathouse, girls" Miss Polleco yelled. And we did!

Even though the lake lost some of its appeal, I still enjoyed other camp activities. Hide-and-seek after dinner was a favorite game. One night Franny, Renee, and I came upon a trail in the woods and decided to follow it. We could hear male voices in the distance and were curious. Even though our bunkmates were hiding elsewhere in the woods, we ventured on, hoping to discover new horizons. We arrived at a fence with a hole in it. On the other side was a golf course, where a group of boys stood talking. "We've found Blairstown Acad-emy," I announced, "and a way out of camp. Let's not tell anyone about this." Franny and Renee just nodded.

A few days later, my stay at camp grew worse. I had a disagreement with another camper—Thomasina Lemon. She was a large, intimidating girl from Newark, who was thought of as a bully. Other campers were afraid of her. I decided not to let her intimidate me after we exchanged words and I taunted, "Fat Thomasina belongs in a circus arena."

Her face grew stormy and she ran after me. I could run faster and sought shelter in the nearest place—my bunk. "Hide me, hide me," I screamed. "Thomasina is after me."

Franny and Renee put two orange crates side by side in the bunk's cor-ner, and I crouched behind them, sweating.

Thomasina threw open the door and yelled, "Where's Libby?"

"She's not here," Franny lied. "I think she went to KP duty."

"You tell her I want to see her," Thomasina said and left.

I shook, hoping she would not discover me. After ten minutes my legs grew tired, and I could not stop sweating. I wanted to come out. But what could I do? I knew Thomasina would beat me up. I crouched there and thought about what I'd said. It was awfully mean and not like me. After another ten minutes, I decided to face the consequences of my words. I came out from behind the crates and announced, "I'm going to apologize."

"I'll go with you," Franny said.

I knocked on Thomasina's bunk and hoped she wouldn't hit me. "I came to apologize. I should not have said what I did. I know what it's like to be teased. I'm really sorry," I said and offered my hand to shake.

Thomasina stared at me. I wasn't sure what she'd do next. I don't know if anyone had ever apologized to her before. "That was really mean," she said. "Don't do that again. You hurt my feelings." She shook my hand and relaxed.

I then realized that the camp bully was just like me. She had feelings, too. I still think of Thomasina and my cruelty to her and feel fortunate she forgave me.

Nature has a way to restore balance in the world, and I got my comeuppance a few days later. I was in the outhouse doing my business, when I felt a fly buzz by my head. I swatted it and felt it fall into my rain boot. I didn't think anything of it until a few seconds later when something stung my ankle. I pulled up my shorts and ran outside screaming, "Something stung me in the outhouse." My friend Franny ran and pulled off my boot. Out flew a big, black wasp. Off we went to the infirmary.

Between my experiences at the lake, my altercation with Thomasina, and my outhouse experience, I became disenchanted with Camp Kalmia. I pondered my options during rest period and decided to take action.

I approached the camp director and asked, "May I call my parents? I really want to go home."

"Libby, you know that phone calls aren't allowed," she replied. "Go back to your bunk and write them a letter."

I did what I was told and then got distracted by other camp activities. The drama class was putting on a play, and I loved drama.

Visiting day came, my parents arrived, and I felt better about staying at camp—until the rain began. It rained for four days straight after they visited. The camp was enveloped in a gray, wet gloom. The glow was gone. All our activities took place indoors.

I felt sad and had had enough. All I wanted was to go home. That night I hatched my plan. I would leave camp the next morning, using the trail that led to Blairstown Academy, climb through the hole in the golf course fence, and walk home. Hillside was a long distance away, but I could not bear to stay at camp any longer.

After breakfast the next morning, the girls in our cabin returned to the bunk to prepare for the day. The rain had stopped, but my mood was as dark as the clouds that threatened overhead. I donned my raincoat and boots, stuck my flashlight in one pocket and my only food stash—twenty packs of Juicy Fruit gum—in the other.

"What are you doing?" asked Franny.

"I'm going home," I announced, trying not to let my fear show. I'd never done anything like this before, and I wasn't sure I could actually go through with my plan.

"If you're leaving, I'm going, too," Franny declared.

Hearing her words, I could no longer back out. Franny thought of me as the leader, and I had to act the part. "All right," I said. "You can come. Let's wait until the other girls leave for arts and crafts, and then we'll head into the woods and take the trail we found last week."

Ten minutes later we were gone. Neither of us were experienced hikers, so we walked along the road facing traffic. We also scanned the ground ahead for the creatures we dreaded most—snakes. The mountains of northern New Jersey were home to rattlesnakes, copperheads, and water moccasins. The latter wouldn't be a problem, and the rattlers gave warnings, but the copperheads were the most troublesome in our minds.

Heading down the road, Franny turned to me and said, "Let's head to my house. Clifton is closer than Hillside. Your parents can pick you up there."

"Good idea," I answered. I knew that Clifton was in the direction of Jersey City, gateway to New York, and at least ten miles closer to camp.

We walked on, carefully scanning the approaching cars. If one looked like a New Jersey state trooper, we ran into the woods beside the road and threw ourselves face down, flat on the ground, the way we'd seen escaped convicts do in movies. We felt so smug.

By midmorning we arrived in Blairstown, which was like many American rural towns in the late fifties. It contained a bank, post office, general store, and a few small businesses along Main Street. Because we had no money, we could not stop to buy something to eat or drink, and both of us felt thirsty. As we exited town, we spotted a young woman walking a few feet ahead of us.

"Hi," I said.

"Good morning, girls," she replied. "Where are you headed?"

"We're just out for a walk," I answered.

"Where are you from?" the woman asked.

"Oh, my family just moved here," I lied. "My friend Franny is visiting this week."

The woman smiled, "My name is Sandy, and I'm on my way home from the post office. My mother lives nearby, and I'm visiting for the week. Will you come in for a snack?"

Franny just rolled her eyes. I hesitated. From the time I was a toddler, I'd been told never to talk to or go off with strangers. Now I was walking down a country road with a young woman I met two minutes earlier, and she'd invited me home. I wasn't sure what to do, but my thirst won out. Sandy seemed safe enough.

"Sure," I replied. "That's very kind of you."

Sandy's mother, Mrs. Covington, lived in a large, two-story, Victorian house just outside of town. The screened-in front porch with its swing and chairs looked inviting after having walked for more than an hour.

Sandy's mother welcomed us. "Come in, girls. I've just baked some cookies, and I'll make you some cocoa."

"Thank you," we said in unison.

We sat and chatted while we munched. The cocoa tasted delicious, but I could barely swallow it. What was I doing leaving camp and sitting in a stranger's house having cocoa and cookies, I asked myself. This behavior was unlike anything I'd ever done.

"Sandy said you just moved to town, Libby. Where do you live?" Mrs. Covington asked.

"Uh, you know we just arrived, and I can't remember the address," I stammered. "Our house is on Main Street." Now I was lying, to compound my mischief. My mother taught me that lying was a sin; I was never to lie—ever. Consequently, I'd always been a terrible liar, and I could tell Mrs. Covington didn't believe my story. I motioned to Franny to finish her cocoa and announced, "I'm sorry. We have to go. My mother will be worried." These were the first true words I'd uttered in the past half hour. "Thank you very much. We really enjoyed our snack."

Franny and I headed back to the road and walked on. "Do you think they believed us?" she asked.

"No," I said. "We have to be even more careful now. But it was really nice to have something to eat and drink, wasn't it?"

Franny nodded, and we walked on. The sun had finally come out, and the morning was growing warm. I sweated under my plastic raincoat, but it afforded me some protection from the sun and forest creatures. My flashlight and gum were in my pockets, so we continued to walk and began to sing to pass the time.

An hour later a tan Volkswagen beetle headed down the road in the opposite direction, but we paid no attention to it. A long walk lay ahead, and it was nearly noon. The car suddenly slowed, made a U-turn, and stopped. An older woman at the wheel leaned over and threw open the passenger door. "Get in girls," she ordered. "We've been looking for you all morning. You didn't make yourselves easy to find."

I took that as a compliment and smiled as I looked at Miss O'Neill, the assistant camp director, who was at the wheel. In a way I felt relieved. We headed to the car and obeyed her orders.

"What did you think you were doing?" Miss O'Neill asked.

"We wanted to go home," I answered. "I asked you if I could call my parents, and you wouldn't let me. So I did what I needed to do to go home."

"You'll get your wish now," Miss O'Neill said quietly.

She drove us back to camp and took us to the infirmary. We were checked by the nurse and given lunch. We could not leave the infirmary or talk to any other campers. We had become the "bad girls," and news of our escape was the talk of the camp.

My mother arrived alone about three hours later. She was pale, and I could see she had been crying. She hugged me for a long time and said, "I'm so glad you're all right. When the camp called, they said you had run away and they'd found you. They didn't say if you were hurt. I've been so worried the entire way here. You must promise you'll never do anything like this again."

"I'm sorry, Mommy," I cried. "I promise this will never happen again. I just wanted to go home and be with you." We left a few minutes later.

Shortly after I returned from camp, I became very ill. My fever soared to 105 degrees, as I lay alone in my darkened bedroom, wondering if this was punishment for my misdeed. I could not eat or drink for days. Once again, my mother worried, making me feel even worse.

After I recovered, I moped at home. I had missed my opportunity to be away and felt sad and lonely. Most of my neighborhood friends were still at camp having a good time.

One warm, rainy summer evening I asked, "Can we go for ice cream?"

Mommy seemed happy that my appetite was back and drove me to Dairy Land, an ice cream store on Liberty Avenue that made freshly churned ice cream in an assortment of flavors. I chose a hot fudge sundae. Mommy had nothing.

I nibbled away as Mommy put the car in gear for the short drive home. We'd gone only a block when a pickup truck veered across the center line on Liberty Avenue and skidded into us head on. A tall, thin man wearing a baseball cap got out of the truck and came toward our car.

"Are you all right?" he asked. "I'm so sorry. The road is slick, and when I braked, I skidded into you."

Mommy sat gripping the wheel and shook her head. A police car and ambulance pulled up a minute later. When the ambulance attendant took Mommy's blood pressure, he said, "You need to go to the hospital. Your blood pressure is 240 over 120. You could have a stroke."

"I'm all right," my mother insisted. "I'd like to go home now."

The emergency crew objected, but Mommy was adamant. I think she wanted to believe she'd escaped the family curse—heart disease—and she ignored the symptoms.

Since our car was still operable, she drove us home—slowly. Suddenly, my ice cream sundae no longer tasted good, and I tossed it in the trash when we entered the house.

Mommy called the doctor, and eventually Daddy came home and drove her to the hospital for a checkup. Her blood pressure was still high, and the doctor prescribed medicine and sent her home. After that, she went to the doctor more often for checkups. I had no clue how ill she really was.

That summer I learned that my behavior had the power to hurt those I loved, and I vowed never to hurt my mother again. It would take time to regain my role as the good girl.

8

The Graduation Dress

"Mommy, can I really have this?" I
asked, as I looked at the dress I'd coveted since 1958.

"Yes, with a few alterations it should fit nicely. Your sister will never
wear it again, and it will be perfect for all the bar mitzvah parties you'll attend
this year."

"Oh, I can't wait to attend my first bar mitzvah."

I adored the dress my mother had bought my sister, Blanche, for her
eighth grade graduation two years earlier. With its fitted bodice, cap sleeves,
and scoop neck, it looked like something a princess would wear. The skirt was
made from yards and yards of filmy, white organza decorated with pink polka
dots, which were also on the bodice. A wide pink satin cummerbund accented
the waist. I'd always loved it, and now it would be mine.

I remember some details of Blanche's eighth grade graduation so well—the arrival of Zayde Berger from Philadelphia, the playing of "Pomp and Circumstance," my parents attending a function together. Other details are a blur. I guess I wasn't paying much attention to Blanche.

I was focused on my own graduation outfit and lack of appropriate accessories. I wanted to wear my pink dress with the sailor collar, but the only dress shoes I had were red patent leather. In 1958 this combination was a definite fashion "don't," but I didn't have any other options. I had one pair of school shoes and one pair of dress shoes, as did most of my friends. Although my parents were upper middle class, they didn't want to "spoil" us, and my mother was careful when it came to buying us things.

During her childhood, Blanche was the ultimate tomboy and didn't seem interested in what she wore. She seemed happier hanging out with the neighborhood boys—Bobby and Sandy Bloom, across the street; Stuie (Stuart) Lieberman, in the house behind ours; and the Schuckman boys on Clark Street. Blanche preferred to ride bikes, climb trees, and throw rocks. My parents took to dressing her in dungarees (jeans) and striped polo shirts (tee shirts) that I eventually inherited.

Blanche rarely spent time with Aunt Pearl and Uncle Moe's daughter Ruth, who was four years older than she and lived next door. Ruth was an auburn-haired beauty who played piano, sang like an angel, and earned good grades. She was always smiling, popular with everyone, and someone I looked up to.

Nor would Blanche give Neil's sister, Ellen, a passing nod. Ellen was petite, with dark curls and a beautiful face that resembled a young Elizabeth Taylor. She was a piano virtuoso, who attended Juilliard while still in high school.

Ruth and Ellen were ladies and my role models, but my older sister had little to do with them.

While Blanche paid Ruth and Ellen little attention, for some reason she hated Sheila Gelfond, who lived in the corner house beside ours and was a year or two older. Sheila was overweight and quiet, always kind, but shy and reserved. One day Blanche was bored and rang the Gelfonds' doorbell. "Can Sheila play?" she asked. The two spent a few hours together, and Blanche came home.

An hour later, the Gelfonds called my parents. "Is Sheila at your house? We can't find her," Mrs. Gelfond said.

My parents helped them search the neighborhood, but no one could find Sheila. It began to grow dark, and the Gelfonds were just about to call the police, when my parents suggested they check inside their house one more time. The adults searched every room, opening closets and looking behind doors. They discovered poor Sheila bound, gagged, and locked in her own closet. Blanche was never invited to play there again.

One day, a few months later, just after my mother returned from the grocery store, Blanche said, "Lib, watch this." She grabbed an apple from the grocery bag, went down three steps to our side door, opened it, and threw the apple directly through the window in the Gelfonds' side door. The sound of shattering glass made me run upstairs.

A few minutes later our doorbell rang. My mother greeted Mr. Gelfond, who stood with apple in hand and asked, "Does this belong to you?"

"I'll check," my mother answered. She quickly returned to the door, embarrassed once more by my sister's actions. After that the Gelfonds barely acknowledged us.

While Blanche did not get along with the neighborhood girls her age, when she reached adolescence, she developed a whole new relationship with the boys. She began wearing more feminine clothes: tight capris, short shorts, pedal pushers, and sleeveless tops that revealed her budding breasts. The neighbors occasionally made comments about her dress and demeanor that were not meant for my ears. I overheard them and did not understand what they meant.

My sister and I were so different that most people did not know we were sisters. I had an average build, blond hair, and my once-blue eyes were now hazel, like my mother's and sister's. I was the people-pleaser, the good student, and the sweet child who always wanted to do the right thing.

Blanche was the rebel and always the tallest in her class, eventually reaching a height of nearly six feet. She needed extensive orthodontia to correct a severe underbite. By the time she was old enough for orthodontia, she developed bad acne to go along with her braces. Her straight, chestnut-brown hair, hazel eyes, and ski-jump nose were clearly her prettiest features. When she began bleaching her hair with straight peroxide, it turned orangey-yellow. Blanche's attempts to make herself more attractive did not seem to work, based on what I saw and what others said.

While walking to school with a friend, I overheard some older girls talking about my sister. One said, "Blanche's hair is so orange and dry that it looks like a bird's nest with shit in it." I was hurt and did not understand how someone could say something so awful about my big sister. Although I was afraid of her, she was still family.

As eighth-grade graduation drew near, my mother took Blanche to the hairdresser for a new style that would complement the lovely dress. He cut Blanche's shoulder-length, over-bleached hair short, added some curl and eliminated most of the split ends that came from a year of putting straight peroxide on it.

Sadly, the hairdresser could not do anything about Blanche's teeth. My parents had begun her orthodontia work when she was only ten, and she had been wearing braces for nearly four years.

One day while Mommy was at the market, Blanche became frustrated with her braces and began removing them with pliers. "Blanche, please stop, you'll hurt yourself," I begged, when I saw what she was doing.

"Get me something to cut this off, Lib," she pleaded.

The scissors I brought did not work, and all I could do was watch in horror until Mommy came home. She burst into tears when saw Blanche standing in the kitchen with a foot-and-a-half of wire protruding from her mouth. Off they went to Dr. Kessler, but the damage had already been done.

Blanche's grammar school graduation was a major event at our house. My parents were celebrating their ability to get their first child through elementary school, despite a number of obstacles. Blanche was smart, but she was not a good student. She greeted authority with hostility. Many of the teachers were afraid of her because she'd threatened to strike one. Her size and her attitude were intimidating.

When I began elementary school four years after she enrolled, my teacher asked, "Are you Blanche Berger's sister?"

"Yes," I said, "but I'm not at all like her."

The teacher smiled, but she wasn't convinced until a few weeks later, after she had a chance to know me.

The school district even hired a psychologist to deal with Blanche's behavior problems, but Dr. Lyon's visits did not help much. My sister did not do her homework or pay attention in class. School was the last place she wanted to be, and she only went because she had to. On the days when she decided not to go, my parents would receive phone calls from neighbors who had spotted Blanche somewhere in town. Hillside was a small community, and the only way Blanche could escape the neighbors' prying eyes was to broaden her geographic base.

She would go "Down Neck," an undesirable area of Newark, and pick up older boys. Some were grown men. She brought one home the year she was in eighth grade, and my parents took an instant dislike to this tall, blond-haired, blue-eyed guy who wore tight dungarees and white tee-shirts with rolled sleeves where he kept his cigarettes. Bob Belachek had an edge. I heard my mother use the word "ex-con" to describe him, and I realized he'd been in jail. She begged Blanche not to see him.

Her pleas only made Blanche more eager to date Bob. I would watch from my second-floor window when he brought my fourteen-year-old sister home at night. It took them a long time to say good night, and I wondered what went on in that car. But I was only ten and not attuned to their world, which was so different from mine.

Mine was a world filled with books and music. I loved school. As soon as I began to read, I joined Weekly Reader Book Club. Each month a book would arrive in the mail addressed to me. I eagerly awaited these packages and savored their contents. By second grade, I had my own library card. Neil and I walked down the street to the library, located inside Hillside City Hall, where I checked out a stack of books every two weeks.

Music played a major role in my early years. Our neighborhood housed some accomplished musicians, who were close friends, and we sometimes gathered at their houses to hear them play. Uncle Moe, Ruth's father, played violin beautifully. Jack Bloom played the cello, and Joe Goodman played the clarinet and piano. These role models made me want to learn to play other instruments, but Mommy encouraged me to take piano lessons as Blanche did.

I began studying piano when I was in first grade. I begged my parents to let me start earlier, but my mother felt I should learn how to read before I learned to read music. I studied classical with Mrs. Pearl Lutzky and practiced every day. I was so proud of my progress. By the time Blanche graduated I was almost able to play "Pomp and Circumstance."

Blanche first studied popular music with Mrs. Lutzky's husband, Harry, who had a small band that often played at local bar mitzvahs and weddings. She then continued her studies with Mr. White, a tall thin black man, who seemed a better teacher for her.

By eighth grade Blanche no longer took piano. Her main focus was boys, fun, and anything that drove my parents crazy. Their goal was to get her through school.

In the months before graduation Blanche put on weight, and my mother began buying larger clothes for her. The graduation dress was one of those items, and it was the prettiest thing she owned. I had no idea what lay beneath that dress.

By late spring Bob Belachek no longer came around to take Blanche out, and I figured they broke up. No one spoke of him in our house.

A few weeks before the graduation, our doorbell rang at three in the morning, awakening our whole family. My parents went downstairs to see who was at the door. Blanche and I stood near the top of the steps, frightened but curious. My parents opened the door to a uniformed policeman. "Mr. and Mrs. Berger, do you know this man? A neighbor spotted him prowling in your back yard."

The policeman stepped aside, and there stood Bob Belachek, all six-feet-something of him. He sneered at my parents and said, "I told you I'd kill her."

Blanche and I ran up to the safety of our bedrooms, and the policeman took Bob down to the station.

I had trouble going back to sleep. I no longer feared the bogeyman. A real monster had arrived at our door.

Graduation day came, and Blanche looked lovely in her new dress. My parents and Zayde were proud, and afterwards we all came home to celebrate with a special luncheon.

That was the summer I went to Camp Kalmia for the first time. On the first visiting day, Blanche was ill and Daddy came to see me alone. When I returned home after a month, Blanche was gone. "Where's Blanche?" I asked. I remembered how she'd been so ill on camp visiting day two weeks earlier, and my mother had had to stay home with her.

"She's gone to Buffalo to spend some time with Aunt Florrie," my mother replied.

"How come she gets to spend the summer with Aunt Florrie, and I don't?" I asked.

"She's older and getting ready to start high school," my mother answered. "Aunt Florrie is going to make a lady out of her."

Whenever I wanted to go somewhere my sister went or do something she did, I was told I had to wait "because Blanche was older." She may be older,

I thought, but I'm sweeter. Why can't I go, too? I didn't voice this last thought because my mother already seemed upset.

I thought of my sweet little aunt and wondered how she would accomplish this. No one in our house had been successful in making Blanche a lady. Aunt Florrie and my mother were close friends, and her daughters, Davida and Mimi, and son, Tim, and his wife, Sue, were special cousins. If anyone could help Blanche, perhaps they could.

Davida was my role model; she was a lady as well as a career girl. After she graduated college, she moved to New York City and often spent weekends at our house in New Jersey. She brought all her weekend necessities in a small train case, which amazed me. Davida was a world traveler and believed in traveling light. I looked up to my cousin, who was tall and slim with a headful of dark curls and large brown eyes. She had the most beautiful complexion, and all she ever used on her skin was Ivory soap. One time when she came, she saw me trying to apply nail polish and taught me how to give myself a proper manicure. Davida was more of a big sister and mentor than my own sister. I hoped she could help Blanche.

After Blanche left that summer, the house was quiet. Although my older sister terrified me with her tales, stole my allowance, and took my clothes, which were several sizes too small for her and she ultimately ruined, I missed her. That summer when I returned to a quiet house that held me, our toy fox terrier puppy, Bonnie Sue, and my parents, I was lonely. I passed the time with Neil and other neighborhood kids or at the swim club.

When school started that fall, Blanche still hadn't returned. "Isn't Blanche going to start Hillside High?" I asked my mother.

"She's decided to stay in Buffalo and go to school there," my mother replied. "She's happy with Aunt Florrie."

I felt sad. I began fifth grade and was assigned to Mrs. Crane, the same teacher Blanche had had. My days were filled with school, friends, and after-school visits to the Jewish Center in Newark. I took Israeli folk dancing, cooking, and drama there.

Thanksgiving came around, but Aunt Florrie did not come to our house that year, as she had in the past. Davida did, but Thanksgiving was not the same without Blanche.

Chanukah and Christmas vacation arrived, and Blanche still had not returned. Over the holidays my mother took me to New York City by train to visit Davida. We stayed in her apartment on East 76th Street in the heart of Manhattan. This was a first, and I was thrilled.

After we arrived at Penn Station in New York, my mother became winded climbing the flights of stairs from the train concourse to the street. She had to rest several times, and a stranger stopped to help her carry our suitcase. I became worried and wondered what was wrong.

We took a cab to Davida's apartment, a fourth-floor walk-up, and my poor mother's face fell. I bounded up the stairs easily. She took them in stages. Eventually she reached the top, and Davida welcomed us to New York. That visit began with foreboding. I'd heard my mother talk about the "family curse," although I wasn't exactly sure what that meant. I worried that she had inherited it.

That afternoon we went to see the New York City Ballet perform *The Nutcracker*. I owned the record album and knew the music by heart, but I was mesmerized by the dancers. The Sugar Plum Fairy was played by Maria Tallchief, a renowned ballerina. I thought she was beautiful with her tall, slender body and striking black hair.

After the ballet we went to dinner at a small neighborhood restaurant, The Wiffenpoof. I thought the restaurant's name was funny but loved the food.

The next day we headed to the Museum of Natural History, my favorite museum, where the dinosaur exhibit greeted us in the entry hall. Even though these great thunder lizards were not alive, they frightened me. I'd seen too many scary movies with Neil.

That weekend in New York City with my mother and Davida was magical, and it made the lonely holiday season special for me. I wondered what my sister was doing for the holidays and figured she'd be freezing up in Buffalo. Perhaps I was the lucky one after all.

January arrived, and one morning at breakfast Mommy said, "I have good news. Blanche is coming home next week."

"Hooray!" I said. Even though my sister often made me miserable, I still loved her and missed her terribly. The day she was due home was a school day, and I could not concentrate in class. Instead, I sat and watched the clock. Finally 3:15 p.m. came around, and I hurried home with Neil.

In our kitchen sat this tall, slender young woman wearing a wool plaid straight skirt and a sweater. Her long, dark hair was styled in a French twist, and she wore some lipstick and powder. She and my mother were having coffee and cigarettes.

Who was this woman, I asked myself. As I got closer, I realized it was Blanche. Aunt Florrie had succeeded. She'd made a lady out of her.

"Hi, Lib. How have you been?" she smiled and opened her arms to give me a hug. My big sister was back.

Mommy made Blanche's favorite foods for dinner that night, and my parents talked with her about enrolling at Hillside High the following week. I thought all seemed well, and we would return to our normal family life.

The following week, Blanche started school as planned. My parents hoped that high school would offer a new start, but on the third day, Blanche came home in tears. Between sobs she said, "Bob Belachek came by school today and asked everyone he saw this question: 'Who started the rumor that Blanche Berger had a baby?' My secret is out. I can't go back to school."

I felt sorry for my sister, but I also felt stupid. So that's why Blanche had grown so large. She was pregnant with Bob Belachek's baby. How could I have been so naive? The graduation dress's full skirt had hidden my sister's growing middle and covered her in a sheath of innocence.

Blanche quit high school by the end of that week. Shortly afterwards, she enrolled in beauty college to become a hairdresser, which began a whole new chapter in our lives. I have pictures that show just how successful she was.

Bob Belachek came back into our lives, appearing in the neighborhood at odd intervals, swearing to carry out his threat to kill Blanche. My parents were vigilant, locking doors, which was not a custom in our small township. Stalkers were unknown in the late 1950s, and restraining orders were rare. There was nothing else they could do. One of them tried to be home at all times.

About two years after Blanche had their baby, Bob Belachek showed up at our door one afternoon. Daddy was at work, and Mommy had gone to the market. Our housekeeper Josephine was home with us. I don't know why Blanche let Bob in, but she did. "Where is my baby?" he demanded. "I want to see him."

"I don't know," Blanche replied. "My parents made sure he went to a good home. They didn't tell me where they placed him."

"You're lying," Bob screamed. "Tell me where he is."

"Get out," Blanche yelled. "Leave right now."

Bob grabbed her by the throat with both hands and started to strangle her.

I stood there screaming, "Stop, stop, you'll kill her," and began trying to pull his hands off her neck.

Josephine ran into the hallway and began beating Bob on the back. He would not let go.

My sister fought back. She was strong, but no match for Bob. Then she grabbed a penknife from Bob's pocket and began slashing his forehead, while he had her in a stranglehold.

"Help, help," I yelled. I did not know what to do. I called Mrs. Goodman, but she told me to call the police. I ran back to my sister and screamed my loudest, "Stop, stop, don't kill my sister."

Bob stared at Blanche, but he was beginning to give up. Between the cuts in his forehead, my screams, and Josephine's pounding, Bob finally let go and ran out the door. We locked it and stood there shaking.

"I told you that man was trouble," Josephine exclaimed, shaking her head. "No way he should ever come near here again."

That incident convinced my parents to obtain a restraining order, forbidding Bob to be within 500 feet of our home. Blanche grew fearful every time she and I were home alone, especially in the evenings. Since Daddy worked most nights, and Mommy often played cards, mah jong, or bingo with her friends, we were home alone at night fairly often. On those evenings, Blanche would go through the house and close the drapes and blinds, make sure that all the doors and windows were locked, and sit in the living room with me watching TV. She locked the door from the kitchen to the basement and would not even go down to the freezer for ice cream.

One Friday night, when I was at a friend's house and our parents were both out, Blanche stayed home alone. She began hearing noises outside and immediately called the police. She feared that Bob was trying to break in and carry out the threat he'd made years earlier when the neighbors spotted him in our yard. He still wanted to kill her, and she believed he would not stop until he had.

Police cars surrounded the house, and when Mommy saw the flashing lights, she returned from her card game, only two doors away. "Why did you call the police?" she asked. "I was only at the Goodmans' house." After that, Mommy did not leave Blanche alone.

Looking back, I find it ironic that the big sister who had spent her childhood scaring me was now the one who felt scared. Seeing how her behavior endangered our family and hurt my parents, I vowed to keep my innocence for as long as I could. Blanche's graduation dress was beautiful, but it held a deep secret, one that took me years to fully comprehend. I hoped that I would never be so naive again.

9
Care Taking

$\mathcal{F}$rom the time I was small, I knew that my mother was colorblind. She had grown up in the same neighborhood as many of Daddy's customers. When her own mother became ill with heart trouble, the family's Negro neighbors had taken my mother and uncle in and cared for them. She learned to judge others by their character and treated everyone with respect.

Because she was a better cook than housekeeper and in her late forties, Mommy had a revolving roster of household helpers. Many were wives, friends, or family members of Daddy's patrons. I recall a few: Mary, our only live-in helper, who we discovered had a drug problem; Edith, a kind, hardworking lady who always smiled but had a drinking problem; Josephine Penny Hawkins, a woman whose self-esteem and opinions were as large as her ample bosom;

and Hey-Ruth, a quiet, kindly woman who arrived occasionally when Mommy called.

Mommy laid down the rules to us regarding her helpers. They were not "maids" but "housekeepers." We were to speak to them with respect and do as they asked, especially if Mommy had to go out, and they assumed child care duties.

All of these women were kind caregivers, but I especially loved Hey-Ruth. Her unfortunate nickname came from me, a child who often said "Hey, this" and "Hey, that." For some reason, I began to say "Hey-Ruth," and the moniker stuck. I realize now that it was disrespectful.

Hey-Ruth loved me, despite the demeaning nickname I'd given her, and we developed a special bond. This soft-spoken woman with a café-au-lait complexion and pleasant demeanor cared for me with love. I remember the day my mother sent me to day camp dressed in white shorts and a white blouse. We made ashtrays and painted them that hot summer day. Being a creative soul, I began to experiment. First I used red paint on my ashtray, added some blue, and then yellow. Before I knew it, my crude creation was mud brown. So were my arms, legs, clothing, and platinum-blond hair! Hey-Ruth took one look at me when the bus dropped me off and said, "Libby, let's get you into the bathtub before your mother gets home." She lovingly bathed me, washed my hair, and soaked my paint-saturated clothes. Mommy never knew.

My memories of some of our family's helpers relate more to their interaction with the many pets that passed through our doors. Earl, my father's bartender, was a loyal employee who helped us out in many ways.

In 1952, when my mother, sister, Poppy, and I went to Florida for the winter, we owned our first dog, Kelly. She was a light brown terrier mix, playful, puppy-like, frisky, and full of fun. I held her in my arms and cuddled her, my own live stuffed animal. I was too young to walk or feed her, and I imagine these tasks fell upon my mother.

Because we were going away and Daddy had to work, Earl and his family offered to take care of Kelly. We gladly handed her over, knowing she'd be safe with them.

Sadly, when we returned, Mommy announced, "Kelly is going to live with Earl's family. They love her, and it wouldn't be fair to take her back. But we can visit her sometime." I never saw Kelly again.

Kelly was one of several pets that did not remain in our home long. Other dogs and kittens came through one door and out the other before we got to know them. There was Ginger, a small mixed breed that Blanche found on her way home from the movies. "Can we keep her?" she asked hopefully, thinking the answer would be "no," as it usually was.

"Once the vet checks her to make sure she's all right, she can stay," Mommy said.

Ginger lived with us for a few days until we could take her to the vet. Daddy took Ginger to Dr. Berkleheimer one morning, but he came home alone.

"Distemper," Daddy declared. "The vet had to put her 'to sleep.'"

I did not understand what he meant.

Each spring Daddy brought Blanche and me baby chicks, although we did not celebrate Easter. We kept them in a cardboard box on the front stoop during the day and in the vestibule at night. The first pair we named Tweety and Sylvester after the cartoon characters. I have no idea how these traditional Easter symbols wound up in our Orthodox Jewish household. Each year after our chicks grew larger, they would be gone when I returned from school. "Where are our chicks?" I'd ask.

"They flew away," Mommy answered.

After a few years of this routine, Mommy declared, "No more chicks!"

Sadly, pets lasted as long as politician's promises in our household. They either died or disappeared.

Kittens fared worse than dogs and chickens. Taffy, a cream-colored feline with blue eyes, was playful and sweet. One day she was there, the next she was gone.

Kitty, a tiger-striped kitten, amused us one summer when Mommy was in the hospital and our housekeeper Josephine Penny Hawkins minded us during the day. Josephine had many strong opinions, and she shared them freely. Each time an airplane flew over our house on its path to Newark Airport, Josephine would say, "I am never going to fly in an airplane. If God wanted people to fly, He would have given them wings."

We liked having Josephine at home with us that summer. We played outside a lot, and she allowed us a bit more freedom than our mother. Unlike the other neighborhood children, we were never allowed to go barefoot if Mommy was home. Josephine compromised and let us play on the grass in our socks.

We thought she was terrific. When Mommy came home from the hospital, she was not pleased and made us go back to wearing shoes at all times—inside and outside the house. To this day, I do not walk barefoot.

I don't remember Josephine's opinions about pets, but because it was her job to keep our house clean, she treated them as a nuisance. Kitty was always underfoot. Her fur clung to the furniture, creating more work for Josephine. One day, Kitty just disappeared. After that summer, Josephine stopped working for us, but she returned when I was twelve. We credit her for saving Blanche's life the afternoon that Bob Belachek talked his way into our house.

Unlike Josephine, our housekeeper Edith was a quiet woman. But she liked to drink. My parents always locked the liquor cabinet when she came to clean. Although she was kind, Edith was not always tactful.

During the period she worked for us, we had a baby-blue parakeet named Pretty Boy, whom we loved dearly. Blanche and I often took him out of his cage, perched him on our fingers, and talked to him. We'd never had a parakeet before, and Pretty Boy was the ideal pet—small and confined to a cage. He made housekeeping easier, which pleased my mother and Edith.

Mommy grew fond of Pretty Boy, and she also took him out of his cage and talked to him while we were in school. He sat on her finger, turned his head, and chirped. He was a loving bird who enjoyed small flights of freedom through the living room before returning to perch on our fingers and coo. Mommy treated him like a baby and enjoyed giving him baths under the kitchen faucet. He loved the attention and his flight through the house to dry off afterwards. Pretty Boy was a keeper, until the day he became too curious.

One afternoon as I walked home from school, I passed Edith on her way to the bus stop. "Hi, Edith," I waved from across the street.

"Your bird's dead," she yelled.

"What?" I asked.

"Your bird's dead," she repeated. "Your mother gave him a bath this morning, he flew around the house to dry off, and then he bit an electric cord."

Tears ran down my face as I rushed home to hear the news from my mother. Sadly, she nodded, and then she became upset after learning how I heard about Pretty Boy. Edith was never one for subtlety. Years later, she went to jail for stabbing her husband.

It seemed that our family was not meant to have pets. Blanche and I grew content with neighbors' pets, especially their dogs Tibi and Mittens. Tibi, a Norwegian elkhound, lived two doors down with the Goodmans. Her grey fur flew everywhere, but Mrs. Goodman didn't mind. Tibi was smart, played with us, and protected the house. Often I heard the Goodmans calling, "Tibi, Tibi," and came running, thinking they were calling me.

Mittens, one of Tibi's offspring with a neighborhood mutt, lived with the Blooms, directly across the street from us. While Mittens had some Norwegian elkhound in her, she was a mixed breed, black with white feet and specks of white around her muzzle. Although not as bright as her mother, Mittens was a friendly dog that we enjoyed.

But Blanche and I still wanted a dog of our own. "Please, Mommy, please," I begged. "I'll feed it and take care of it. I promise."

By the time I was in fourth grade, my mother began driving, and she relented. "All right, girls," she announced one morning. "We're getting a dog."

We could not believe our good fortune. Our parents had decided they wanted a small, short-haired dog that wouldn't shed too much. Little did they realize that short-haired dogs actually shed more, and their tiny hairs cling to clothing with tenacity. They chose a toy fox terrier and located a breeder in Pompton Lakes, several miles away. When we went to the kennel, we found that the puppies each weighed less than five pounds. They'd been given

Bonnie Sue was loyal to the end.

girls' names: Mary Lou, Bonnie Sue, and Sally May. Their mother, Peggy Sue, was named for the Buddy Holly song.

We chose Bonnie Sue, a featherweight bundle with a white body, black head, traces of tan on her muzzle, and a stub of a tail. She was a cuddly pup who cried constantly the first night, despite the alarm clock and hot water bottle we put in her basket to imitate the heartbeat and warmth of her mother.

Bonnie proved to be an active puppy with a mind of her own, a true terrier. She took to nipping our feet when we walked past and chewing on things she shouldn't. One day Mommy came home and found Bonnie on the kitchen table chewing her mother-in-law's tongue plant. A multitude of slippers and socks also succumbed to Bonnie's incisors.

As she outgrew her chewing phase and became house-trained, Bonnie Sue was allowed to sleep upstairs with us. She wiggled beneath the covers and licked my feet until she fell asleep. If I rolled over, she growled to let me know I'd disturbed her.

Mittens became Bonnie's nemesis, although the two never met. When she saw Mittens through the living room window, the hair on Bonnie's back stood up, and she barked unceasingly. I think she had that "Little Napoleon" complex that small dogs exhibit when they see big dogs. She didn't behave this way with Tibi, who acted like her mother from the moment they met.

One day Mittens got out and stood right in the middle of Highland Avenue, just as Mommy walked out the front door. Bonnie Sue spied Mittens and scooted by Mommy, barking and growling. She leaped on Mittens with all of her ten pounds but missed her mark. Mittens just stood there. Blanche and I ran outside yelling, "Stop, stop," but before we could reach her, Bonnie calmed down. When she jumped, she glanced off Mittens's back and landed directly beneath the forty-pound dog. She stood there cowering and shaking until I picked her up. Mittens never moved. Tears of laughter ran down Mommy's cheeks as she scooped Bonnie up.

Bonnie preferred Blanche's room to mine because the smells were better. My sister often left piles of dirty clothes lying around, which made perfect nests for a small dog. Every so often, Bonnie piddled on a pile.

Blanche also gave Bonnie more freedom than the rest of us did. She removed the screen from her window one spring day, and Bonnie ventured onto the roof. The small dog stood there surveying the neighborhood below until a neighbor spied her and frantically rang the doorbell to warn us of Bonnie's whereabouts. Edith Bloom stood on the lawn in case Bonnie jumped, while Blanche and Mommy coaxed her back inside with dog treats.

Bonnie reached her nadir the morning she came into Blanche's room and jumped on the bed, where Blanche sat cross-legged. The determined dog began sniffing and spinning, as if she planned to sit down. Then she took her stance and had a bowel movement on Blanche's foot. My sister just sat there, as I watched in horror.

When Bonnie was three years old, our lives changed dramatically. She remained with us and lasted the longest of any of our pets. I learned that pets can become part of the family and enrich people's lives. Bonnie was a devoted guardian to the end. Like so many others in my life, her presence was temporary.

10

The Decade of Decline

The year 1960, which commenced on a high note, began nearly a decade of decline as our family secrets slowly revealed themselves. With each new revelation, I lost a bit of my childhood. By the time I was twelve, I had to behave like an adult and accept grown-up responsibilities, although my emotional maturity remained that of a teenager.

The first secret came to light one gray March day in 1960 when I was in sixth grade. That year I was assigned to Miss Frannie Focken's class. Miss Focken was a young, thin woman with dishwater-blond hair, worn in a page boy, and watery blue eyes shielded by wire-frame glasses. She was kind, but stern and serious most of the time, and she wore no makeup and dressed conservatively in a straight skirt with a tailored blouse and jacket most days. I liked her and knew that to do well in her class I just had to follow her rules.

Most of us did, but one or two students always seemed to cause trouble. Celia was one of them. She had a chip on her shoulder and was not particularly popular. When she became angry, she did terrible things. One morning she placed a thumbtack on Miss Focken's chair during recess.

When we returned to class, Miss Focken stood before our class, red-faced and ordered, "Everyone sit down immediately and be quiet." My classmates and I just looked at each other questioningly and did as we were told. None of us understood why our teacher was so upset—until she held up a large thumbtack. "Does anyone know who put this on my chair?" she asked stonily. "It was a very dangerous thing to do, and I got hurt. You will all sit here quietly until the person who did it comes forward."

We sat in silence. After about ten minutes, Celia went up to the teacher's desk and admitted what she had done. As we watched her make her amends, we all grew angrier because we bore the brunt of her spiteful deed.

At lunch I asked, "How could you do something so mean?"

Celia replied with a sneer and a taunt, "I know something about you that you don't know."

"What is it?" I asked.

"You're adopted!" she screamed.

"You're wrong," I yelled back. "You don't know what you're talking about." I ignored Celia for the rest of the day, but it was a blur. I could not concentrate on anything except her stinging words, "you're adopted," which echoed through my mind.

I couldn't wait until the school day ended and I could go home and hear the truth from my mother. Celia's words stirred a distant memory—a fuzzy recollection of a day ten years earlier when Blanche and I were told we were adopted. What if Celia's words were true? What if I wasn't really Ruth and Harry's child?

As the afternoon dragged, I tried to recall early childhood events. Had I been told I was adopted? Why couldn't I remember? During my youth, some unusual encounters signaled I was different, but I was either too young or too naive to notice.

When I was about six, my mother and I spent a day in downtown Newark shopping and going to lunch. I loved these excursions with Mommy, who would take me to the four main department stores in Newark: Bamberger's, Kresge's, Klein's, and Ohrbach's to buy fall or spring clothes. "Here, Libby, try on this suit. It will be perfect for the High Holidays," Mommy said. Whatever she picked was perfect in my eyes. New clothes were a treat. They were certainly better than wearing Blanche's hand-me-downs that looked like boys' clothes but were practical for playing outside. I preferred girls' clothes: dresses and skirts, flannel-lined corduroy pants with matching tops, and Mary Janes instead of sneakers. Mommy indulged me when special occasions arose, but most of the time she watched the budget carefully. She did not want to "spoil" us.

On this one downtown outing, Mommy went to the restroom while our waitress brought the lunch bill. "You're so lucky to have a grandmother who takes you out for the day," she said, laying the tab on the table.

"That's my mother," I replied proudly. I thought the waitress was silly to confuse my mother with my grandmother, especially since both my grandmothers died before I was born.

After lunch, I asked Mommy, "How old are you?"

"Forty-eight," she replied.

"Oh," I answered. I had no concept of age. I thought all parents were in their forties and fifties, like my parents, and saw nothing unusual about having a mother who looked older than my friends' mothers. I thought my good friend Gail lied to me when she said her mother was twenty-eight.

After Celia's announcement that morning in sixth grade, I thought back on that day when I was six. When I got home from school, I did not know how to ask the question that had haunted me all afternoon. Mommy asked about my day, and I said, "Fine," although my voice quivered. She did not question me further, but she could tell I was upset.

Mommy returned to the den with her coffee to watch her soap operas, and after fifteen minutes, I came in and sat down next to her.

"Mommy, Celia Poland and I had an argument at school today. She said something very mean to me." Tears began to fall as I asked, "Am I adopted?"

"Yes," she replied. "You and Blanche are both adopted, and Daddy and I told you that many years ago. I was afraid you had forgotten because of some of the questions you've been asking lately. You were adopted because I wanted you. A friend called and said a baby girl needed a home. I went to the hospital, saw you, and said 'I must take this baby home.'

"Daddy didn't really want another child, but I made him come with me. Once he saw you, he wanted you, too. So we took you home and made you ours. In one way that makes you more special than all the other babies in the world because we picked you. That's something other parents don't get to do."

By this time, my cheeks were flooded, and I felt sad, but relieved. Now I knew the truth. I put my arms around my mother and hugged her for a long time. My day had been filled with conflicting emotions. Her words made me feel much better. I was their child, no doubt about it. Ruth and Harry Berger were my parents.

Mommy said, "Your adoptions are not something we talk about with other people. I don't know how Celia found out, but she wasn't very nice. Be careful when you're around her. Our family life is none of anyone else's business."

I understood, and we did not discuss my adoption again.

Another secret was revealed two months later, when my parents took me aside one morning after breakfast. "Libby, we need to tell you something," my mother began. I thought: What's wrong now? What have I done?

Daddy looked at me and said, "We have to sell our house."

I doubled over, as if someone had punched me in the stomach, and my eyes began to water. "What do you mean 'We have to sell our house.'?" I asked. "I love this house. It's the only house I've known. I don't want to move."

Mommy added, "We have to move. We need the money. Daddy's business is not doing well, and we owe people a lot of money."

"But we're rich," I countered. "We have lots of money. We're the richest people on the block."

"Not anymore," Mommy said quietly. "I know you're upset, but we thought you should know before the sign goes up outside."

That morning Mommy only told me part of the secret. I would not learn the whole truth for another year.

A few weeks later, Mommy packed her suitcase and left. We did not know where she went, had no way to contact her, and were not told when she would return. Daddy said, "Your mother needed a break. I'll take care of you." I loved my father, but I was closest to my mother. As a child, I constantly followed her, even to the Goodmans' house where she would often go for a coffee and cigarette break. Mrs. Goodman would say, "Libby, leave your mother alone. She needs some time to herself. She'll be home soon." Reluctantly I'd leave, but I did not understand why my mother needed to be away from me.

During her unexplained absence that spring, I cried every day she was gone. Blanche tried to console me. "Don't worry, Lib. Mommy will be back. She's just tired. It will be all right."

Her attempt to calm me did not work. I missed Mommy terribly.

My parents celebrated their wedding anniversary in
New York during happier days.

Five days passed, and Mommy returned. Things were not the same in our house. She and Daddy barely spoke, and in the evenings they went their separate ways. Mommy chose mah jong, bingo, and card playing as her favorite pastimes. Daddy liked boxing, wrestling, and one or two card games a week. His favorite pastime was horse racing, but he did not go often anymore.

From my perspective as a child, I never questioned my parents' relationship. Our life seemed normal enough. Daddy worked at the bar and kept odd hours, compared to my friends' fathers, while Mommy stayed home and took care of Blanche and me. She was a typical, middle-class 1950s housewife who had many good friends in the neighborhood, was involved in charity work, and spent her spare time playing bingo, cards, or mah jong.

Some evenings that Mommy went out to play, Daddy held poker games at our house. Blanche and I greeted his friends and then were sent to watch TV in the den, while the men smoked cigars, ate sandwiches, drank, and placed their bets. When Mommy returned, she opened all the windows in the breakfast room to clear the house of smoke.

A few times Daddy went to Florida alone, and Mommy stayed home with us. Other times, she took us on trips to Florida, Buffalo, and New York City. The only times we went away together as a family were when we went to Philadelphia to visit Zayde or the Bronx to see Aunt Evelyn and Uncle Arthur and their son Elliot. I thought all parents behaved this way.

I did not know that the problem between my parents began five years earlier when my mother's father, Morris Dickstein, our Poppy, died. He had gone to the hospital one summer day and never came home. I remember the morning I walked into the kitchen for breakfast and the phone rang. My mother answered, listened for a minute, and then began to sob. "Mommy, Mommy, what's wrong?" I asked.

My mother just shook her head as the tears flowed down her cheeks. She never told me what happened, but I knew it was something bad because Ruth Goodman came over a few minutes later. "Libby, why don't you go to my house and play with Neil? Your mother needs some time alone."

I quickly got dressed and headed down the street. Two days later, Blanche and I spent the day at the Goodmans' house while my parents attended Poppy's funeral. No one ever told us he died.

After Poppy died, my mother was very sad and could not concentrate on anything. Poppy left his estate to my mother and her brother. But she had not seen her brother for nearly thirty years and was unable to find him in 1955, despite advertising in newspapers around the country. Consequently, she became sole owner of the bar, but she left its management to my father. Now she regretted her error.

After Daddy tired of running the bar himself, he decided to sell it and purchase a package liquor store on Morris Avenue in Union, a suburb closer to our home in Hillside. My mother begged him to let her share in this new mom-and-pop enterprise. "Harry, we could take turns working at the store and really make a go of this business," she pleaded.

"Never," my father declared. "You will not go to work as long as I'm around."

The sad truth was that Daddy "was not around." Perhaps my father wouldn't allow my mother to work by his side because he didn't always go to work. Instead he went off to play and hired help so that he could indulge his favorite pastime: gambling. Many days he frequented Monmouth Park, Aqueduct, and Yonkers, placing big bets. If he lost, he bet more, hoping to win his money back. When not at the horse races, he satisfied his addiction by playing cards. My father was a compulsive gambler. No one recognized this as a serious addiction in the 1950s and 1960s.

Some of Daddy's help was honest, but many were not. My father often left for the day and returned to missing inventory. Most days the receipts did not equal the amount that disappeared from the shelves, yet he persisted. Finally he decided to sell the liquor store.

I was sorry to see that liquor store go. There were many Friday nights when my mother went to play bingo at St. Antoninus Catholic Church and couldn't find a babysitter. Occasionally, I accompanied her, but I was bored sitting in the parish hall without any other children.

Sometimes my father took me to work with him. Right next door to his liquor store was a candy store, or soda fountain, where he bought me comic books and bubble gum to help pass the time. I sat behind the counter in his store reading "Archie" or "Superman" while he waited on customers, proudly introducing his little girl. After he closed for the night, we stopped for ice cream on the way home. It was our time out, and I thought it was great fun.

After he sold the liquor store, my father purchased a foundering tavern on North Broad Street in Newark. Dark and dank, it was always empty. I hated to go there because the place seemed so down at the heels. Sadly, I think my father knew that the tavern didn't have a chance when he purchased it.

He must have given up. He was often absent when my mother called the tavern, and she was never sure of his whereabouts, I learned later. Perhaps he was visiting a lady friend or off to the racetrack; he wasn't at work. Ships without captains go under, and the tavern sank quickly, especially after Daddy sent his cook to buy supplies in his Oldsmobile convertible. That afternoon the phone rang at five o'clock. When Mommy answered it, Daddy asked, "Ruth, can you come pick me up? I sent the cook out to buy food several hours ago, and he hasn't returned. He's driving my car."

Mommy and I hopped in her 1956 Plymouth Belvedere and headed to Newark. We brought Daddy home for dinner, and he drove the Plymouth back to the bar afterwards. By closing time, he realized his cook wasn't coming back—and neither was his car.

My father eventually sold the bar on North Broad Street, but he could not deal with defeat. Rather than find a new job, he stayed home, watched TV all day, and smoked his cigars as our fortune diminished.

When Mommy realized that Daddy no longer could provide for his family, she defied him and sought work. She was nearly fifty-five years old and had not worked outside the home for her entire marriage, but she could not bear to have no food on the table or cash in hand. After thirty-four years as a stay-at-home wife and mother, she applied for a job as a cashier at a local discount chain store with a branch on nearby Route 22. She pawned her engagement ring and accepted minimum wage, all to feed her family. Instead of supporting her efforts, my father asked, "What are you doing working in a place like that? Don't you think that's beneath you?"

"I need to keep food on the table, and I'll do whatever it takes," my mother stoically replied. And she did.

One day she returned from work and gave me a dollar. "Go to the corner grocery store and buy a pound of ground round and some potatoes," she said.

I looked at the dollar, wondering how that could buy dinner for a family of four, but did as I was told. The kindly grocer knew our family well, and he accepted my dollar and filled our order. My mother did not serve her usual abundant meal that night, and I recall wanting seconds, but there weren't any. Life in our house had certainly changed.

My father continued down his self-destructive path, continuing to gamble and hoping for a big payoff. One morning when I was thirteen, I went out to the Plymouth for a ride to school and was shocked by what I saw. The driver's seat had been slit open, and the knife remained in it. Spindled on the knife was a note that read "Next time it will be you. Pay up, or else..."

I was too young to understand what was going on. Busy with my seventh- grade classes and my friends, I did not realize that my parents rarely spoke. One day seventeen-year-old Blanche enlightened me.

"Daddy tried to sell Mommy's mink coat to Mrs. Schuckman today," she whispered. "I saw him carrying it down the street when Mommy was at work."

"How could he do that?" I asked. "He bought that coat for Mommy."

"But he's broke, and we need the money," Blanche replied.

"No, no," I protested. "He can't be broke. What are you talking about?"

"Why do you think Mommy went to work?" Blanche asked.

"I don't know," I answered. I'd always had problems believing Blanche, but this time I realized that our lives were not as they seemed. I had been protected by my youthful innocence, yet surrounded by unpleasant truths. My father had made a series of bad business decisions, was addicted to gambling, and refused to work. Now the reasons why we had to sell our house became clear.

"Why aren't you working?" I asked my big sister.

"Lib, can't you see that I'm pregnant? I was raped a few months ago, and now I can no longer work."

Her response made me recall the Sunday morning she sat sobbing on her bed while Mommy tried to console her. I had no idea what really happened to my big sister, but I felt sad that she had been violated with no recourse.

"What about my savings account?" I asked. "I can help."

Blanche just shook her head.

"That's not fair," I screamed. "That was my money. He's taken it just the way you used to steal my allowance." I ran to my room, locked the door, sat down on my bed, and cried.

Our house sold in the spring of 1961, almost a year after my parents announced we would have to sell it. The buyers paid several thousand dollars less than the asking price. As a result, many of our possessions had to be sold to make up the difference and help pay off our debt. The new owners agreed to buy my piano, a refurbished Brambach baby grand that I'd played on since the time I began taking lessons at age six. They also bought the built-in bedroom set that Joe Goodman carefully crafted for my room. My mother divided her antique collection among her friends, allowing each to choose one she wanted. She sold the remainder of the collection to dealers.

Because it was midsemester and I wanted to remain at Hillside Avenue School, I went to live with the Goodmans during the school week and shared a room with Ellen. Many nights Neil and I stayed up talking way after bedtime. We shared secrets and talked about our school friends, as a brother and sister would. Despite our "divorce" years earlier, we were just as close as ever.

My mother stayed in an old hotel in East Orange, and I spent weekends with her until we left for California. I hated the hotel and found excuses to spend my weekends with friends whenever I could. I did not understand how hard this move was for Mommy.

Seventeen-year-old Blanche often stayed with friends following the birth of her second child shortly before our move. She put the baby girl up for adoption and left the hospital alone only three years after she'd done the same with her baby boy. We went to see Blanche in the hospital, and when I looked at that little girl, I turned to my mother and asked, "Mommy, can we keep her?"

Mommy shook her head. Now, more than ever, she felt the need for a fresh start.

I stood outside that spring day and watched the movers remove our household belongings one by one—the antique black lacquer Chinese chair with

The carved, lacquered dragon chair was sold along with other treasured possessions.

dragon heads carved into the arms, where Blanche and I hid playing hide-and-seek; the china cabinet and buffet; our dining room table and chairs, kitchen set, two sofas, chairs, beds, my books, and boxed sets of leather-bound editions of Shakespeare and Dickens from the attic. I would never see these things again.

As the movers carried the last of our family's belongings out of the only home I'd ever known and closed the doors to the moving van, my parents came out of the house and walked in opposite directions. My father hugged and kissed me one last time and headed for his car. My mother took me by the hand and led me to the Goodmans' house, where I would live for the next two months until my mother's brother arrived to drive us to our new life in California. Our family's decade of decline had begun.

Part II

The Promised Land

California is a wonderful place to live—
if you happen to be an orange.

—Fred Allen

11

Heading West

$\mathcal{M}$y family left New Jersey on Monday, May 22, 1961, heading for the Promised Land—California—where we would start new lives. Bonnie Sue jumped into the car first that morning, claiming her space in the backseat. My uncle took the wheel of my mother's pink-and-black 1956 Plymouth Belvedere, while my mother rode shotgun. All five feet, eleven inches of Blanche shared the backseat with me and Bonnie Sue.

We made one last stop on Highland Avenue in Hillside to say good-bye to our former neighbors. Aunt Pearl and Uncle Moe came running out, "We'll miss you, Ruth. The neighborhood has not been the same without you."

Ruth Goodman stood nearby, waiting her turn. "Who will I take my morning coffee break with?" she asked my mother. "Girls, you take good care of your mother."

Edith Bloom was next. She had tears in her eyes as she hugged Mommy good-bye.

After we had our final hugs and kisses, Uncle Richard pulled the car away, and I cried. I did not want to leave Hillside, my home for my entire life. Now that our house and most of our possessions were gone, I did not want to leave the only people who sustained me through this awful time—our neighbors and friends.

My friends had given me a surprise going-away party a few weeks earlier and teased me about going to Hollywood. This became the running joke: Libby was going to Hollywood to become famous.

The reality did not come close.

Our journey across the country took seven days. From New Jersey we drove through Pennsylvania and across the Appalachian Mountains. My mother was at the wheel when we crested a steep hill. As she maneuvered the car down the incline into the Ohio River Valley, her hands began to shake and her face grew pale. Uncle Richard looked over at her and asked, "Ruth, what's wrong?"

Mommy just shook her head and concentrated on getting us down the hill safely. At the bottom, she pulled off to the shoulder. "I thought I could do it, but I can't," she said, perspiring heavily. "I only started driving again three years ago. I guess I never got over my accident in the mountains more than thirty years ago!" My mother moved into the passenger seat, and my uncle drove for the remainder of the trip. Our plan was to drive about 500 miles per day.

We reached Zanesville, Ohio, the first night and found a comfortable, inexpensive motel that allowed dogs. During the day Bonnie Sue stayed in the car when we stopped for lunch. She spent her nights in our motel room beds, licking our feet. We were inseparable.

The second night we headed through Indianapolis and Terre Haute, Indiana, where the whole state was preparing for the Indy 500 on Memorial Day the following week. By that time we'd already be in California.

After settling in, we headed to the coffee shop next door to the motel. Dinner was good, but I liked the desserts best, delicious house-made tarts in my favorite flavors: cherry, blueberry, and chocolate cream. We each ordered a different flavor and shared bites.

That night in Indiana, my mother hung the new robe my sister and I had given her for Mother's Day on the back of the bathroom door in the motel. The next morning we hit the road early. By the time Mommy realized she'd left her new robe behind, we were too far away to turn back. She announced the loss with tears in her eyes, knowing we had no money to replace her lovely gift.

From Indiana we turned south through Illinois until we arrived at the famed Mississippi River and the city of St. Louis. I was surprised that the great river's water looked like coffee with skim milk, a muddy brown, and that the river was so wide. Now I understood how it got the moniker, the "mighty Mississippi," but I'd expected the water to be crystal clear.

Many of my expectations changed during this journey, which essentially became my introduction to the real world. In St. Louis we picked up Route 66, the renowned road to the West that took us through Missouri, Oklahoma, Texas, and New Mexico. This was my first exposure to Middle America, and I felt that I was being transported back in time. In Missouri, we traversed the Ozark Mountains, where the women and teenage girls wore long skirts with bobby sox and saddle shoes and the men dressed in dungarees and work shirts. Their clothing seemed so old-fashioned and unsophisticated compared to that in the New York metropolitan area, where I'd grown up. There were no Jersey girls here.

To break the boredom of our long daily drives, we'd play the License Plate Game that Unc introduced. "Girls, when cars go by, try to see what state their license plates were issued in. Count how many plates you can identify from each state." One variation of this game was to find other cars with New Jersey plates. There were fewer the further west we headed.

The landscape changed as we headed west. Mountainous Missouri gave way to flat Oklahoma with its oil wells staggered across the state. With little to attract our interest as we drove, we made up new games to play while driving. Our trip proved the best geography lesson. I'd always loved this subject in school, and maps fascinated me. Now I experienced them and recalled the descriptions in my school books. The Northeast and Midwest had been filled with green foliage with roads bordered by wooded areas.

As we passed through the Texas Panhandle, trees and grass gave way to more arid landscapes. By the time we reached New Mexico, we were in the desert, and I spied cacti along the road.

When we stopped for lunch in Tucumcari, New Mexico, I tasted my first Mexican food. Before ordering, I looked around at what others had on their plates. The red sauce I saw reminded me of catsup or the tomato sauce on Italian food. I decided to order enchiladas. Unc ordered a tuna salad and tried to warn me, when I placed my order, saying, "You may not like the red sauce. It's hot and not what you think it is."

"I'll be fine, Unc," I replied and insisted on completing my order. When the food arrived, it smelled different than I thought it would. The enchiladas were made with corn tortillas, and I did not like corn. I poured red sauce all over them, thinking it might help, and took my first bite. My mouth burned, not from the food's heat, but from its spice, and my eyes began to water. I could not chew it and wanted to spit out what was in my mouth but knew it wasn't polite. So I sat in the booth with tears in my eyes and swallowed.

Unc looked at me and said, "What did I just tell you? It's not catsup." Then he pushed his tuna salad toward me and asked, "Would you like my lunch? I'll eat yours."

"Thank you," I mumbled, embarrassed by my actions, but grateful for his help.

We proceeded across New Mexico into Flagstaff, Arizona, gateway to the Grand Canyon, where we found a motel for the night. This was the one site we'd stop to visit along the way and would be the highlight of our trip.

None of the books I'd read prepared me for the vastness of this sacred space; carved by wind and water, it was majestic, timeless, and humbling. I stood at the rail-less canyon rim, frightened that I could fall over the edge into the deep gorge, yet transfixed by the beauty that surrounded me. Even Blanche, who'd found most of the journey boring and uncomfortable, was awed by the canyon. For once she realized there was something bigger than she was in this world. This trip to the Grand Canyon offered respite from our emotional journey and calmed our weary souls.

After visiting the canyon, we ate dinner and prepared for the following day's drive, which would be shorter than the others. The next morning we left a little later than usual and headed to Kingman, Arizona. Once there, we'd stop for dinner and go to a drive-in movie, preparing for the final leg of our trip across the Mojave Desert. Unc had driven this route many times, and he believed it was safer to cross the desert at night, especially with an older car. He did not want to take the chance of breaking down during the day's heat, when temperatures could exceed 100 degrees and the nearest town was forty miles away.

Unc napped during the movie so that he could stay awake and drive. My mother nodded off in the front seat as well. When the movie ended around eleven o'clock, Unc started the car and began the final leg of our journey. Blanche and I lay across the backseat, our feet in each other's faces. Blanche had the advantage, since she was seven inches taller than I. Bonnie Sue snuggled between us, curled in a tight ball, pressed against our bodies. Eventually we dozed off. My mother tried to stay awake to keep her brother company.

I awoke about five o'clock in the morning and found us winding our way through the San Bernardino Mountains into the Los Angeles basin. The sky was beginning to lighten. As the night sky turned from an inky black to gray, I realized we were driving through a heavy mist. I looked around and asked, "Is this the sunny Southern California that you told us about? Where's the sun?"

"This time of year we don't get much morning sun," Unc answered. "It will come out later today."

I was upset. Was the sun's failure to appear a sign? Was this land of opportunity as hollow as the image of glitz and sunshine it showed the world? Disappointed, I rolled over and went back to sleep.

About two hours later we arrived in Alhambra, where Unc lived in a trailer park adjacent to a small motel on Garvey Avenue. Alhambra is a suburb in the San Gabriel Valley that's an easy commute to downtown Los Angeles. By the time we arrived, the sun had come out, as promised. Unc checked us into the motel, and the owners ran out to welcome us. "Welcome to California," they said in unison. "Your uncle has told us so much about you and we're happy you arrived safely. You must be tired from your long trip." The owners were fond of my uncle, who'd lived in this park for many years. He kept to himself, paid his rent on time, and was always pleasant.

Unc had reserved a large room with a kitchenette for Mommy, Blanche, Bonnie Sue, and me until we found an apartment. After we unpacked the car, we explored the trailer park with Bonnie on her leash. She sniffed at all the new smells. Afterwards Unc took us to a local market to stock up for breakfast and lunch the next day. We put the groceries away, washed up, and went out to dinner. That night we turned in early, exhausted from the journey.

The next day was Memorial Day, a national holiday, and Unc offered to take us all to the beach. Blanche and my mother begged off, still tired from our trip. I was eager to see the Pacific Ocean for the first time and hopped in Unc's old Pontiac sedan.

He drove for more than an hour until we arrived in a place called Redondo Beach, where the sun shone brightly. We found a parking space and headed down to the beach to look around. I stood there staring at the people hanging out around the beach. They looked like people in sun tan lotion ads, not like the people down the shore in New Jersey. Unc asked, "Do you want to put on your bathing suit and go in the ocean?"

I shook my head.

"Are you sure?" he asked. "We drove all the way to the beach and now you don't want to go in? I don't understand it."

Unc had no idea how awkward and uncomfortable I felt standing there with my fifty-three-year-old uncle, while all these teenage boys and girls walked by. I was out of my element—a pale-skinned, hook-nosed, dishwater-blond from New Jersey standing amidst bronzed, bikini-clad California girls and the guys who hung all over them. They all seemed so tan and confident.

I sat silently on the long ride home, brooding about my first California encounter and feeling like I'd never fit into this strange, new world.

A few days later my first "California" experience reinforced this belief. That morning Kathy, a young mother who lived in a trailer near my uncle, knocked on our door.

"Hi, I'm Kathy," she said. "I was wondering if you would babysit for me today."

Eager to earn some extra money, I said, "Sure. How long will you be gone?"

"Oh, just a few hours. I have some shopping to do, and it's hard with the baby," she added.

I nodded and agreed to watch Richie, her two-year-old son, until she returned. He was an adorable little boy, and I figured I could keep him entertained for a few hours, although babysitting was never my strongest skill.

I played with Richie all morning, and when noon came around, I took him to our room for lunch. He ate the peanut butter and jelly sandwich we offered, and my mother and Blanche seemed to enjoy having him around. I even put him down for his nap in our room because his mother had not returned.

As the day wore on, Kathy did not call or reappear. She hadn't left a phone number or said where she was going, and it was nearly five o'clock. "Let's walk Richie back to his trailer and see if his mom came home," Mommy suggested.

We did, but found Richie's trailer unlocked and empty. We walked through the compact living space and came across a note addressed to Richie's father. My mother opened the unsealed envelope and read Richie's mom's part-ing words. "I couldn't find an easy way to do this, but I have to leave," it said. "Richie is with the neighbors. Please take good care of him."

My mother and I could not believe it! Kathy had left her husband, and we were unwitting accomplices. This would never have happened in New Jer-sey, at least among the people we knew. I began to wonder just what type of place this land of California was.

12

Life in the Golden State

$\mathcal{M}$y first few days in California showed me what I would face in the year ahead. I was different—the girl from New Jersey with an accent that wouldn't quit. I "wawked the dawg" (walked the dog) and drank "cawffee" (coffee). I "tawked" (talked) funny. People were amused every time I opened my mouth.

Mommy, Blanche, and I each had to make adjustments, and we each dealt with them differently. My mother scanned the local newspapers to find an apartment we could afford. She had some money left from the sale of our home, but no job, and would have to keep expenses down. After a brief search, we found a two-bedroom, one bath, second-floor apartment on Bushnell Avenue in Alhambra. I had to share a room with Blanche, but our move would get us out of the motel.

We had no furniture. When we sold our house, special furniture items had been sold, but the rest were too expensive to move. Our budget kept shrinking, so Unc found a discount furniture store in Hawthorne that sold four rooms of furniture for a set price. It was cheap, but new, and consisted of an orange Naugahyde sofa and a serviceable chair for the living room, a dinette set, and two bedroom sets that consisted of beds and dressers. Mommy would sleep in a double bed, and Blanche and I chose twin beds.

Shortly after we moved into our apartment, Mommy began looking for work. I don't think she realized how hard it would be. There were few jobs for former housewives in their midfifties with little work experience. Each time my mother stated her age on the application, she was not asked for an interview. She finally resorted to lying, something that was nearly impossible for my mother.

Blanche also began looking for work and encountered her own obstacles. Because she was only seventeen, she needed a work permit, although she'd worked full time since she was sixteen back East. She also discovered that her beautician's license did not transfer from New Jersey to California. She would have to go back to school for more training and take another state exam.

Blanche hated school, and the thought of taking another exam was too much for her. She agonized over the requirements. "They're unfair," she screamed. "Why won't California accept my work experience for the additional hours required?" No one could calm her, and within a month of our arrival, she hitched a ride back to New Jersey with two young men who lived in the apartment next door. When my mother said good-bye to her, she did not realize that she would never see her older daughter again.

Right after Blanche left, my mother found work at a men's clothing store in downtown Los Angeles. It paid minimum wage, $1.25 an hour, and the hours were long. She left early in the morning and returned after six in the evening.

For the first time in my life, I was on my own all day. Bonnie Sue was my only companion. The days dragged, but Bonnie was around to amuse me. She was small and cuddly—truly my best friend.

California was new territory for Bonnie, too. For the first time in her life, she developed fleas, because the weather was warmer and the neighborhood not as well tended as ours was in Hillside. She also had more freedom. I'd walk her when I could, but she would often wander around the cul-de-sac on Bushnell Avenue alone, exploring and piddling, if I was busy. She always returned home.

Summer had begun before I had a chance to meet my new schoolmates, and I was so lonely after Blanche left and my mother went to work. I tried to befriend some of the neighborhood kids, but they already had friends and few were my age. I did spend time with an older girl named

Bonnie Sue was my only companion that first summer.

Sandy, mostly at her house, where she was responsible for cleaning and ironing while her mother worked. Sandy walked around barefoot, even outside, and spoke with a twang. Someone referred to her as an Okie, but I had no idea what that meant.

A lot of boys lived on Bushnell Avenue, but they did not consider girls friends, only girlfriends. I really missed Neil.

I was so different from the neighborhood kids, and these differences further isolated me. I sat and wrote copious letters to all the friends I'd left behind—Wendy, Rona, Ronnie, Neil, Helene. My list was endless. When I didn't write, I read or ate. There was nothing else to do.

Bushnell Avenue was different from anywhere I'd ever lived. Inexpensive, wood and stucco, two-story, post–war apartments filled the long cul-de-sac street, and families with little money dwelled in them. We had become one of them. Some seemed normal, but others were more colorful. Angie, the woman who lived directly beneath us, entertained men at all hours and ignored her young children. We would hear them banging on her door, hungry, dirty, and crying to be let in. Occasionally, one of the men who came to visit would slap Angie around, and we'd hear screams. But she kept letting them in—and locking her children out.

Teresa, a friend of hers who lived down the street, asked me to babysit her little boy one Saturday evening, and I agreed because we needed the money. Her little boy was about three, a blond-haired, blue-eyed angel of a child—a real sweetheart. He was already asleep when I arrived. All I had to do was sit and watch TV until Teresa came home.

Teresa was not as angelic as her son. She and my neighbor Angie spent many nights drinking and entertaining in the apartment beneath ours. Both women were divorced at least once, and Angie may have had many husbands. Because it was a warm evening, I left the door to Teresa's ground-floor apartment open, but latched the screen door.

About half past nine, I looked up and saw a man standing at the door. I jumped and then realized it was Teresa's ex-husband. I'd seen him in the neighborhood to pick up his son. "Open the door," he ordered.

"I can't," I replied. "Teresa's not here, and no one is allowed to visit."

"You know me. I'm the boy's father, for God's sake, not a guest. Please open the door," he begged.

Reluctantly, I did. When he stepped into the apartment, he reeked of alcohol and quickly stumbled to the other armchair and sat down. Then he undid his belt.

"What are you doing?" I asked, feeling foolish and frightened.

"I'm just getting comfortable," he answered.

"You know, my mother is not well. She asked me to check in with her, so it's important that I run home for a minute," I said.

"Okay, but you'll come back, right?"

"Oh sure. I'll just be a minute, but I've really got to go home right now," I said and headed for the door. I ran up the street the fastest I'd ever run in my life. "Mommy, Mommy. Open the door," I wailed.

"What's wrong?" she asked. "Did Teresa come home?"

"No, Mommy," I explained. "Her ex-husband came by and insisted that I let him in. Now he won't leave. He undid his pants and scared me, so I made up an excuse to come home."

My mother turned white. She was no match for a drunken man. "Let's see if Bernie will help."

A family from Pittsburgh, Pennsylvania, had rented the apartment next door to us shortly after the previous tenants took off with Blanche. It seemed like everyone was searching for a new life in California in the early 1960s. Jane, the wife, was a nurse at Los Angeles County General Hospital, and her husband, Bernie, was a big, burly man with a kind nature. They had three young children and were good parents. When Unc and I went on outings, we often took the older children with us.

My mother saw their light on and banged on Jane and Bernie's door. When they opened it, she explained what had happened. Bernie said, "C'mon, let's go get that guy out of the apartment."

When we returned to the apartment, the ex-husband was fast asleep in the chair. Bernie shook him, but the guy didn't stir. Finally, Bernie said, "Leave Teresa a note. You can't stay here. The baby's asleep and should be all right until she comes home."

Teresa was furious when I stopped by the next morning with Bernie. Although I explained what had happened, she'd have none of it. She didn't pay me or ask me to sit again.

While I found it hard to make friends, Mommy felt isolated and alone. She reached out to Daddy's cousins, Shirley and Lou Kaplan, who had moved to East Los Angeles from Philadelphia to live near their son Milton and his family. Milton practiced cardiology at a hospital in Downey and lived nearby. Stanley had moved to California with his parents, hoping to get his big break in show business. In the interim, he earned a degree in psychology at a California state college.

Aunt Shirley and Uncle Lou welcomed Mommy warmly, and they developed a strong bond, despite my parents' separation. Since Mommy and Aunt Shirley both worked in downtown Los Angeles, they sometimes met for lunch. Aunt Shirley was in "foundations" at the May Company, and she possessed a talent for fitting women into the right bras and girdles.

It took a bit longer to make friends among the neighbors. Bushnell Avenue in Alhambra, California, differed greatly from Hillside. Filled with inexpensive apartments, the street was densely populated by working people who had little in common with our former neighbors.

Our second-floor apartment grew hot on summer evenings, and we resorted to our East Coast habit of sitting on the stoop. One evening we looked at the building across from ours and saw a younger woman also trying to escape the summer heat. She lit a cigarette and said, "Hello, my name is Gene. Did you move here recently?"

"Yes, we just arrived from New Jersey in May. I'm Ruth, and this is my daughter Libby."

"I'm from New York," Gene replied. This announcement created an instant bond. They were two easterners far from home. "I like to sit out here in the evening after I put my children to bed," Gene continued. "I have three: Robin, who's five, and Richard and Dorothy, who are only a year apart."

"You have your hands full," my mother said. "I enjoy little ones and would love to meet them. Does anyone help with the children?"

When we first moved in, we saw a man leaving Gene's apartment each morning, but we had not seen him lately.

"One morning last month my husband left for work, and he never returned," Gene said. "I tried to find him, but he's gone. He was my second husband, and the father of my two little ones. I'm all alone here. My mother lives in L.A."

Mommy and I felt sorry for Gene and vowed to help her. Sometimes my mother went over to assist after work. She especially liked Robin, the older child, and would often read to him. He called her "Bergie" and developed a deep affection for her. I babysat for the little ones when I could, but I was not very good at it. Mainly, I changed their diapers and held them when they cried. Gene appreciated our help and would return our favors in many ways.

My attempts to befriend the neighborhood kids proved fruitless. In August Uncle Richard decided I needed something to do. He knew how much I loved makeup and fashion. "How would you like to go to modeling school?" he asked. "I'll pay for it."

"I'd love it," I replied. "When can I start?"

A week later, I enrolled at John Robert Powers, located across the street from MacArthur Park in downtown Los Angeles. MacArthur Park had once been a lovely urban garden, but by the early sixties it attracted more transients than families. Unc warned me not to walk in the park.

To get to John Robert Powers, I took a bus to the main terminal at Sixth and Los Angeles streets in downtown Los Angeles each Saturday morning. There I transferred to a second bus that dropped me off near the school, which was located on Seventh and Alvarado. I was only thirteen, but I'd navigated the streets of Newark, New Jersey, and New York on my own, so my mother figured I could manage this trip. One day, after I'd been accosted by one of the transients, I wasn't so sure.

I loved being a Powers girl and learning how to become a model. My teachers taught me how to walk, talk, dress, stand, apply makeup—everything

I'd always dreamed of doing. They emphasized the bandbox look (clean, fresh, and stylishly dressed as if you've just stepped out of a gazebo in the park after a performance) and how important it was to always look your best.

Secretly I hoped to become a model and earn enough money to help my mother pay the bills. In reality, I was not model material—too short, too heavy (at least for a model), and not pretty enough. But I still enjoyed spending my Saturdays at school and learning how to improve myself. I didn't realize that my classes at Powers would make it even more difficult for me to make new friends.

This photo was taken when I was thirteen, just after I completed my course at John Robert Powers.

I anticipated the start of school and then learned that the first two days fell on Rosh Hashanah. "Libby, these are the High Holy Days, and you'll have to stay home," Mommy announced.

"But Mommy, these are the first two days at a new school. I want to be there," I whined.

"Sorry, but I can't let you do that. Daddy would be furious with me," Mommy answered.

"He won't know," I said. "He's in Philadelphia, and besides, he doesn't care about us anymore."

"That's not true," Mommy retorted. "Don't ever say that. Your father loves you."

We did not belong to a synagogue, because we could not afford to join. I could not understand why I had to stay home from school and sit around all day, but Mommy insisted.

When I arrived at school on day three, I discovered that other kids were talking about me. To my amazement, I found out I was the only Jewish student in the entire eighth grade. One more thing to make me different, I thought.

My clothing also separated me from the other kids. I wore dresses to school that were far nicer than what the other girls wore, despite our frugal budget. I styled my hair, often back-combing it to new heights, and applied lipstick before going to school. The other students stared at me as if I were an alien from space. What had been normal in New Jersey stood out in Alhambra!

I attended Northrup Elementary School and was assigned to Coral Schneider's classroom. Mr. Fields was the other eighth grade teacher, and like me, he was Jewish. Mrs. Schneider was a gray-haired old crone who believed that Communists lurked under every desk and behind every door. She thought it was just a matter of time before they took over Alhambra and the entire United States. She trusted no one, especially an easterner who thought she was smarter than the teacher. Mrs. Schneider set me straight on that matter right away.

While correcting an assignment in class, I raised my hand. When called on, I said, "Mrs. Schneider, I don't think that's the right answer. If it is, I don't understand."

Mrs. Schneider glared at me and said, "I'm the teacher, and I'm not going to be questioned by you from New Jersey or anyone else."

The rest of the class sat there silently, while I fought to keep back tears. I had never been spoken to by a teacher that way.

The material we covered in eighth grade in Alhambra I had already learned in seventh grade in New Jersey. I was bored. In New Jersey, we changed classrooms and saw different teachers for each subject. Not so in Alhambra. I was stuck with Coral Schneider all day long.

My classmates thought I was a "brain," and they did not like how I spoke or dressed. They'd even make fun of what I ate for lunch. While they chomped on bologna and cheese or peanut butter and jelly, I lunched on cream cheese and olive or date nut bread sandwiches. My classmates would gobble their food and run off to play tether ball and get sweaty. I would use my lunchtime as my social hour, or at least my attempt at one. I certainly didn't allow myself to get hot and sweaty or mess up my clothes or hairdo.

Once or twice I arrived at school, and Mrs. Schneider sent me home to change because my skirt was too short. No one had ever checked the length of my skirt in New Jersey. I decided that Northrup Elementary School was repressive and backward. I couldn't wait to graduate and move on to high school. My mother even tried to convince the school to allow me to skip eighth grade because I was so far ahead of my classmates academically. But school officials said it was too big a leap and would not hear of it.

Besides, the principal seemed to enjoy driving me home to change my clothes. One day he turned to me in the car and said, "I don't think your skirt is too short; I like it." After that I wore longer skirts.

I really dreaded going to school and often got sick, just to avoid Coral Schneider, the lecherous principal, and my classmates.

Then one day I met a shy, smiling girl named Julie. She introduced herself at recess and was the first person who seemed kind and sincere. When she invited me over after school, I was happy to

Julie Frank made life bearable when we became friends.

say "yes." Julie lived on Seventh Street, only a few blocks from Northrup, in a yellow house with a big yard. Her mother was a warm, welcoming housewife, and her father was a gruff postal worker. Julie was the youngest of three. She had an older sister, Chris, and a brother, Robert. Best of all, she had a dog—a Dalmatian-mix named Duchess, who went everywhere with Julie's mother in their VW Beetle.

I loved going to Julie's house after school to spend time with her—and to play her piano, since I no longer had one. I would go in and play Rachmaninoff's *Prelude in C Sharp Minor* and "Malagueña" and whatever else I could remember. Julie was always up for a duet of "Heart and Soul" or "Chopsticks." We usually found something fun to do, even if it was just sitting around and talking or doing each other's hair. Pretty soon we became "best friends." She came to my house; I went to hers. We stayed overnight sometimes, and best of all, our mothers got along, too. They'd sit and drink coffee while they smoked their cigarettes and visited. It was a great arrangement.

Sometimes Mrs. Frank took us to a drive-in movie, which was a real treat. I'd always thought drive-ins were special when I was a child. I never figured out that it was our parents' way to see a movie and take the kids. They had worked out a routine that made missing our regular bedtime less painful. Sometime after the movie started, my mother changed my sister and me into our pajamas, and we lay down on the backseat and fell asleep when we got tired. This is what I thought people did at drive-in movies. After the third or fourth time I fell asleep at the drive-in with the Franks, Julie's mother said, "Libby, I'm sorry, but I'm not taking you to any more drive-in movies."

I was crushed. What had I done? I looked at Mrs. Frank and gulped, "Okay, but why? Did I do something wrong?"

"Well, you always fall asleep. Why bother going to a movie?" she answered.

In my own attempts to adjust to a new life, I never realized how unhappy my mother was. Yes, she had lost most of her material possessions, but more importantly, she had left behind all of her friends. She had no support system and very little money. She couldn't even call back East to talk with them, because long distance phone calls were very expensive.

My mother and I had each other and my uncle, a bohemian bachelor two years her junior, who tried to be as supportive as possible. On Sundays, my mother's only day off, he took us on outings, showing us the Southern California he'd come to know and love. Secretly he hoped we'd come to love it, too.

Because my mother was at work all day, my life changed a lot. I now had to do housework and help prepare dinner. I was thirteen, old enough to help, but I had little experience. One night my mother yelled at me when she saw the salad I prepared. "You used cabbage. You were supposed to use lettuce. I bought the cabbage to make coleslaw," she screamed.

I did not know the difference, and tears ran down my cheeks. "Why are you yelling at me?" I sobbed.

"I'm tired, I'm just so tired," she said softly. "I shouldn't have yelled."

"I'm sorry, Mommy," I answered. "I didn't know. I love you and will do better next time." I did not realize how much more I would be responsible for the household in the months ahead.

13

Too Many Changes

On our first Thanksgiving in California, Mommy insisted on preparing her traditional dinner: turkey with stuffing, homemade giblet gravy, sweet potatoes, and blueberry and apple pies. The small kitchen with a single oven would prove a challenge, but Mommy loved to cook and bake. Thanksgiving gave her the opportunity to show off her exceptional culinary skills. This year only Mommy, Unc, and I attended her feast. None of us realized it would be the last Thanksgiving meal she ever made.

The next day Mommy returned to work selling men's clothes at a store in downtown Los Angeles. As the holiday season began, her hours grew longer, and she became exhausted. Unc and I worried about her health, but my mother was stoic and determined to make a new life for us, no matter what it took. She vowed to keep her promise that she made the first time she saw me—to love and care for me all of her life.

We found the holiday season in California so different from that in New Jersey. The weather was bright and sunny out West, with no sign of winter-gray skies or snow. We enjoyed occasional rainstorms, which reminded us of home. But those could not make up for the absence of family and friends or Chanukah activities we relished in the East.

Unc noticed how sad we were, and one Saturday morning when he stopped by to pick up the batch of chicken my mother prepared for him each week, he asked, "Ruth, would you and Libby like to go the Rose Parade this year? It's your first year in California, and it's unlike any parade you've ever seen."

My mother responded, "I'd love to go, especially because it's nearby in Pasadena. But it's expensive, and I can't afford tickets."

"My treat," Unc replied. "It will be your holiday present."

"Please say 'yes,' Mommy," I begged.

My mother smiled. "It sounds wonderful. Let's do it. Thank you, Richard."

Uncle Richard purchased grandstand seats on Colorado Boulevard, and we sat among throngs of people on January 1, 1962, basking in the California sun. I was amazed by all the floats covered in flowers and seeds and adorned with California's most beautiful people. I could not believe my good fortune to attend the Rose Parade. Afterwards we looked for a place to eat, but it was New Year's Day and all the restaurants were closed. Finally, we headed home to Alhambra, where Mommy prepared a meal. The Rose Parade differed greatly from my experience two years earlier with Mommy and Uncle Richard on Times Square. I preferred the warm sunshine and glamour of the parade to that freezing night in New York City two years earlier and thought, "What a wonderful way to begin the New Year!"

I had no idea what lay ahead. I guess I was naive, or just a typical thirteen-year-old. My mother was deteriorating. She worked hard all day, too hard for a woman who smoked nearly two packs of cigarettes daily and was overweight. She worried constantly about money, fretted about Blanche, missed her friends back East, and was saddened by the collapse of her thirty-five-year marriage.

The second week in January, eight months after we arrived on the West Coast, Mommy became ill. Unc rushed over and called a doctor. In those days, doctors still made house calls. The young doctor who showed up at our apartment hospitalized her immediately. She'd had a heart attack.

Since we had little money and no medical insurance, he sent her to Los Angeles County General Hospital, a place so full that patients lay on gurneys in the hallways for hours and sometimes days.

The first time we went to see her, Unc and I had to navigate around the gurneys in the hall. As we were leaving, we passed a group of prisoners with their hands cuffed and feet shackled being herded to the prison bus. I grabbed my uncle's arm in fear.

While my mother was in the hospital, I was on my own. I went to school, came home to an empty apartment, ate dinner with Gene, and slept on her couch at night. Mommy came home after a week, but she lost her job at the clothing store with her absence. Now she was old, sick, and unemployed. We were fortunate Uncle Richard helped us out.

Despite our lives not working out as we planned, we tried to remain cheerful and anticipate a brighter future. I looked forward to my fourteenth birthday in February, although birthdays were not big occasions in our household. Usually I'd receive a gift, such as a book or record album, and Mommy would order a small cake. There was no party or big dinner to mark the passing of another year. That's why I was thrilled when Uncle Richard stopped by and said, "Your birthday is in a few weeks. How would you like it if I bought you a piano?"

I ran and gave him a big hug. The smile on my face was the only answer he needed.

Although he didn't play an instrument, my uncle was a music lover. He'd built shelves throughout his small trailer to house all his record albums, which numbered in the hundreds. He especially loved opera and owned original recordings of Enrico Caruso.

We set off for Burbank, where Unc knew a used piano dealer. After playing several models in the showroom, I settled on a dark wood upright with a mirror across the top, a former accompanist's piano. When it was delivered, I was thrilled to be able to practice once again. Out came all of my sheet music that I'd carefully packed away. Soon I would begin taking piano lessons. Life began to look brighter.

But one month later, life changed once more. I'd finally made some friends at school, and I brought a classmate home without first asking permission. Mommy usually welcomed my friends and was not deterred by surprise visits. She always offered them a snack and sometimes invited them to stay for dinner.

But this day was different. When I walked in the door, I was surprised to see Uncle Richard there. The mirror over the sofa in our small apartment was covered, and my mother stood in the living room beside my uncle. She looked as if she'd been crying.

"Hi, Mommy. Sandy came over. Is that all right?"

"She'll have to go home," my mother sobbed. "Your father died this morning. He had a heart attack."

I stood still, my mouth open, not knowing what to say. Two weeks earlier I'd written my father an angry letter, telling him how much I hated him for what he'd done to our family. Now I would never see him again.

My mother began to cry openly, something she rarely did in front of me. "Now we'll never see him again. We lived apart for ten months, but we still talked. Neither of us filed for divorce. I can't believe he's gone," she said through her tears.

Uncle Richard stood nearby, trying to console her, but nothing he said helped. My parents had been married more than thirty-five years and separated for less than one. Mommy had never removed her wedding rings once she got them back from the pawnshop. She never considered meeting any of my uncle's unmarried friends and would admonish my uncle by saying, "I'm still married."

"Ruth, why are you so upset?" Unc asked. "Harry was responsible for all that has happened the past few years. Surely you're not considering going to his funeral."

Through her tears, my mother said, "I have no money to fly back East. Even if I did, I would not be welcome. But he was still my husband."

She turned to me and explained, "Your father began having chest pains last night. He didn't tell anyone until this morning. When the pain became so bad that they took him to the hospital, it was too late. Zayde said your Daddy died of a broken heart, and it's our fault."

I stood there dry-eyed, unable to cry for a man who had left my mother, Blanche, and me in such dire circumstances. Blanche had returned to New Jersey and had even seen Daddy once or twice. I had not seen him since we left New Jersey, and I was still very angry with him.

My hateful letter had been the last straw. Filled with sadness and anger, I told Daddy that what he did to our family was terrible, leaving us without a home, furniture, and very little money after his gambling debts were paid off.

Now I felt responsible for killing my father and making my mother even more miserable.

"We can't go to his funeral, but we will honor Daddy as is our custom," Mommy said. I dutifully did what she asked, covering the remaining mirrors in our small apartment and staying home to sit *shiva* for a week. We did not turn the television on, and only Gene and Uncle Richard came to sit with us. Our little apartment in a run-down neighborhood 3,000 miles away from those we held dear was filled with sadness.

When I was a child, I adored Daddy.

That week I thought about the last year with my father. Not all of my memories were happy, but I began to understand how he got into so much trouble. Always a generous soul, he wanted to please everyone, especially me.

One night the fall before we moved out of our home, Daddy picked me up from a friend's party. "Can we stop for ice cream?" I asked.

Always one to indulge me, Daddy obliged. I bought a double-dip chocolate cone and was still eating it when we walked in the door. Daddy had nothing.

Mommy stood there and glared. "Harry, what have you done?" she asked angrily.

"I bought Libby an ice cream cone," he answered.

"We can't afford an ice cream cone!" she screamed. "We can't afford food. What were you thinking?"

Daddy looked at her in surprise, and they began arguing in front of me. I'd never seen them argue and felt guilty for requesting the ice cream. Suddenly Mommy picked up a dinner plate and threw it at my father. When he ducked and the plate shattered against the wall, I ran to my room crying.

Anger pervaded our household after that night, spreading across all of our daily interactions. My father spent his days out with friends while my mother worked at a minimum-wage job. Blanche worked and I went to school, preferring to go to friends' homes after school rather than return home.

In the evening, Mommy and I watched TV in the living room. Daddy locked himself in the den, watching TV and inhaling his beloved cigars. Occasionally, he'd open the den door and poke his head out to see if anything was going on. One of Mommy's friends referred to him as "The Turtle."

The morning that President John Fitzgerald Kennedy was inaugurated, January 20, 1961, I stayed home from school because it was a snow day. On January 19, a major snowstorm blanketed the entire East Coast, shutting down roads and air traffic. Workers in Washington, D.C. labored furiously to clear the streets and venues for the president's inauguration.

I sat down on the living room sofa to watch it on television. Like so many people of that era, I was enamored of the handsome young man about to become the leader of the free world. I turned on the television, and Daddy came into the room and switched it off.

"I want to see the president sworn in and the parade," I said.

"Get dressed and go to school," Daddy answered.

"There is no school. It's a snow day," I replied.

"Don't get fresh with me," Daddy said. Then he strode across the room and spanked me, something he rarely did.

I stood there and began to cry. "Go away," I yelled. "I hate you. Why are you always so angry?"

Daddy stalked out of the house, and I was relieved.

Two months later, we left our home for the last time and Daddy was no longer part of my life.

To this day my memories of him are hazy and somewhat suppressed. He was responsible for a major turning point in my life—our family's financial losses, which led to the sale of our home, its furnishings, my mother's jewelry and furs, my beloved piano, and many other treasured possessions. This reversal of fortune made my mother seek a new life in California, one where we could start over. But we left our lifelong friends and all that was familiar. His actions caused the dissolution of their marriage, but they also resulted in two broken hearts.

Looking back on that painful time in my life, I realize that I only knew my father for thirteen years, but I never really knew him at all. He was born in Russia on October 18, 1900, the beginning of the twentieth century. His parents named him Harry Berger, and when he was three or four years old, his entire family—father, Isaac; mother, Anne; and brother, Joseph—emigrated to America.

Aunt Rose and Uncle Joe, Poppy, Daddy
and Mommy were once close.

As Jews, they were subject to the pogroms that ravaged their homeland. My father's family was fortunate to obtain papers to leave. One cousin said that my father behaved so badly on the passage to America that they almost threw him off the boat. I can believe that. He remained a child for most of his life.

After the family arrived in the United States, they settled in Philadelphia. My grandfather, a painter by trade and a very religious man, became a cantor at an Orthodox synagogue. His brother's family found housing nearby. When my father grew up, he entered the retail clothing business on Market Street. Uncle Joe, my father's brother, became a pharmacist.

The Berger boys eventually married young women from New Jersey. My father married my mother, Ruth Celia Dickstein, on July 25, 1926. Uncle Joe married Rose Bierer, an Austrian immigrant. They became close friends, along with another couple, Rose's sister, Pearl, and her husband, Morris Gast, who became my Aunt Pearl and Uncle Moe.

To me my father was Daddy, the go-to guy for fun, the man who showed me off at work by placing me on the bar, took me down the shore on Sunday afternoons, or picked me up from friends' houses after school.

My mother thought he spoiled Blanche and me and continually tried to constrain him. The December evening that he brought home two small, blue-flocked Christmas trees and told her they were Chanukah bushes was typical. Daddy wanted to have some fun, to bring a little joy into the house. Mommy was all business and told him to get rid of them. Jews did not have Christmas trees.

Because my mother didn't drive, my father more than made up for it. He bought a new Oldsmobile every year, and he made sure that everyone knew it. He proudly parked the latest model out front and invited all the neighbors over for a look-see.

One year he bought a convertible, an unusual car for Hillside, New Jersey, in the midfifties. Because he owned a convertible, he was invited to drive it in our town's annual Little League Parade. Hillside resident Phil Rizzuto of the New York Yankees was his guest of honor. I felt so proud to see my father at the wheel of his car while the New York Yankees' great sat beside him. I ran alongside the car cheering Phil Rizzuto and pointing at Daddy.

Not long afterwards, his car was stolen by his cook at the tavern he owned. He had to drive the 1956 Plymouth he bought for my mother when she began to drive again. We could not afford another car. Six months after the theft, a Hillside policeman rang our doorbell. "Is Harry Berger here?" he asked.

"He's not home," Mommy answered. "What's wrong?"

"We found an Oldsmobile registered to him in Coatesville, Pennsylvania. It was towed away as an abandoned vehicle."

"That car was stolen months ago," Mommy replied. "We filed a report with the Newark Police Department."

Daddy was delighted when he came home and heard the news. I remember the day his friend Arnold drove him to Pennsylvania to pick up the car. He was elated and still owned that car when he died.

My father was nearly fifty years old when I was born, not the ideal age for fathers in the late 1940s. Although he did not want another child, he acquiesced after my mother got the call. It seems a fifteen-year-old had given birth, surprising her parents one Sunday afternoon in February 1948. They needed to find a home for this child immediately. My parents' doctor began making calls. I remember when I was in sixth grade and my classmate told me I was adopted, my mother said, "I wanted you the minute I saw you, but Daddy didn't really want another child. I made him come to the hospital with me, and once he saw you, he wanted you, too."

Daddy doted on me and my sister, although children never fit his agenda. He was having too much fun being a child himself. He loved good times— card games, horse races, trips to Florida—anything but work. Yet he owned a business, thanks to my mother and her family, who'd struggled for years to buy a neighborhood bar in Newark and build it into a prosperous enterprise.

Daddy sold the bar and then lost two other businesses while he was out having fun. Because of his childish ways, he lost everything—his livelihood, his home, his belongings, but most of all his family. I wonder if he ever thought about the consequences of his actions.

After we moved out of our house in Hillside, I did not see my father again. When I learned to what extent he was responsible for our family's misfortune, I was too angry to talk to him. He was no longer the man in the photo, lovingly standing beside me while I sat on a pony for the first time, buying me a doll after I broke two bones in my right arm, buying me lobster dinners down the shore, visiting me at summer camp when Mommy stayed home to take care of Blanche, picking me up from friends' houses after parties, and being the man I ran to hug and kiss when he walked in the door each evening. The Daddy I knew died long before he left this world on March 19, 1962.

Because she lived back East, Blanche attended Daddy's funeral and cried the loudest, according to reports from our Philadelphia cousins. She ingratiated herself to his side of the family by showing up. It took me years to realize how much my sister and my father were alike. All I knew now was that my mother and I had become outcasts.

14

Mommy

My mother was still recovering from her heart attack in January when my father died in March. Ten days later we received news that our dear Uncle Charlie also passed away. Poor Zayde and Aunt Bessie only had each other now. I wonder if my mother worried that she might be the next to die.

She struggled to regain her health and gradually gave up smoking, something she had done since she was nineteen years old. When she began smoking, she thought that it was sophisticated and modern, because that is the image the tobacco companies portrayed. Sadly, she experienced the toll it took on her heart, which had already been compromised by family genes.

But she persisted and searched for a new job. Not many positions appeared for fifty-six-year-old former housewives, but she promised to do whatever she could to care for me.

She eventually found work as a cashier in a nearby car wash owned by an Italian family. When she came home and told me, I thought that my mother had come a long way from Hillside, New Jersey. I remembered her full-length mink coat, mink and fox stoles, large diamonds and other jewels, weekly visits to the beauty salon, lovely dresses, and our large two-story home in an upper middle-class neighborhood. We'd even had a live-in maid. Now Mommy sat in the cashier's booth of a car wash on Valley Boulevard with the sun beating down on her all day.

The job offered other benefits: kind owners, friendly customers, and a chance to be off her feet. My mother grew tan from the constant sun, and she began to look healthy once more. With her olive skin and dark hair, she was often asked if she was related to the owners. In her more playful moments at home, she would talk with an Italian accent, something she did often in New Jersey. But she was rarely playful anymore. The fun had gone out of her life, and she devoted herself to me and to getting by.

I helped as best I could. I became a decent housekeeper and spent each Saturday cleaning house, a habit that continued until I left for college. I learned a little bit about cooking, and even accepted some babysitting jobs to earn a little cash. I was never a great babysitter because I had no idea what to do with children. I'd never learned how to play, and at best I was a careful monitor, nothing more.

As eighth-grade graduation approached, Mommy searched for an affordable white dress for me to wear. All of the girls were required to wear white at the commencement ceremony. Because I was such a good student, I was asked to read the opening prayer. Our class would sing a few songs and then receive our diplomas.

The day Mrs. Schneider asked the class what songs we'd like to sing, I suggested "Stranger in Paradise," because we'd learned it in music.

Mrs. Schneider glared at me. "That song was written by a Russian composer and talks about the steppes of Asia. We are not going to sing a Communist song at graduation."

Mrs. Schneider had blinders on when it came to literature, art, and music. I recalled the day I'd brought *Gone With the Wind* to school to read in my spare time. "Does your mother know you're reading this book?" my teacher asked.

"Yes, she gave it to me," I answered.

"Well, you may not read it in my class," announced Mrs. Schneider.

I was puzzled but complied. I'd learned how mean my teacher could get that year.

On graduation day, Uncle Richard had to work, but Mommy and Aunt Shirley had the day off. When Mommy went to pick Aunt Shirley up, my aunt emerged

Mommy smiled proudly when I graduated from eighth grade.

from the bedroom wearing a two-tone gray knit dress with a jacket. Underneath the dress, she wore one of her foundations, known as a Merry Widow. The Merry Widow was a strapless corset with stays that pushed everything up, including my aunt's ample bosom.

Uncle Lou, who was unable to join them, looked at his wife and said, "Shirley, I think your bust is a bit too high today. Go in the bedroom and take it down."

Mommy asked to use the bathroom to suppress the laughter that she felt coming after Lou's remark. When she told me about it later, tears rolled down her cheeks as she laughed once more.

These comic moments made our daily lives more bearable. Finances became a greater worry after Mommy's medical bills our first year in California. To ease the burden, Uncle Richard suggested we move in together and share the rent.

In July 1962 we rented half of a duplex on Hidalgo Street in a better area of town. Our side of the duplex had only one bedroom, which we assigned to Unc, and my mother and I slept in the area designated as the dining room. Apartment dwellers on the East Coast often transformed the dining room into a bedroom, similar to what Aunt Bessie and Uncle Charlie had done in their house in Philadelphia. This wasn't a novel idea, but it was new to us.

Moving into a home with us was a major concession for my uncle, a nonconformist construction plumber who lived in a robin's-egg-blue trailer and played opera on his state-of-the-art high fidelity system. When he agreed to move in, he towed the trailer to the back of our driveway and used it for respite. He was with us in body, but not in spirit. At times, he played his music so loud that his trailer shook and the neighbors complained.

Uncle Richard made many changes for us those first two years. Before he brought us to California, he lived alone with the philosophy that he would only work when he needed to. He earned money, lived simply, and saved most of his salary. Then he'd take a few months off to pursue his writing, hiking, and other pastimes. He rejected the middle-class lifestyle popular in the fifties and sixties and lived more like a bohemian or Beatnik.

I think he was a nonconformist his entire life. He had been politically active in the 1930s and was arrested picketing the German Embassy in Washington, D.C., toward the end of that decade. He had also been a member of the Communist Party, which was why he changed his name from Abraham Dickstein to Richard Stein.

I'm not sure why he felt so generous toward us now. Perhaps he was trying to make up for his thirty-year absence. I never quite understood the reason for that either.

My grandmother Blanche Owsowitz married a man named Goldstone when she was young. She gave birth to my mother, Ruth, in 1906 and my uncle two years later. Unc was born with a club foot, and treatment was limited at that time. Although he'd had corrective surgery, he always walked with a pronounced limp. I think my grandmother treated him differently because of his "imperfection," and he never felt accepted.

When my mother and uncle were little, my grandmother divorced, which was rare at that time. A few years later, she married Morris Dickstein, and her children took his last name.

"My mother had big plans for me, but I had my own plans," Unc told me. "Once she insisted that I become a doctor. I told her that I would rather be a plumber. A doctor is merely a plumber for people's bodies. If I'm going to be a plumber, I'd rather work on buildings."

"I never got along with my stepfather either," he added.

I did not understand how anyone could dislike my beloved Poppy, whom I adored. Surely, Unc did not tell me the whole story.

"My mother always favored my sister, and I became the 'black sheep' of the family," Unc continued.

I knew that my grandmother and mother were close. They bore a strong resemblance to each other, traveled together frequently, and were often mistaken for sisters. My uncle resented their relationship and left home as soon as he was able.

Although our new living arrangements were a major concession for Unc, I liked our new neighborhood much better than the old one. Other families lived nearby, and I could walk to high school with my classmates, as I had with my friends in New Jersey. Life seemed a lot better.

Once we started high school, Julie and I went to football games and dances. We spent a lot of time together, except when she had a date.

That same year I met Rickie Berns, who became my other close high school friend, in synagogue on Yom Kippur. A mutual acquaintance introduced us, and Rickie and I instantly liked each other. I recall how funny she was on that High Holiday. "Look over there," she said, turning her head to the side. "Do you see that man? I call him *The Red Velvet Yarmulke* because of his unusual skullcap. He doesn't wear a black satin *yarmulke*, like the other men in temple." We began to make up stories about *The Red Velvet Yarmulke* and his exploits, as if he were a superhero.

We also listened to impassioned pleas to help Israel, a struggling young nation filled with our own people, during the break in prayers. I knew my parents

Uncle Richard believed his mother favored his sister.

My grandmother and mother traveled together often.

had purchased Israeli bonds to support the Jewish homeland, as had Rickie's family. After all, Rickie and I were born the same year Israel became a nation.

Rickie lived with her divorced mother and her mother's parents in adjoining houses on Atlantic Boulevard in Monterey Park. Mrs. Berns operated a nursery school behind their homes. Rickie's grandparents, Adam and Sadie Rubin, were sad, but kind, people. They still mourned the death of their son in the Black Forest of Germany during World War II. They and Rickie's mother hated Germans and all things German. Rickie would not even ride in Mrs. Frank's Volkswagen, her bitterness was so deep. They conveyed their biases to me, and I, too, became wary of people with German backgrounds.

When I first met Rickie, I asked, "What high school do you go to?"

"Mark Keppel," she replied, "but I want to transfer to Alhambra High. The kids there seem nicer than where I am."

Within weeks, Rickie changed schools. Julie and I invited her into our circle of friends. We often spent time with her after school, when she was not working at her mother's nursery school. If her mother needed extra help at the school occasionally, Julie and I would go over there and work. Mrs. Berns was so kind to the children. She fixed them hot lunches every day and even served them kosher meat.

Julie, Rickie, and I were assigned to different classes at Alhambra High. Rickie and I took college preparatory courses, while Julie took general education, having no great academic aspirations. I was assigned to advanced placement within the college prep sector, so Rickie and I never had a class together either. But the three of us managed to find each other at lunchtime, when we sat and talked.

Our freshman year Rickie and I joined B'nai Brith Girls (BBGs), a Jewish social organization that included some service to the community. BBGs held dances with their male counterparts, who belonged to Aleph Zedek Aleph (AZAs). Once or twice Rickie and I invited Julie to attend a dance. Before we could blink, she started dating Phil Pressman, a nice Jewish boy. Julie really liked him, and he liked her. Phil's parents were not thrilled because Julie wasn't Jewish. "How could you bring a *shicksa* [a non-Jewish young woman] to a Jewish social gathering?" they asked me.

"I didn't mean any harm," I replied. "Julie's a very sweet girl from a nice family."

"But she isn't Jewish!" they screamed.

Meanwhile, Rickie had been asked out by Rick Solis, a Latino football player at Alhambra High. Her mother had a lot of questions, but her grandmother, Mrs. Rubin, asked the critical one, "Is he Jewish?"

Rickie hemmed and hawed. She liked Rick, but she knew her grandmother would say no if she told her his real name. Instead, when questioned, Rickie said, "His name is Rick, Rick Solistein."

Her mother and grandmother relented. Rickie went out with Rick once or twice, but she realized she couldn't keep up the pretense at home. Julie was happy to step in and rescue her, and she invited Rick to the Sadie Hawkins Dance. Julie and Rick began dating, and after that, religious discussions quieted down for a while.

Alhambra was primarily a Christian town in the 1960s. There were numerous churches and only one small synagogue. The Jewish kids sometimes got together at school, but there weren't enough of us, and many of us had nothing in common except religion.

We also had many Christian friends, who came from Caucasian, Latino, and Asian families. I enjoyed the mix, which was far more diverse than Hillside.

The social clubs at school were called Y clubs and were affiliated with the Young Women's Christian Association, or YWCA. You had to "try out" for a club; you couldn't just join. Neither Rickie nor I even tried out because of the YWCA affiliation. Julie hung out with us and didn't join a club either. We were The Three Musketeers for a while, and life was good.

About a week before Thanksgiving, my life changed once more. I came home from school to a ringing telephone. When I answered it, a woman asked, "Is this the Berger residence?"

"Yes," I answered. "Who is this?"

"I'm calling from Los Angeles County General Hospital. Is Ruth Berger your mother?"

Again, I answered yes.

"Your mother came in for a checkup this afternoon, and the doctor discovered she'd had a heart attack. He has put her in the hospital. Is there an adult at home who can take care of you?"

"My uncle will be home from work shortly," I answered. "Please give me a phone number where he can call you. I'll be fine." Then I hung up the phone and cried. More tears flowed later that evening when Unc and I drove to County

General Hospital to see my mother. She was asleep in a room by herself, heavily sedated. The doctor took my uncle aside to talk, and I could see him shaking his head. I cried all the way home, fearing the worst. Mommy looked so small and so still.

Having survived the night, my mother was moved to a critical care ward the next day. There were at least twelve patients in the room, all seriously ill men and women. Tubes snaked from beneath their bedcovers, carrying bodily fluids. Although it appeared to be clean, the ward reeked. I'm not sure if the smell emanated from the sick patients or the body-fluid bags attached to them. I hated going there to visit.

Each evening I was afraid to look at the other patients hooked up to different types of medical equipment as I entered to see my mother. I'd try to be cheerful and say hello to everyone, but they all looked so sick that it frightened me. Every few days I'd spy an empty bed and ask my mother where the person was. "He died today," she would answer, tears in her eyes. I saw fear in her face for the first time and realized I had to be brave for her sake. She thought she might be next.

One evening my uncle and I went to visit, and my mother's bed was empty. We ran to the nurses' station, panicked. "Where is Ruth Berger?" my uncle yelled.

The nurse looked up and said, "I don't know."

"What do you mean you don't know? She was here yesterday and now she's gone. What happened?"

A supervisor stepped in and located my mother's medical chart. "We moved her to a rehabilitation facility today. Didn't anyone call you?"

My uncle and I rushed to get to the new hospital before visiting hours ended. The rehab facility was on the other side of downtown Los Angeles, and my uncle sped away. When we finally found my mother alone in her room, we all cried.

"I thought you forgot me," she said.

"I could never forget you," I answered, trying to gain my composure.

A few weeks later, I turned fifteen. My mother was still in the hospital, nearly three months after she'd been admitted. On my birthday she leaned over and kissed me. Then she removed the small gold Star of David from her neck and handed it me. "I want you to have this as your birthday present," she said. I was thrilled to receive something so special.

At the beginning of March my mother came home, three-and-a-half months after she'd first been hospitalized. For most of that time she'd lain in bed, dosed with Phenobarbital and milk of magnesia, not allowed to move. In the early sixties, that was how they thought the heart should mend.

That spring everything began to change. Julie and I were still close, and Mrs. Frank and my mother became better friends. Rickie had little to do with us, and I did not know why. She was distant at school and never available when I called. I was dealing with enough at home and tried not to let her behavior bother me, although many times it did.

Shortly before my mother planned to return to work, my uncle announced, "I'm moving out, back to the trailer park."

I guess three-and-a-half months caring for me made him want his freedom once more. He and my mother talked, and reluctantly she agreed he should go. I did not understand, but I knew my mother and I could no longer afford the larger portion of our duplex. The smaller side had recently become vacant, and our landlord agreed to rent it to us.

Since we had acquired little during our stay in California, the move went smoothly. But after Uncle Richard moved out and we moved next door, he and my mother rarely spoke.

"Mommy, why doesn't Unc call or come over to see us anymore?" I asked one evening.

For the first time, my mother treated me like an adult and answered, "Your uncle is angry with me. He doesn't understand why I didn't set aside his half of our inheritance, why I let Daddy take over the bar. I tried to find him. I put ads in newspapers all over the country, but you know that he was gone for thirty years. What else could I do? I didn't even know if he was still alive."

"How can he still be angry over matters that occurred so long ago?" I asked. "Mommy, this doesn't make sense, especially now. What's wrong with Uncle Richard? I don't understand," I said.

My mother was my role model. I knew she did not hurt people intentionally, and she was painfully honest—a trait that I learned from her. She would never keep something that belonged to someone else. She just shook her head, trying to keep from crying. She rarely showed emotion with me, and this talk was the closest we ever got to so many family secrets.

In June my mother went back to work at the car wash part time, thanks to the lovely family who owned it. They sent a Thanksgiving turkey and Christmas ham when she was hospitalized and called often to check on her during this bleak period. Each time they said, "Tell Ruth we're holding her job for her when she's ready to come back."

By July, Mommy was back at work full time, and I began to feel like a normal teenager again. I had just completed my freshman year of high school, received high grades despite my nightly commutes to the hospital, and enrolled in summer school to learn typing. After school I spent time with Julie while my mother worked. The weather was warm, and a long, fun-filled summer stretched ahead.

One day when I was home alone and feeling bored, I found a large envelope filled with my mother's papers. I began to go through it, curious about what she kept. After sorting through many documents, I came to a birth certificate. It listed "Baby Girl Scaglione" with my birthdate. So that was my birth name? I read on and discovered someone named Angela Scaglione had given birth to me. I also found a second birth certificate with my present name and adoption papers signed two years after I was born. I began to cry and put the papers back in the envelope, never telling my mother what I had found.

A few days later, on July 12, 1963, Julie and I went to see the new movie *Bye Bye Birdie*, and she spent the night. We came home singing the songs and dancing around the house, laughing and being silly. In the morning Julie's mom came to pick her up, and she and my mother had coffee and visited. It was a beautiful summer day.

That evening I agreed to babysit for a young couple who lived in the apartment next to our friend Gene on Bushnell Avenue. They were going out for their anniversary, and I promised to care for their two little boys.

Gene had moved from Bushnell Avenue before we did, and now lived near her mother in midtown Los Angeles. Mommy had called her several times since she'd returned from the hospital, but Gene only spoke briefly and then said she needed to hang up, especially when Mommy asked if she could say hello to Robin. Mommy turned to me one night and said, "I don't know what's wrong with Gene. I can't seem to get her to talk." Sadly, I would find out all too soon.

Babysitting had never been my favorite activity, especially since I'd moved to California, and that night was the last time I babysat.

About ten o'clock I called my mother, "Hi, Mommy, what are you doing?" I asked.

"I'm watching TV and getting ready to go to bed. I'm feeling very tired and will probably be asleep by the time you get home," she answered. "Are you all right?"

"I'm fine," I said. "I'll be quiet when I get home so I won't wake you. I wish they'd come back, because I'm pretty tired right now."

"You can doze a little if you need to, but listen for the boys," Mommy added. Before she hung up, she said, "I love you."

"I love you, too," I responded. "Good-bye, Mommy."

About half past two in the morning, the couple returned. They thanked me, paid me, and the husband drove me home. He dropped me off, waiting until I was inside before he drove away.

When I entered the house, I sensed something was terribly wrong. I walked into the bedroom that my mother and I shared and saw her lying on her bed with Bonnie Sue curled up beside her. My mother's lips were blue.

I ran to her yelling, "Mommy, Mommy, wake up."

She did not respond. I began shaking her, my voice growing louder, "Mommy, please wake up. I need you. Don't leave me." Tears streamed down my face as I wailed. I grew cold with fear.

I could hear a television blasting next door, and I rushed to the other side of the duplex, banging on the front door. "Help me, help me! Please open the door."

No one answered. Frantically I rang the bell. The TV continued to blare in the background.

I returned to our house and tried to rouse my mother once more. Then I grabbed the phone, not knowing whom to call. My uncle was angry with us, but I tried him first. "Unc, Mommy is lying in bed and her lips are blue. She's not moving," I whined.

"What do you want me to do?" he replied.

I put the phone back on the receiver and then called Julie's mother.

She arrived within minutes, looked at my mother, and called an ambulance. When the ambulance pulled up, I felt hopeful. Perhaps they could save my mother. The adults made me go into the other room, and Mrs. Frank held me as we waited. An attendant came in and shook his head.

A police car and a hearse pulled up next. My worst fear was confirmed. My mother was dead, and I was alone.

15

The Child that Nobody Wanted

With my mother's death I became "the child that nobody wanted" for the second time in my life. The first was shortly after my birth. The story I was told by my mother's best friend, Ruth Goodman, after my mother died went like this. I was born to a large Italian family that had a lot of children and could not afford another, so they gave her up for adoption. The family asked their physician to find a home for the little girl.

Their physician called the three Ruths—Kaplan, Goodman, and Berger— to enquire if any would like a baby girl. Ruth Kaplan had just given birth to Ned and had an older son as well. "No, thank you," she replied.

Then the doctor called Ruth Goodman. Her son, Neil, was less than six months old, and she also had an older daughter. "We can't do it," she said, thinking of her husband's salary as a high school teacher.

The doctor next called Ruth Berger, who became my mother. She had to do some talking to get her husband, Harry, to agree. After adopting Blanche in 1944, Harry didn't want any other children. But Ruth asked Ruth Goodman to drive her to the hospital to see the baby. She came home that night and said, "I want that baby, even if I have to raise her myself." Shortly after that I became their daughter.

The day they brought me home, my name was changed from Baby Girl Scaglione to Libby Jewel Berger. Libby was after my great-grandmother, Shima-Libby Owsowitz. Jewel was after my mother's Uncle Jule, who died shortly before I was born. It actually took two years for my adoption to become final, but on that day shortly after my birth in 1948, Ruth and Harry Berger became the only parents I ever knew.

When my mother died that July morning in 1963, the enormity of my loss overwhelmed me. I had lost two mothers and fathers, one set known, the other strangers. My sister was 3,000 miles away, and I had no one. At times I wasn't sure if I wanted to live or die. I felt completely alone. I was also frightened and did not know what would happen to me. I recalled the policeman who arrived at our house on Hidalgo Street in Alhambra the night Mommy died.

"Do you have someone to take care of you?" he asked.

"Yes," I lied, fearing I would be placed in an orphanage.

Mrs. Frank put her arm around me and said, "She's coming home with me."

I was relieved, but my relief was only temporary. The three Ruths were no longer around. I did call Ruth Goodman a few hours after my mother died and asked if I could come back to Hillside. "I'm sorry, Libby," she said. "It's just not possible." I knew she was right, but I secretly wished I could go back and live in the only place I knew as home.

I'd also hoped that the Franks would take me in, but that was a dream, too. Julie's father was a postal worker, and her mother cared for the family and her own parents. They did not have the means, the time, or the desire for a "new" family member, especially someone they'd only known for two years.

Blanche was now nineteen and about to marry Vinnie, her on-again/off-again boyfriend since she was fifteen. She was finally able to care for herself and did not need to care for her younger sister, too.

Uncle Richard had mixed feelings. He was almost fifty-five years old, divorced, and childless. Although we'd grown close since he arrived on our doorstep in December 1959, he had no experience as a parent. He thought I should live with a family and have the semblance of a "normal" life.

My cousin Milton, a successful cardiologist with four children, and his wife, Leila, had invited me over several times during my mother's illness. I enjoyed time with them and their children. One night, while driving me home, Leila said, "Libby, if anything happens to your mother, you can live with us."

I thought her offer odd, and at the time, I was shocked. It never occurred to me that my mother might die. "Thank you," I said and put them out of my mind.

When Uncle Richard called them to tell them that Mommy died, Milton did not offer what his wife so generously had. He suggested that my uncle call his younger brother Stanley.

Uncle Richard called Stanley, who was indeed eager to help. As a child, I'd adored my cousin Stanley. I thought he was so handsome, and he had a beautiful singing voice. When he sang at our monthly family circle gatherings in Philadelphia, the family referred to him as the next Mel Tormé. He aspired to be just that, but he also wanted to become a psychologist and earned an undergraduate degree from Cal State L.A., the local state college. (California State College, Los Angeles, became California State University, Los Angeles.) He was a social worker in Los Angeles County, and music was his avocation.

Now thirty, Stanley had married his girlfriend Carol the previous year, and I was happy for him. My childhood crush now had a wife I looked forward to meeting. Mommy had told me about her when she'd attended Carol's baby shower only a few weeks earlier. "She's very pretty," Mommy reported. "She has a lovely smile, big blue eyes, and dark blond hair. She's also very sweet. I think you'll like her."

Aunt Shirley and Uncle Lou (my father's cousins) welcomed Carol to the family. But in July 1963, Carol was only twenty-three, and Stanley was thirty. Their first child was due any day. I wondered why they opened their home to a grieving fifteen-year-old, but I was grateful they had.

When Unc told me the news, I was thrilled that my cousins wanted me. "But you can't bring Bonnie Sue," he added.

I began to cry, something I did easily and often after my mother died. "But Unc, Bonnie made the trip with us across the country and is the only member of my family left. She curled herself around Mommy the night Mommy died. How can I give her up?" I protested.

"I'm sorry, Libby," Unc said softly. "Stanley and Carol live in an apartment, and the building does not allow dogs. What choice do we have?"

I thought I was all cried out, but Unc's announcement brought more tears. Fortunately, my mother's employers, the kind Italian family who owned the car wash where she was cashier, offered to take Bonnie Sue. They promised I could come see her.

But a few weeks after Bonnie Sue arrived in their household, she nipped their two-year-old daughter and was banished. I was told that she went to live with an older lady who pampered her to the end. I never saw her again.

Once Unc found a place for me to live, we began to plan my mother's funeral. It was the hardest thing I'd ever had to do.

Eight years earlier, my beloved Poppy, who had lived with us all my life, died. I was not given the chance to say good-bye to him. In our home, death was never discussed in front of the children, and adults used hushed tones when dealing with the subject. On the day of his funeral I played with Neil Goodman as if nothing had happened.

My parents had shielded me from death my entire life, and my mother's death was not a good introduction. Another big problem added to the emotional aspect: we were poor. At her death, my mother's assets consisted of some family jewelry she'd managed to salvage from the pawnshop, crystal, china, a few antiques, a 1956 Plymouth Belvedere, and $200 in cash that I'd found in her sewing basket.

Fortunately, traditional Jewish funerals are not elaborate affairs. Religious Jews are wrapped in shrouds and buried in plain pine boxes. They wear no shoes or jewelry. These traditions would make the monetary aspect easier, but I could not bear to put my mother in a shroud.

Because she'd lost sixty pounds through illness in the past year and money was scarce, her wardrobe was limited. I was able to find one dress in her closet that was appropriate. She had worn it only thirteen months earlier to my eighth grade graduation. We had no choice but the plain pine box. We could not afford anything better.

I called my mother's employer and her small group of friends. Gene was at the top of the list.

"Hi, Gene," I said. "It's Libby. We haven't talked in a while, but my mother died early Sunday morning. Her funeral is on Tuesday. I hope you'll come."

"Oh, Libby, I'm so sorry," she replied. "I haven't been able to call her lately. I just couldn't bear to tell her what happened, but I knew she sensed something was wrong."

"What happened?" I asked, recalling my mother's concern over Gene's distance.

"Robin died," Gene answered. "You know how active he was and how he did not always listen. Well, we were walking down Pico Boulevard, and I had Dorothy and Richard by the hand. Robin was beside us when he saw a ball in the street. He ran into the street before I could stop him and was hit by a car. He lived for a few days, but he was too far gone. I sat by his bedside saying, 'Breathe, Robin, breathe,' but his little body just gave up.

"I didn't tell your mother because I knew her heart couldn't take it," Gene added. "I'm so sorry."

We were both crying by the time our conversation ended, and I felt glad that my mother had been spared the death of the little boy she loved so much.

Blanche and Vinnie flew in from New Jersey for the funeral. I was surprised that Blanche had actually come on an airplane. The last time either of us had flown was in 1954, and we each vowed never to fly again.

I had not seen my sister in two years, and she seemed much more grown up than the last time we met. We arranged for her and Vinnie to stay at the duplex where my mother and I had lived. I could not bear to stay there after finding my mother two nights earlier and had already moved in with Stanley and Carol.

I borrowed my friend Julie's sister's black dress to wear to my mother's funeral on that warm July morning. My new "family," Stanley and Carol, did not attend. They said it was "bad luck" for a pregnant woman to attend a funeral. I didn't question their reasoning. I could barely make it through a few hours without bursting into tears.

The mortuary was on Venice Boulevard, close to a freeway ramp near downtown Los Angeles. A small group gathered to bid my mother farewell. She'd been in California such a short time, and only a few neighbors, friends, and her employer attended.

My uncle, sister, Vinnie, and I filed slowly into the area reserved for family, hidden behind a sheer curtain to allow us to grieve privately. My mother had not known the rabbi who performed the service, as we did not have enough money to join the local temple. He was kind and did a beautiful job describing her, based on what my uncle and I had told him. I could not understand many of the prayers, which were recited in Hebrew, but I followed along as best I could through my unending tears.

After the service, people were invited to view the open coffin before they drove to the cemetery. When it was time for our family to say farewell, Blanche screamed as she took one last look at Mommy. She had not seen our mother in two years, and she could not get over how thin she had become. Blanche's shrieks could be heard in the parking lot, Julie told me later.

The ride to the cemetery seemed endless. Our motorcade headed up Interstate 5, through the San Fernando Valley, and into the foothills surrounding Kagel Canyon. Mommy would be buried in Sholom Memorial Park and lie in a pauper's grave far from the affluent cemeteries of Los Angeles.

My uncle, sister, Mrs. Frank, and Julie surrounded me as we prayed by the gravesite and the rabbi led us in the mourner's *kaddish*. Then they began to lower my mother's coffin and invited each person to shovel some dirt over it. My hard-won composure dissolved when my turn came. As I poured the dirt into the grave, I wanted to jump in after it. Life was no longer worth living.

16
New Life

*N*ew life brings joy after sorrow. My joy arrived in the form of a baby girl, born to my cousins Carol and Stanley one week after I moved in. They named their blond-haired, blue-eyed first-born Suzanne Frances and called her Suzie. I loved this little girl, so sweet and innocent, and hoped we would be friends.

My cousins' lives centered around her, and I often wonder why they offered to give me a home when neither of them was prepared to parent a teenager. Their years of parenting had just begun, and although we were related, we were essentially strangers.

Logistically, they were unprepared. Their two-bedroom, one-bath apartment in Montebello could comfortably contain their little family unit, but my presence complicated matters. There simply wasn't room for one more. In the months ahead, I'd realize this in more than one way.

I lived with Stanley and Carol for one week before their little girl arrived, and they kindly gave me the second bedroom they had decorated for the baby. She would stay in their room temporarily.

While Carol and Stanley adjusted to a newborn's schedule, they also had to deal with the realities of having a teenager, especially one who had just been orphaned.

My first few days with them, I cried often and sat around doing nothing. My parents were dead, my sister had returned to New Jersey, Unc retreated to his trailer, and Bonnie Sue had been given to a new family. I felt like someone who had landed in a new place and taken on a new life, one that I had not wanted or chosen.

Each afternoon about five o'clock, I waited for my mother to return from work. I longed to hear her voice once more and hoped to see her walk through the door. By six o'clock, I realized that she was not coming home and started to cry, grieving for the one person I truly loved.

I wanted to call her on the telephone, like I did that night I babysat. But I knew if I called our home number, no one would be there to answer it. The phone had already been disconnected.

Because I no longer lived in Alhambra and had missed the entire week of school after my mother's death, I had to drop out of summer school. I was enrolled in only one class—typing—and I would not learn how to type until years later. My days dragged in the hot, crowded apartment miles from my friends and an eternity away from my family.

My nights were endless. I wanted to die and be reunited with Mommy, yet I feared going to sleep, because Mommy had died in her sleep. I was so conflicted and grief-stricken at a time when no one talked about grief or death. Everyone around me expected me to carry on and keep my emotions contained. I tried to do just that, but tears fell when I least expected them.

A few weeks after Suzie was born, Stanley called my uncle and invited him over while I was at Julie's house. Later Unc told me about their conversation.

"Richard, we didn't anticipate having two children when we expected one. There's not enough room in this apartment, and we'd like to buy a house. It had always been our plan, but we did not anticipate moving so soon after our baby was born. Could you lend us money for a down payment?"

Uncle Richard said his mouth fell open and he stared at them for a few minutes before responding, "I don't have that kind of money. I live in a trailer. My needs are minimal, and my savings are limited.

"When Ruth died, she left $200 in cash in her sewing box, her 1956 Plymouth, and a few household possessions. Harry spent her family's fortune. That's why she and the girls came to California. The only money Libby has is the Social Security check she'll receive each month."

Unc later told me that he should have seen their request as a warning. My cousin must have thought that my mother was still well off when she died. Perhaps that's why he offered me a home.

Unc remembered why he did not care for my father's family. He'd called them *shnorrers*, the Yiddish word for beggars, after meeting them at my parents' engagement party in 1925. My father's family viewed my mother's family as wealthy, and Unc believed they only liked them for their money.

Despite Unc's inability to help, Stanley and Carol managed to scrape together a down payment. They found a three-bedroom house in Covina that would suit their needs. It was further away from my uncle and my friends in Alhambra, but it was affordable. My parents' Social Security benefits—$88 per month—would be my contribution to the family budget. I also offered to babysit and help with the housework.

The small house they bought looked neglected. Ivy overtook the front yard, and the grass in the backyard had died from lack of water. The inside needed work: a thorough cleaning to remove the layers of grease and dust that had settled upon everything, removal of the Shoji screens (translucent screens made from rice paper stretched on wooden frames) from the windows and between rooms, and new paint before we could move in. The room sizes were adequate, and lovely hardwood floors ran throughout.

As I scrubbed grease from the kitchen walls, I wondered what type of people had lived in this house. I was put off by the dirt in every room and vowed never to let my home get that dirty.

I think Stanley really wanted to make this house our home. He and Carol sat down and planned the paint colors for each room, consulting me when it came to my room. They wanted something modern for the dining room. They settled on bright orange and called it "pumpkin." The baby's room would be pink, and most of the others would be pastel tones. I chose baby blue, which mirrored my feelings.

Stanley's father, sixty-year-old "Uncle" Lou, who was really my father's first cousin, pitched in to help with the painting. I recruited Julie to join the crew, and Stanley worked beside us. We only had one week to clean and paint the entire house before we moved in. The rigors of painting made me miss my old life even more, but I tried to be cheerful and help. I saw this little house as an opportunity for a new life. I desperately wanted a story with a happy ending.

At fifteen, I was too young to realize that too many changes at one time can be stressful. I was grieving. The past two years had been filled with losses: the sale of our home, loss of our upper-middle-class lifestyle, a cross-country move that left my childhood friends behind, then my sister's departure, my parents' deaths, and giving up my beloved dog. All that was familiar in my life was gone.

Now my "family" consisted of my father's cousins, an uncle I'd only known for three years, a distant sister, and a handful of new friends. The comforts and security of my childhood had disappeared.

I was completely absorbed in the new direction my life had taken during the summer of 1963 and totally unaware of what was taking place in the world outside. As we prepared to move into the house in Covina, Dr. Martin Luther King Jr. was leading the March on Washington, a peaceful demonstration for civil rights and economic equality that drew 250,000 people to Washington, D.C. in August. The march culminated at the Lincoln Memorial, where demonstrators prayed, sang, and gave speeches. This tremendous gathering became the prototype for the free speech and antiwar demonstrations that would occur later in the decade. Dr. Martin Luther King Jr. delivered his rousing "I Have a Dream" speech at this march that was televised to millions. My mother would have been proud and cheering Dr. King on had she lived. Unc may have been watching, although I don't recall him mentioning the event. He advocated equal rights for all people, but he had too much on his mind that summer. My cousins never mentioned the March on Washington. Like Unc, they were otherwise occupied.

Soon after I moved in with them, I became Stanley and Carol's ward in a courtroom proceeding. It was my first visit to court, and I recall raising my right hand and taking the oath about telling the truth. The judge reviewed the paperwork and when he saw that my sister had been given money and I, at age fifteen, had been given a car, he balked. "Why are you giving this child a car?" he asked my uncle.

"Because it's the only asset left in her mother's estate," he answered.

The law considered me a child, but I soon discovered that Stanley and Carol expected me to behave like a grown-up: helping to cook, clean, baby-sit, and maintain academic excellence. In some ways, I was the au pair they dreamed of but could not afford. I accepted my new role as best I could, although I was very much a child inside.

In September 1963 my cousins enrolled me at Northview High School, which was within walking distance of our home. I had always been a good student, with high grades, and I looked forward to starting school. It was my solace, a place where I could lose myself to learning. I was eager to begin my sophomore year. I remember signing up for English, journalism, history, and geometry in addition to the mandatory physical education.

From the day I entered kindergarten, I had always loved school, and I vowed to enjoy my new high school even though I was adjusting to a new family, a new home, and new classmates. For the second time in two years, I had to try to make new friends.

Northview High School was only a few blocks from home, and I walked to school daily, eventually making friends on the way. Since Covina was rural and we had no sidewalks, we stuck to the side of the road. One property we passed each day had geese, and one goose would chase us and nip at us on our way to school. I never realized geese could be so hostile.

After ten weeks, the school sent out progress reports, which indicated that I was doing fine. I'd always done my homework without having to be reminded. Yet I dreaded coming home at the end of the day.

Stanley felt the need to check on me all the time. "Have you read your book for your book report? How are you doing in geometry? Did you study for your history test?" he asked.

"Yes," I answered to all his queries. Ironically, the book I had read for my book report was Fail Safe, a novel about American bombers that had gone beyond the point of recall and were about to bomb Moscow during the Cold War. One review said that this book reflected the apocalyptic attitude that pervaded American society after the Cuban missile crisis. People felt that disaster could strike at any minute.

I'd experienced my own apocalypse, and my anxiety had only intensified. My cousin's constant badgering made it worse. He expected me to act like a grownup, but he treated me like a child. My parents had never done that, and I resented his constant monitoring and endless questions.

Carol never explained her expectations, but she relayed them to Stanley, who would say, "Carol thought you would clean the kitchen when you got home from school today, but you didn't."

"I didn't know she wanted me to," I answered.

Life became a constant guessing game. I was never good at games, but I was always a people-pleaser, and I desperately wanted my cousins to like me. I just could not figure out how to do it.

The only one I looked forward to seeing after school was baby Suzie. She always smiled when I walked in the door, and I loved holding her and talking to her. She was a sweet baby, someone to love who brought comfort to my life.

I thought that by helping with Suzie, I'd endear myself to my cousins, but they were wary of my attachment to her. I wanted her to be the little sister I never had; they suspected I might harm her, although I'd never done anything that could be considered dangerous or harmful to anyone in my life. If I sneezed, I was not allowed near her and was sent to my room immediately. If I said I didn't feel well, I received two different responses: I was faking and didn't want to go to school, or I was ill and must be kept away from the baby. Sometimes these responses followed each other so closely that I was completely confused.

On Saturday mornings if I awoke early and heard Suzie in her crib, I'd go in and change her. Then I'd heat a bottle and feed her while we watched cartoons so that my cousins could get a little more rest. She'd lie contentedly in my arms, and I'd feel good.

I treasured these times when it was just Suzie and me and dreaded the moment when her parents awoke. I never knew what I would be reprimanded for each day, and I become wary and hesitant around them. As hard as I tried, I just didn't fit into their lives.

At dinner each night my uncertainty always came out. I was hesitant to take food without asking, although Stanley and Carol assured me that I did not have to ask. Sometimes Stanley became playful at dinner and started performing for us. When he was "on," he could be very funny. He'd start telling jokes and saying one-liners until I could not stop laughing. Occasionally I lost it and snorted my milk out my nose.

Stanley was actually very talented. He'd written a musical revue called

Take a Chance and hoped to have it produced. During the day he worked as a social worker for Los Angeles County, but he dreamed of making his living in show business, like so many others who moved to Los Angeles. Although he had a bachelor's degree in psychology and called himself a psychologist, I saw little evidence of his ability to understand people when he was at home.

Uncle Richard visited me each weekend. He'd often bring Julie with him, and the three of us would go for a ride and out for lunch like we did before my life changed so dramatically. I looked forward to his visits, complained bitterly about what had occurred at home that week, and cried when he left. I felt so trapped.

Fortunately, I'd made a new friend, Carolyn, someone I'd known slightly from the Southwest Region of B'nai B'rith Girls (BBGs). Carolyn was president of the West Covina chapter. Her family was warm and welcoming, and I spent many weekends with them. Her home became my respite, and she became a dear friend and mentor.

I cried a lot during the time I lived with my cousins in Covina, but I shed the most tears on November 22, 1963, the day President John F. Kennedy was assassinated. It was a Friday and only four months and eight days after my dear mother died. I was finally making friends at my new high school.

Between classes my friend Kenny approached my locker and said, "Somebody just shot the president."

"That's not funny," I replied. "That's a terrible joke!"

"I'm not kidding," he added, before hurrying to his next class.

I rushed to journalism, wondering if my friend's words were true. Our teacher, Mr. Schwartz, a hardened old journalist who rarely showed emotion, was in tears. The class filed in somberly, and he delivered the awful news. "President Kennedy is dead. He was assassinated in Dallas this morning. School will be dismissed at noon." Then, like a true journalist, he provided what details he knew.

After school got out, I rushed home and turned on the TV. All the stations showed footage of what had happened, and I watched in horror and cried each time I saw Jacqueline Kennedy standing next to Lyndon Johnson on Air Force One as he was sworn in as president.

That weekend I was scheduled to go to a Southwest Region BBG conclave at Camp Hess Kramer in Malibu. The planners could not cancel it, and so I went and joined many other Jewish teens from around Southern California.

Although we were supposed to conduct business, we spent a great deal of time talking about our dead president and wondering who could do such a thing to this handsome young leader who had offered so much promise. We prayed a lot that weekend and met with more shock on Sunday morning when told that someone had shot the president's alleged assassin. Would the sorrow never end?

Monday, the day of the president's funeral, was a national day of mourning. I sat glued to the TV and sobbed.

Stanley looked at me and said, "You seem to care more about our dead president than you did your own mother."

I just stared at him through my tears, wondering how anyone who claimed to be a psychologist could say something so mean. Even I realized that my tears were for my dead family, although I was deeply saddened by the president's death. His funeral was only the second one I'd ever attended, even though it was on TV. It brought back all the grief I'd felt after my mother's death and burial only a few months earlier, a sorrow that has remained with me my entire life.

Shortly after President Kennedy's funeral, I received a letter from my cousin Davida in New York.

"Dear Libby, I am so sorry to tell you that my brother Tim died from a heart attack in April. He was playing in the yard with Mike when he keeled over. At first Mike thought Tim was playing, but then he realized that something was terribly wrong and yelled for Sue. We are all devastated..."

After reading her letter, I realized that the Family Curse had struck once more. Everyone in my mother's family died from heart disease. I sat down and wrote a long letter to Davida and Aunt Florrie. Tim's death at age thirty-nine was so unfair.

In early December, Stanley and Carol asked to speak with me. I became nervous. What had I done now, I asked myself. We sat around their dining room table, and he began, "Do you remember before you came to live with us that we said we'd give it a try?"

I nodded, fearing the worst.

"This arrangement is not working out," he continued. "You don't seem happy, and your time here has been difficult for all of us."

I continued nodding as my tears began to flow.

"We've spoken with your uncle, and he's agreed to take you in. After the semester ends in January, you'll move back to Alhambra and live with your uncle. You can return to Alhambra High and be back with your old friends."

I smiled through my tears. Although I was unwanted for the third time in my life, I was also free. I would return to a familiar place and be among friends. "You're right," I said. "This isn't working out. I think the new arrangement will be much better." I felt so relieved. At least I would not be sent to live with strangers or placed in an orphanage, a continuing nightmare that had once been proposed.

During Christmas vacation I spent a great deal of my time with Carolyn and her family. Uncle Richard had liked them instantly, and he was happy to see me among people who were kind and caring. We all spent New Year's Eve at Carolyn's house, and Uncle Richard offered to take Carolyn and me to the Rose Parade on New Year's Day. We left her family's house after midnight and staked our claim to some sidewalk on Colorado Boulevard in Pasadena.

I loved the idea. I'd heard from Julie that the Alhambra High School band and drill team would be marching in the parade. It would be great fun to see the floats and some old friends.

Before we left for the parade, we drank screwdrivers that Carolyn's brother had made. I'd never had alcohol before, but cloaked in orange juice, vodka didn't taste too bad. I felt pretty mellow when we headed out the door.

Several hours later I awoke on the sidewalk of Colorado Boulevard and vomited. I guess having a New Year's Eve drink wasn't such a good idea. I certainly didn't want another. Unc bought us some Cokes, and I perked up enough to watch the parade and say hi to old friends.

January 1, 1964, brought sunlight and celebrations. As I watched the parade participants march down the street, filled with smiles and energy, I became hopeful that 1964 would be a much better year.

17

Unc

Life is filled with ironies! Less than three years earlier, the thought of living in Alhambra, California, repulsed me. When I first arrived, I felt that I had landed on an alien planet, where people talked and dressed differently and were shallow. I missed my home and friends in New Jersey terribly and spent my entire first summer writing to them all.

In January 1964, I was thrilled to be moving back to the small San Gabriel Valley town that I had initially shunned. It had become the only home I'd known since our move to California, and it now felt familiar.

I'd made some changes so that I'd fit in better, too, beginning with the way I talked. I lost my Eastern accent within a year of my arrival in California and quickly picked up the nondescript inflection of the West. I also toned down my hair and makeup and saved my nicer clothes for special occasions. People did not "dress" in Alhambra, and I did not want to draw attention to myself with my clothing.

Uncle Richard and I began looking for a place to live in Alhambra just after the holidays, so that I could begin my second semester of tenth grade at Alhambra High. I was eager to return to familiar faces and surroundings after living in Covina for the past six months.

Unc and I found a lovely three-bedroom home for rent in a quiet, family neighborhood only blocks from school and Julie's house. Its yard was large enough for Unc to park his trailer, and it seemed ideal. One of my classmates lived next door.

I was ready to leave Stanley and Carol, but despite my unhappiness while living in their home, I would miss Northview High, where I finally felt comfortable. School had been my solace during this difficult period, and I wanted my grades to show how well I'd adapted that semester, despite the radical changes in my life. My English grade bordered between a B+ and an A-, and I hoped to earn the higher mark. I met with my teacher, Miss Yvonne Vaughn, to find out what I needed to do. She had been especially kind to me that semester, and I really liked her. She was everything I aspired to be—pretty, trim, kind, and bright—and became my role model. She advised me to study as hard as I could, and I followed her advice.

When I received my final exam back, Miss Vaughn had written, "You did an excellent job. You should become an English teacher." Her words remained with me, and only eight years later I did become an English teacher.

Shortly after I became a teacher, I saw a pretty young woman singing on TV. Her name was Donna Fargo, but she looked exactly like Miss Vaughn and sang "I'm the Happiest Girl in the Whole U.S.A." When the song ended, I discovered it was indeed Miss Vaughn. I was happy for her but sad that she would no longer teach others. What an inspiration she had been to me!

When we moved into our small rental house in February 1964, Unc and I became this unlikely father and daughter team—a bachelor uncle and his orphaned niece. When people heard that I lived with my uncle, they always brought up the 1950s' TV show, *Bachelor Father*, with John Forsythe. Unlike the fictitious family, we had no money or servants or others to help us out. Unc worked as a construction plumber during the day, when work was available, and I went to high school. His salary and my parents' Social Security survivor's benefit—$88 per month—were our only income.

We divided the household duties. He shopped and cooked; I washed the dishes each night and cleaned the house every Saturday. We divided laundry duties, and somehow the work got done. Our house was clean, because cleaning was my obsession, but it was not a candidate for *Better Homes and Gardens*.

Returning to Alhambra High was difficult at first. Other students asked where I'd been. In those days when a high school girl was gone for a semester, she was sequestered in another city having a baby out of wedlock. I explained that my mother had died during the summer, and I was sent to live with relatives, since my father had died the previous year. That recitation usually brought me close to tears, but I became more composed each time someone asked. The questions didn't last long, as word of my return spread quickly. Oddly, few teachers knew of my circumstances, which may have been to my benefit. They treated me the same way they treated the other students.

I was placed in honors English and geometry classes, but I could not enroll in biology, a two-semester course, because I'd missed the first semester. I also missed mythology, the focus of English that first semester of sophomore year. I never studied either subject, and my lack of knowledge in those areas always makes me recall that time in my life and wish I could have a do-over.

The typing course I began in the summer of 1963 was not part of my college prep curriculum. It would take me five more years and my first clerical job to teach me to type.

Back in Alhambra, I led a sad, quiet existence. School occupied my days, but my social life was minimal. My nights were spent at home in front of the TV, while Unc read and listened to opera in his backyard trailer.

Many evenings the doorbell rang while he was out there. When I answered it, our next-door neighbor stood on the porch very upset. "Could you ask your uncle to turn down his music, please?" she'd ask. "Our entire house is shaking from the vibrations."

"I'm so sorry," I'd reply. Then I'd go outside and relay the request.

"Oh, that old crone doesn't understand that you need to turn up the volume to truly appreciate music," Unc said. "It's my yard, and I'm going to listen to my music the way it was intended to be heard."

I went back inside, but within the hour, the doorbell rang once more. Sheepishly I opened the door, and the same scenario unfolded. I always felt caught in the middle.

On weekends I hung out with Julie or Rickie if they were available.

On those few occasions when I went out with friends or left the house to go to school, I engaged in some unusual rituals before departing. I'd enter each room, look around, as if I was memorizing it, straighten pictures and knickknacks, touch doorknobs, and make sure everything was in order before I left. Today I'd be called obsessive-compulsive. In 1964, I was just odd.

Unc and Julie laughed at me and said, "There she goes again. Hurry up, Libby, we need to leave."

I felt foolish, but I could not stop myself. I was superstitious and needed to reassure myself that when I returned everything would be just as it was. I later learned that this was my meager attempt to assert control, since my life had been so out of control. Fortunately, I gave up this practice after a year or two, but I had to work hard fighting those obsessions, just as I worked hard to lose my accent.

My friends were much more socially acceptable and a lot prettier than I. With her light brown hair, sparkling blue eyes, sprinkle of freckles, pretty smile, trim figure, and sweet personality, Julie attracted many boys. She also had a strong circle of girlfriends. She was busy, but she always kept me close within her circle.

Rickie was pretty, but she'd grown distant since my return to Alhambra. I couldn't figure out why. Occasionally, she and I attended BBG-AZA parties together at temple, but most times we only saw each other at school.

Many weekends were spent alone at home watching TV in my room until I fell asleep, sometimes fully dressed, and woke up to the white noise. My uncle was out in his trailer, reading and listening to music. He might as well have been on Mars.

In all fairness, my uncle was not used to having another person in his life. He was married and divorced many years earlier and never had children. Suddenly, at the age of fifty-five, he became mother and father to a fifteen-year-old girl. I might as well have been a Martian.

But he did try. On Friday nights we often went to the movies together. I especially remember how we roared at *The Pink Panther* with Peter Sellers. Unc's favorite movie was *It's a Mad, Mad, Mad, Mad World*, which we must have seen three times because it made him laugh. He also loved popcorn and Nestlé Crunch bars, which were forbidden because of his diabetes.

On Sunday evenings we went out for dinner, usually to a place called Preble's on Atlantic Boulevard. It was a glorified coffee shop, but we ate a decent meal without having to cook or spend too much money. Another Sunday favorite was Beadle's cafeteria in Pasadena. Unc loved cafeterias because he could pick and choose.

One Sunday, Unc became adventurous and took me to a restaurant in downtown Los Angeles that had monkeys in cages hanging from the ceiling. We loved the novelty and also enjoyed the food.

Sometimes I found Unc amusing with his unusual names for things. He referred to Westinghouse as W.E. Stinkhouse, Montgomery Ward became Monkey Wards, and former United States President Ulysses S. Grant as Useless Grant. When I applied makeup, he referred to it as War Paint. He called Aunt Shirley an old Powder Pigeon and described her shape as five-by-five. He was irreverent and truly different from any other adult I'd known. Perhaps that is why he considered himself his family's "black sheep." Sometimes his irreverence made me laugh; other times it embarrassed me.

Despite my grief over losing my parents, my lack of a social life, and adjusting to life with my uncle, I found two things on which to focus—school and learning how to drive.

That was Mommy's legacy. On the night my mother died, her assets consisted of a 1956 Plymouth Belvedere and $200 in cash that I found in her sewing basket. Blanche got the cash, and I got the car, a decision my uncle made that several people questioned. "Why would you give a fifteen-year-old a car?" they asked.

When I moved in with cousins Stanley and Carol, I brought the car with me. Shortly after I turned fifteen and a half, I took the written driving test, scored 100 percent, and received my driver's permit. On weekends Unc began teaching me how to drive in Covina's vacant parking lots.

"The first thing you need to learn is how to back up in a straight line," he declared. "If you can do that, going forward isn't very hard." Then he demonstrated his technique, changed seats, and let me have a turn. At first I could only zigzag across the asphalt in reverse, but after many attempts, I got the hang of backing up. To this day, it's something I do well. The day Unc said I could drive forward, I finally felt like I was going somewhere.

My driving lessons continued after I moved back to Alhambra with my uncle. Sometimes he let Julie join us, and she sat quietly in the backseat. Julie was two months older than I and already had her driver's license. Like her mother, Julie was an excellent driver—and she drove a stick shift, something I did not even attempt. Whenever her mom lent her the Volkswagen Beetle, we would go off on adventures. I couldn't wait for my own adventures to begin.

My sixteenth birthday drew near. Unlike some of my friends, I would not have a Sweet Sixteen party, and I didn't feel much like celebrating. My mother had been dead seven months. The one gift I wanted the most—my mother's presence—would never materialize. I recalled my fifteenth birthday when I received my mother's gold Star of David, which I now wore. Although she gave it to me from her hospital bed, I wished I could go back to that day just to see her alive one more time.

At night I dreamed of my mother often. In my dream we had a conversation, and I reached out to hug or kiss her. Then the alarm rang, and I suddenly awakened. Often I awoke in tears, trying to will myself back to sleep, hoping my mother would reappear. The dreams seemed so real, and I desperately wanted her back—if only to say good-bye and tell her how sorry I was that I wasn't home and couldn't help her on the night she died.

I felt so guilty. I truly believed that if I had been home I could have saved her. In my mind I pictured a scenario that went like this. My mother began having a heart attack in her sleep. She cried out in pain. I heard her cry and called an ambulance. It arrived in time to take her to the hospital, and she lived. I never shared these thoughts with anyone for fear that they would have confirmed what I thought. It was my fault she'd died. Then I would have felt twice as guilty.

The reality was that my mother suffered several heart attacks, and nothing I or anyone else did could have saved her that night. I didn't know that at the time, and it has taken years to accept the truth. I realize I had engaged in magical thinking by believing I could have saved her. We all do at times to try to change what we cannot.

Because I could no longer have my mother on my birthday, I decided that the only other thing I wanted was my driver's license. That was not to be. My birthday was on a Saturday that year, and the Department of Motor Vehicles (DMV) would not be open until Monday. Another wish went unfulfilled, but only temporarily.

On the morning of my sixteenth birthday Julie arrived with a gift and a huge smile. Julie is full of smiles, even when life is not going well. We didn't usually exchange gifts, because neither of us had much spending money, and I was surprised. But this was a special birthday, and Julie knew better than most people how I would feel.

I carefully unwrapped her package. "The Beatles' first album! How great is this? How did you know that's what I wanted? Thank you so much," I said and gave her a hug. I loved the Beatles, a quartet from England who wore shaggy haircuts and had a great sound. The Beatles were considered *avant-garde* in 1964. When I hear songs from that album, I always think of Julie's gift and the love that came with it.

The Monday after my birthday Unc picked me up right after school, and we drove to Covina so that I could take my driving test. I was nervous. It was one thing to drive with my uncle and my best friend in the car, quite another to have someone watching my every move and scoring it.

The DMV official got in the car and ordered me to drive. I felt pretty relaxed until we went under a freeway underpass and he spotted another DMV employee walking back to work. "Pull over and park," the first official ordered.

I followed his instructions, but I thought his request was unusual. My hands began to perspire, and I wondered what he was up to. The second official approached the car, and the men began chatting. What were they talking about, I asked myself, and became more anxious. Finally the first official turned to me and said, "You don't mind if we give my friend a ride, do you?"

What could I say? "Of course not," I mumbled, my stomach fluttering. Now I would have two people judging my driving. Great, I thought!

The second official hopped into the backseat, and off we went. My hands began to tremble. Why was I taking my driving test with two DMV officials in the car? I asked myself. This was not normal.

The one in the front seat instructed me to turn, change lanes, and make various other maneuvers before we arrived at the ultimate challenge—parallel parking. I pulled the car alongside four plastic posts and began to back up. Parallel parking had always been difficult. It was not at all like backing up in a straight line. My angle was wrong, and I hit a plastic post that substituted for a car.

"Try again," the man from the DMV said.

I did but could not maneuver into the spot a second time. I was allowed one more try, and I put my best effort into it. I started to back up slowly. The DMV official in the backseat helped by either nodding or shaking his head as I inched my way backwards. Eventually I parked the car. My clothes were soaked in perspiration from the effort, and I managed to drive back to the DMV office fearing the worst.

When we arrived at DMV headquarters, the second official got out of the car when we reached the edge of the parking lot. The first man handed me my score: 75 I had failed parallel parking, rolled through a stop sign instead of making a complete stop, and changed lanes for no reason, although I had signaled. "Congratulations, you passed," he said.

Instead of being elated, I was disappointed by my low score. I was used to excelling in everything I did, and a 75 was mediocre in my book. But I had a driver's license and a car, and I believed my adventures would finally begin.

18

The Newlyweds Arrive

*I*n March 1964, my twenty-year-old sister married Vinnie DeCicco. After they wed in New Jersey, they drove across the country on their honeymoon. No one we knew attended the ceremony, and years later we learned that there may not have been one. They decided to move to California to start life over, just as my mother, Blanche, and I had done three years earlier.

Although I was scared to death of my big sister throughout my childhood, she was the only other member of my nuclear family still alive. We'd been through a lot together, and I was happy she had returned to California. My uncle and I both wanted to believe that Blanche had settled down after her colorful childhood and wild teen years.

Vinnie, her dark-haired Italian husband, still drove his black Cadillac El Dorado with fins, the one he stood on five years earlier to try and see Blanche through the window of the mental hospital. Vinnie was a few years older than my sister, and his looks were part teen idol part Mafioso. With his black hair slicked back, he resembled Sylvester Stallone as "Rocky." Unlike the actor, Vinnie was not smart or particularly athletic, but he was kind. He said he'd been married once, and the marriage ended with a Mexican divorce. We never knew if this was true.

My most vivid memory of Blanche and Vinnie occurred in August 1959. My mother and I had spent the day at the family swim club in East Hanover with Ruth, Neil, and Richie Goodman. East Hanover was about an hour away from Hillside, and going to the swim club during the summer was a big event. We packed picnic lunches and were gone several hours, as was our custom. Neil and I loved the Olympic-sized pool and spent hours swimming and diving until our lips and fingernails turned blue with cold. We were usually pooped by the time we arrived home.

When we returned to Hillside and my mother and I entered our house, it was dark and quiet. Bonnie Sue came bouncing out to greet us, jumping and wagging her tail. "Blanche, we're home," we called in unison. No one answered.

We began going through the rooms, one by one, searching for my sister. When we walked into the downstairs bathroom, the countertop was littered with empty, sample packets of Excedrin and Bufferin, painkillers usually taken two at a time. There must have been at least fifty empty packets. Our family always used sample packets, rather than buying these products because my mother's good friend Anne worked for Bristol Meyers and readily supplied them to us.

My mother's face grew pale, and her eyes widened when she saw the mess. She grabbed the telephone and began to dial, but the doorbell rang just at that moment. I ran to the door, and there stood Jules and Ruth Gast, my cousins who lived next door.

"Aunt Ruth, we saw your car and rushed right over," Jules began. "Blanche and Vinnie broke up today. Afterwards, she said she wanted to die. Then she locked herself in the house and took all those pills. She called her best friend, Eileen, to say good-bye, and Eileen came right over. Blanche wouldn't let her in, so Eileen ran next door for us. We all pleaded with Blanche to open the door for almost an hour. After she became drowsy, we slit the screen door, unlocked it, and took her to the hospital. She's in Elizabeth General. They pumped her stomach."

My mother had to sit down when she heard their story. Our bright, sunny, fun-filled day with the Goodmans had been overtaken by darkness and gloom.

Jules drove my mother to the hospital to see Blanche. Ruth stayed with me to clean up the evidence. My hands shook as I grabbed the empty pill packs, fearing that my sister might die. I began asking questions: "How could she do such a thing? Why does she make life so hard for all of us? What is wrong with her?" But I knew there were no answers.

This was the sister who brought home boys from "Down Neck" in Newark, who'd had a baby with an ex-con a year earlier at age fourteen, who'd beaten up teachers in elementary school, and who staged a robbery of our parents' home when we were younger. Half the town was afraid of her, and they didn't have to share the same house. I lived in fear.

Blanche looked awful when Mommy brought her home the next day. She eventually recovered, although her heart was still broken, and she spent the rest of the summer pining for Vinnie.

Two months later, she had to appear in court for a hearing with our parents, which was standard after a suicide attempt. The state of New Jersey found her guilty of attempted murder for trying to end her own life. They sentenced her to Roosevelt State Hospital, a mental institution where she remained for six months. I hated visiting her there.

Although she and Vinnie eventually became friends again, they did not begin dating until Blanche returned to New Jersey in the summer of 1961, two months after we brought her to California to begin life anew and she abandoned us.

Now eight months after my mother's death, they came to California together as husband and wife. The plan was that Vinnie would look for work, and once established, they'd find an apartment nearby. Unc agreed that they could stay with us until they were settled. He gave them his bedroom, and he slept in his trailer at night.

Vinnie sought work and Blanche stayed home, helping around the house. Despite our contentious relationship during childhood, I found her being there comforting. I was lost, floundering, grieving, and I'm sure she was, too. We were both so young—I was sixteen, she was twenty. Our parents died within sixteen months of each other. We felt we had to behave as grownups, but inside we were each very sad children. Our pain manifested itself in different ways in the years ahead.

After a few weeks, Vinnie found a job in a bakery, similar to the job he'd had in New Jersey. He'd always worked in Jewish bakeries and made the best bagels in the East. Now he complained that this bakery did not use the same ingredients as his previous employer. "Can you believe they make cream pies with meringue instead of whipped cream?" he'd ask. "How cheap is that? And no one out here knows how to make a decent bagel."

My Italian brother-in-law made me laugh, something I had not done in a long time. One morning he was very tired and getting ready to go to work at five o'clock. Barely awake, he grabbed the red Lavoris mouthwash, which looked a lot like the hair tonic he used, and rubbed it into his hair. Blanche spotted him, but it was too late. His hair went flat that day, but it sure smelled good.

Blanche was a hairdresser, but she could not help Vinnie. His head was his own domain. She also could not work in her chosen field in California because she lacked a high school diploma. She'd dropped out in her freshman year, shortly after her ex-con boyfriend, the father of her first child, spread rumors at Hillside High and began stalking her, threatening to kill her. Afterwards she'd enrolled in beauticians' college and obtained her cosmetology license in New Jersey. She'd had years of experience as a hairdresser, with lots of trial and error, but she preferred to find a new source of work rather than return to school, a place she associated with all that was wrong with her life.

Secretly I was happy she'd no longer be doing hair after her many mishaps with our family's hair. Giving up hairdressing would not be a terrible sacrifice for Blanche, and it might save some poor souls the embarrassment my mother and I had experienced a few years earlier.

The summer before I entered sixth grade, Blanche promised to give me the latest hairdo, as she was a budding beautician and needed practice. I was self-conscious when I entered puberty and hoped she could make me more glamorous. My nose had become my most outstanding facial feature. Blanche's solution was to chop my bangs and sides very short, which only accentuated my prominent proboscis. While I waited for school to begin, I hoped my hair would grow back quickly. I never let her cut my hair again.

Sadly, I was not her only victim that summer! One morning I walked into the kitchen, where my mother was perking coffee. She had just removed permanent rod rollers from her hair. Blanche had given her a home permanent the previous day and told her to leave the curlers in all night. Mommy stood in the middle of the kitchen floor, her long dark hair sticking straight out, as if she'd put her finger in a light socket. I stopped short—speechless. Blanche walked in and screamed. Mommy plastered her hair into a bun for months afterwards and had regular trims until her once-smooth auburn hair began to look normal again.

At least my mother's hair did not fall out. Earlier that same summer Blanche gave herself a permanent on her over-bleached hair. When she removed the permanent rods, her hair came out with them in big clumps. By day's end, her shoulder-length, platinum-blond page boy had shrunk to a shriveled white pixie. Blanche dyed her remaining hair black a few days later, and the it contrasted with her pale skin, making her look ghastly.

After two months with us, my sister and Vinnie grew quite comfortable in our home. Blanche could not find work, and the couple made no attempt to move out.

Unc became irritable. He wanted his space back and thought they should have their own place. One morning he asked them to sit down, explained it was time to look for an apartment, and wrote them a check. That week they found a one-bedroom apartment nearby, but we saw them often.

On weekends Blanche and Vinnie began exploring their new state. They viewed themselves as wild westerners and discovered the sport of shooting. Vinnie bought a .22 caliber revolver, and he and Blanche drove into the San Gabriel Mountains each weekend.

I'm not sure what they planned to do with the gun, but they got their first opportunity when they encountered a rattlesnake. Blanche grabbed a stick and poked at it. The snake began to strike at her. Vinnie rushed to her aid, aimed his gun, and blew it away.

Although I did not like snakes, I hated what my sister and her husband had done. They had invaded the snake's territory and then killed it when it tried to defend itself. Guns were not my thing, and I thought it ironic that the two least bright people I knew owned one.

This thought came back to me one Sunday afternoon a few weeks later when Blanche and I were visiting at their apartment. Vinnie had gone hunting in the mountains with friends that day. He left around six that morning, and it was nearly five in the afternoon. Blanche expected him home for dinner, but she hadn't heard from him. "Where is he?" she asked.

"Oh, he probably ran into some traffic," I replied, trying to keep good thoughts. I always imagined the worst, after the events of the past few years, but I tried to keep a brave face for my sister. "He'll be home soon, and we can all have dinner together."

About twenty minutes later, Vinnie's friend Fred came to the door.

My sister looked up and asked, "Where's Vinnie?" fear creeping into her voice.

"Don't worry, he's all right. He had a little accident, but he'll be fine," Fred answered. "He accidentally shot himself."

Blanche panicked. "Where? How? What happened?" she screamed, rising to her full height of nearly six feet.

"He had holstered his gun and then remembered that he forgot to put its safety on," Fred said. "So he tried to put the safety on when the gun was holstered, and it discharged. He shot himself in the foot."

We almost laughed, except the situation was serious. We'd heard of people shooting themselves in the foot but never actually met one. Now Vinnie had brought the cliché home.

"Where is he?" Blanche asked.

"He's in the car. We just came from the hospital, but he wanted me to come in first and tell you what happened. Help me bring him in."

Blanche and I rushed outside to help a pale, shaken Vinnie out of the car. He was given crutches at the hospital, and he stumbled as he stood and tried to use them for the first time.

"No more guns," Blanche said as she helped him inside. Vinnie just sat there, staring in a drugged stupor, and I went home to tell Unc the news.

Vinnie's gunshot wound was more serious than we thought. He shot himself between the big toe and the second toe. The wound became infected, and he could not work for months. His disability checks did not cover their expenses, and now Unc had two more people to provide for. Eventually Vinnie's foot did heal, but from that Sunday forward, we referred to him as Quick Draw, much to his chagrin.

By Christmas his foot had healed, and we joined them at their apartment on Christmas Day. I looked forward to a big dinner cooked by my sister. We all sat down, and Blanche pulled a lasagna from the oven.

"What's this?" I asked.

"It's lasagna," she answered. "This is what Italians eat on Christmas. Vinnie's mom taught me how to make it." That was my introduction to an Italian heritage that I would not really discover for another forty years.

The following year, 1965, the gun did go away, but not as I imagined. Early one morning a neighbor went out to get his newspaper and saw the screen to Blanche and Vinnie's apartment lying on the sidewalk. Vinnie's pants lay in a heap nearby. He banged on their front door, afraid of what he might find.

Blanche answered, still half asleep. "What's the matter? Why did you wake us up?" she asked.

Her neighbor showed her the screen that had been jimmied and Vinnie's pants lying on the ground. "Vinnie, get up," she yelled. "We've been robbed."

Sadly, they had been robbed, and they didn't own much to begin with. Vinnie's wallet was gone, and so were the guns. Sometimes things just work out for the better.

19

Metamorphosis

*T*he doorbell rang after dinner in the spring of 1965, second semester of my junior year. I was dressed in my bathrobe, scrubbing our dinner dishes, when I opened the door to several Alhambra High classmates. "Congratulations," they yelled. "You're now a member of Laule'a."

I flushed, feeling elated about being accepted into a good club, but I was embarrassed by my appearance. "That's great news," I said.

"Get dressed," they ordered. "We're going to pick up other new members and go out for sodas."

I hurriedly changed my clothes, brushed my hair, and hopped into the waiting car. I had arrived.

The pecking order at Alhambra High School consisted of five main groups: the Soshes, Jocks, Brains, Performers, and Others. The school offered two courses of study: general education and college prep.

The Soshes were popular, the ones everyone wanted to befriend. They were good-looking and served on student council, as queens and princesses for homecoming and prom, and as cheerleaders, songleaders, majorettes, or members of the drill team at sporting events. They also belonged to Y and service clubs and proudly wore their clubs' colors on designated days. Many planned to attend college.

Supermodel Cheryl Tiegs was a Soshe, although she was quiet and shy. She was also kind to everyone, no matter where they ranked in the social strata. When I was a freshman, I sometimes walked to school with her. I recall her cheering me on in the locker room before I tried out for cheerleader between my junior and senior years. I did not make the cut, but it was great to have her on my side. She began modeling her junior year but enrolled at Cal State Los Angeles after she graduated from Alhambra. After that, she went to New York, but Alhambra still claims her as one of its most famous alumni.

The Jocks were the athletes—football, basketball, and baseball players, as well as members of the track and cross-country teams. They often dated the Soshes, and one could become a Soshe by dating a jock. Julie dated several Jocks, but she never considered herself a Soshe. She was always sweet, lovable Julie, someone who was kind to everyone. The Jocks were an entity unto themselves, focused on winning. They were the Big Men on Campus, or BMOCs, as we referred to them. I knew few of them, as I was not a big sports fan in high school, and we were not in the same classes.

The Brains were those who took advanced placement courses and were good students who planned to attend college. Most belonged to the California Scholarship Federation, the Junior Statesmen, and several other academically oriented clubs. They took classes together and formed in-class friendships through the years. Most graduated, attended good colleges, and became successful professionals.

The Performers were those with talent: acting, singing, dancing, instrumental, and speaking. They joined the Glee Club, performed in student plays, played in the band and orchestra, or attended debates.

I belonged to the Brains, although I ventured into the Performers and Soshe territory occasionally. My goal in high school was to get good grades and earn a college scholarship. Our finances made that imperative. But I also wanted a social life, and our high school counselors encouraged us to participate in school activities to boost our chances of being accepted to college.

Freshman year I ran for class vice president and won. When the class president became ineligible to serve because of poor grades, I took over. I referred to myself as class president from that day on, which did not endear me to other classmates. I was a bit too full of myself, and I learned that arrogance was not a characteristic to embrace when I ran for student council two years later.

When I began my sophomore year at Northview High School in Covina, I concentrated on getting good grades. Making new friends was not a high priority, since I was grieving and adjusting to my new home life.

I moved back to Alhambra to begin the second semester of my sophomore year and had to reacquaint myself with classmates. Considering that I'd just lost my mother and had switched homes and guardians for the second time since her death six months earlier, I was not very sociable. I was fortunate that Julie was there for me, my one constant among so many changes.

But by my junior year in high school, I decided to "try out" for a social club. I had little confidence and was uncertain of the outcome.

Rickie, my second closest friend, questioned my behavior. "How can you try out for a Y club? It's associated with the YWCA. Do you know what the 'C' stands for? Christian! You'll have to go to church!"

I paid her no heed and was thrilled that club members dropped by to take me out this evening to celebrate my acceptance.

Nearly four years after arriving in the Golden State, I longed for the social connections and close friendships I'd had in New Jersey. My time here had been tarnished by tragedy.

As it turned out, Rickie was right. As a member of a Y club, I had to attend "Go-to-Church Sunday" twice a year. Since most of my club's members were Catholic, we always went to one of the Catholic churches in town. Years later I discovered that Catholics weren't supposed to attend any other denomination's services.

I was always a bit put off by these Sundays, uncomfortable with my surroundings and worried that they'd try to convert me. At this point in my life, I didn't know what I believed. I was an orphan, and I was very angry with God for taking my parents away. Where was *He,* and how could *He* let this happen?

Uncle Richard was agnostic, so he offered little religious direction.

Actually, I wasn't really religious in the sense that I'd attended Hebrew school, made my bat mitzvah, and attended services regularly. That had not been an option in our oddly Orthodox Jewish household. My parents stopped keeping kosher after Blanche was born, although they kept two sets of dishes for Zayde's occasional visits.

I now realize that we were secular Jews. We celebrated the major holidays and attended bar mitzvahs, but our family belonged to the Orthodox synagogue a few blocks from our house.

Daddy walked to services on Saturday mornings, but he went alone, carrying his bag containing his *tallis* and *yarmulke*. Mommy only went to synagogue on the High Holy Days.

I can't blame her. In the Orthodox synagogue, women were second-class citizens and had to sit separately from the men in the back or the balcony, separated from the men. On the few holidays my parents sent me to *shul (a synagogue)*, I hid in the bathroom, afraid to enter the sanctuary alone, unsure of what was expected.

My parents sent Blanche to Hebrew school and thought she went willingly. A few weeks after she started, one of the neighbors called. "Ruth, why is Blanche attending the Presbyterian church?"

When confronted, Blanche admitted that she hated Hebrew school and would continue to go to church. Her religious education ended abruptly.

Blanche's behavior made my father more determined to educate me, and he insisted I attend the same Orthodox Hebrew school Blanche had shunned. I preferred the Conservative congregation, since part of its service was in English. Even my deeply religious *zayde* (grandfather), who was a cantor at his Orthodox temple in Philadelphia, gave his blessing. But Daddy said, "No!" Consequently, I did not have any religious training, but I identified myself as a Jew.

When I arrived in Alhambra and discovered I was the only Jewish person in the eighth grade class, I sought my Jewish roots. We could not afford to join the local synagogue, but my mother still would not let me attend school on the High Holy Days. Because I missed the first two days of the school year in my new school, the other students wondered who this mystery girl was. I felt the consequences throughout the year, but one incident in particular reminded me that Alhambra was no place for Jews.

My classmate Mary, a blue-eyed blond, who was pretty and athletic, decided to let me know how people felt about Jews in Alhambra one day after school and picked a fight. A circle of students gathered around us on the playground, cheering her on. I had never been a fighter and was shocked when Mary swung and hit me in the face with her broken hand—which sported a plaster cast. I ran home crying, swearing never to return. I did go back and ironically was asked to read a psalm at eighth grade graduation. Apparently Alhambra did not know about separation of church and state.

After I started high school and befriended other Jewish kids, I vowed to embrace my religion. I would sneak into synagogue on the High Holy Days, since tickets to services were very expensive, and in the process I made new friends, like Rickie.

Sometimes I went to church with Julie, who was a Missouri Synod Lutheran. I found the service cold and boring, much as I viewed the Catholic Mass as perfunctory. Neither showed the great emotion I had witnessed in synagogue, although I could only understand a portion of the service.

Belonging to a minority religion in a small town further isolated me socially from many of my classmates. Looking Semitic did not help. Consequently, some of my friends who clung to their Jewish roots tried to erase their Semitic looks. They straightened their hair and had their noses bobbed.

I was a blond, but I certainly had a beak, which first made its appearance when I was about twelve. If I styled my hair properly, my nose seemed less prominent, but this ploy only lasted a few years.

By the time I was fifteen, my proboscis became more prominent. Shortly after my mother's death, when I was emotionally vulnerable, I received comments from classmates, such as, "Is that your nose, or are you eating a banana?" Later that year the Beatles became popular, and my taunts included, "You look just like Ringo."

At the beginning of my junior year, I'd dressed in my favorite blouse, styled my hair, and carefully applied makeup for student pictures. After school, I was driving home and stopped at a traffic signal. My car window was open, and two guys stopped beside me in the next lane yelled, "What a scag!" I took off the minute the light changed, crestfallen from their words.

Life was miserable, and my aquiline hook became the focus of my attention. I hated my looks and could not bear the teasing.

That year I became better acquainted with my classmate Nancy, a sweet Jewish girl whom I knew casually. I was surprised when she returned to school that September with a new nose. Although Nancy had always been petite and pretty, her nose had overpowered her delicate features. Now it was adorable—short and turned up just a touch at the end. I loved it and thought she looked beautiful.

"Nancy, you look great!" I said.

Her beautiful smile showed her pleasure. "Thank you," she answered. "I feel great."

"You have the cutest nose. Did it hurt to have a nose job?" I ventured.

"A little, but it was worth it," she answered and gave me her doctor's name.

Afterwards, Rickie's mother recommended another excellent plastic surgeon.

I came home from school and said to Unc, "Can I get a nose job? I hate my nose, and I'm constantly being teased. One of my friends had one last summer, and she looks like a whole new person."

Unc looked at me and said, "I think your nose looks fine. But if you really want to do this, let's consult a doctor and then decide."

Unc and I made an appointment with the surgeon recommended by Mrs. Berns, and I pleaded my case. He looked at me and said, "I can help you. Let's schedule your procedure for Christmas vacation. You can discuss the cost with my assistant." When we left the examining room, we discovered that the doctor agreed to do the procedure at a sizable discount. It was clear he felt sorry for me, an overweight orphan with a huge inferiority complex.

Nancy and I became good friends that fall, and she worried that I didn't have a mother to take care of me after the surgery. She was an only child, and her parents were dear. They invited me to stay with them post-surgery, since Unc had to work.

When December arrived, I was ready, although a bit nervous about getting a new nose. At that time, doctors performed the procedure in a hospital, and Midway Hospital in Los Angeles was where many nose jobs were performed. I was assigned to a room with an Israeli woman who owned a Jewish bakery on Fairfax Avenue. She was there for a hysterectomy. When she heard about my surgery, she said, "Why do you want to take the bump out of your nose? You're beautiful. I don't understand it."

I thought she was very kind. Unc added, "It's like gilding the lily. One day people will go to the hospital to have bumps put in their noses." He may have been right.

I didn't want to hear their words. I was worried about two things—surviving the surgery and being recognized by my mother after I died and went to heaven. The first fear was real, but the chances of not surviving were slim. The second fear was less certain, since I had been told Jews did not believe in an afterlife. Yet I had conjured up an image of my mother in heaven, because I believed that's where she belonged. To me she was "up there" watching over me, and that image sustained me for many years.

My surgery was educational. I was awake but given mild sedation and local anesthesia. After the first shot, a stinging injection at the base of my nose, I felt no pain. But during the procedure I had to swallow the blood and mucus that resulted from the reconstruction, because they did not use the suction devices in use today. At times I felt I was choking. The worst part was the sound—as if they were filing fingernails inside my head.

My surgeon played classical music while he worked. I heard the strains of "Scheherazade" and "Procession of the Sardar" while I lay on the table. The music soothed me and diverted my attention from what was going on. After a while, the doctor asked, "Well, how does it look on that side?" I could hear him walk around the table, stop, and look. More filing ensued. He walked around the table again and again, making sure that he did the best job he could.

Afterwards I went back to my room and slept, although it was hard to sleep with my nose plugged. For the next week, sleeping was the most difficult challenge, since I had to breathe through my mouth. The pain was minimal, and everything else was delightful.

Mrs. Greene was such a wonderful mother. She made me special meals, grinding up my food, since I had trouble opening my mouth to chew, and she made sure that I had lots of ice chips to suck on. I felt special, being taken care of by a mother once more.

The day they took the bandages off, I was delighted. I no longer had a hook. Now I had a pug. Blanche and Vinnie stopped by to see the results. "You look like a pig!" she screamed. "How could you do this to yourself?"

"I'd rather look like this than have a big nose," I shot back, although inside I was crying. Leave it to Blanche to say the wrong thing. Vinnie just smiled his big goofy grin and assured me that it would be all right.

Pedro wore his "blue baby" jacket to the prom.

The swelling went down, and after Christmas vacation I returned to school. "You look different. Did you get a new haircut?" classmates asked. "Have you lost weight?" I answered "yes" to all their questions, delighted that they even noticed me.

That spring I met Pedro, our foreign exchange student from Chile. "Hi," he said, and smiled, "would you like to go out on Friday?"

"Yes," I answered, and suddenly I had a boyfriend.

Pedro lived with Bruce, a burly football lineman on the Alhambra High School team, who was a Jock. I'd never socialized with members of the football team before and soon discovered that Bruce was a great guy. His steady girl was Debbie, a sweet, shy, pretty blond. Soon Pedro, Bruce, Debbie, and I were a foursome, enjoying weekend outings together. One day Pedro asked, "Would you like to go to the prom with me?"

I could not contain myself. "Yes," I responded and hugged him. "What color is your tuxedo?"

"Blue baby," he answered.

I tried not to laugh. I knew he meant baby blue, but in Spanish the modifiers come before the nouns. Whenever I think of him, I think of the color of his prom jacket.

That spring we had a whirlwind romance—prom, barbecues, miniature golf, movies, picnics, and family visits. Pedro Nery Belaunde Bernal was a perfect gentleman, stealing a kiss now and then, but always very proper.

At school my popularity meter rose. Soon I was asked to join an elite service club that many girls in my Y club belonged to. I was also called into the Dean of Girls' office one day.

Nervously, I awaited her arrival, wondering what I had done. "Libby, do you know what Girls' State is?" the dean asked.

"I think so," I answered. "Isn't it a government leadership training program?"

As mayor of Jordan's Jolly Giants, I wore the Girls' State
sweatshirt to look official.

"Yes," she replied. "Each high school in the state selects one girl from the junior class to attend. We would like you to represent Alhambra High School."

I worked hard to contain myself. I had been chosen. Of all the students in my class of 568, half of which were male, I had been chosen. "Yes," I said. "I'd be honored."

The Sunday after school ended in June, Unc drove me to the bus that would take me and other girls from the San Gabriel Valley to Sacramento for our week-long stay at the University of California, Davis, site of California Girls' State.

Pedro came to see me off. We talked, and when I hugged and kissed him good-bye, I knew I'd never see him again. By the time I returned, he would be back in Chile, headed to university to achieve his goal of becoming a doctor.

My heart felt heavy as I boarded the bus and waved good-bye to Unc and Pedro.

New adventures lay ahead.

20
Working Girl

One July morning between my junior and senior years in high school, Unc was reading the newspaper when he said, "Libby, you're going to need extra spending money now that you're driving and going out with friends. Bullock's department store has an ad here seeking temporary employees for its August sale. Why don't you go downtown and apply?"

"I've never done anything but babysit, and I wasn't very good at that," I answered. "Besides, what if I have to work nights? I don't mind going to downtown Los Angeles during the day, but I'm afraid to be down there by myself at night."

"If you get the job and have to work nights, I'll pick you up," Unc replied.

"But I don't have any experience," I said.

"You'll never get experience unless you try," he answered. "Get dressed, and let's go downtown."

"Don't I need a work permit?" I asked, bringing up one more excuse why I should not venture into the working world. My only previous employment, babysitting, had not been impressive. I was an adequate caretaker but not much fun with children because I'd never learned how to play with small children. I was the younger child in my family, and my parents were older when they adopted me, so play was not a big part of their lives.

Richie Goodman was the only baby I knew while growing up. He was born the summer we returned from Florida on the repaired airliner and was seven years younger than Neil. Occasionally, I played with him but not often. Once I spent the night at the Goodmans because my parents went out, and in the morning Neil and I tried to change Richie. His parents were still sleeping, and we thought we could help, but neither of us knew what to do with an infant. When Neil undid Richie's diaper, he got sick on the living room carpet. I witnessed the mess and gagged, trying not to follow suit. Richie began to cry, which woke their parents. They became angry, and we decided not to attempt diaper changing again.

Since the night I returned from babysitting and found my mother dead, I had not sat for anyone.

My childhood insecurities had multiplied substantially since my mother's death, and I was afraid to try new things. The world I once knew no longer existed, and my new world was filled with uncertainty. All I really wanted was for someone to take care of me, as my family had. Venturing into the working world seemed ominous.

"No, you're sixteen and old enough to work," Unc replied. "I'll drive you to Bullock's to apply. If you get the job, you can take the bus."

My interview went smoothly, and suddenly I found myself in sales training class. The first rule Bullock's stated, "The customer is always right," dictated how I should behave with customers. During training, I learned how to fill out forms and spot shoplifters. After that I was assigned to the Sundeck, located on the mezzanine, where high-end cruise and leisure wear were sold. When I saw the clothing prices, I was shocked and realized I could not afford to buy the merchandise Bullock's sold—until I found out about the employee discount.

I arrived early the day the sale started and stood on the Sundeck with my fellow employees, staring at the store's locked doors. People had lined up twenty across and ten deep. They looked intent. My manager, a slim, young blond who had worked in retail for years, found the scene amusing and began humming the *William Tell Overture* as the clock struck ten, the doors opened, and people raced through pushing babies, like runners seeking the finish line.

When I realized the Sundeck was the finish line, I began to perspire. All these people suddenly appeared, and only two of us were there to write up sales. The sales slips had to be handwritten, filled out in triplicate, and they took forever to complete. While most of the customers were patient, recognizing that I was young and new, a few grew irritable as the line grew longer. "What's taking so long?" "Hurry up, honey, I haven't got all day," they'd snort. That's when I'd make a mistake and have to start over. My stomach churned, but I kept on writing.

Meanwhile, the three dressing rooms filled up fast, and lines formed in our limited space. Customers became determined to get the best deals before they left, and one person was so intent on her purchase that she remained in the dressing room and made a bowel movement on the floor rather than sacrifice her space. Fortunately, I was not assigned clean-up duties, but I learned that retail sales could be filled with surprises.

One day I approached a woman in a blazer sauntering on the Sundeck and asked if I could help her. She put her finger to her lips, indicating that I should be quiet, and then motioned me away from the dressing room. Then she revealed her badge and nodded toward the dressing room area. "Get out of here now," she whispered. I hurried off, feeling naive and not wanting to see the outcome.

While those were low points of working in retail, aside from picking up piles of clothing, refolding and restocking it, being assigned late shifts, and standing on my feet for eight hours straight, there were some benefits. One was that I could buy merchandise at a one-third discount. Since it was already on sale, the expensive merchandise I initially thought was beyond my budget became more appealing. Consequently I spent most of my earnings before they made it home.

Unc consoled me on the nights when I worked late and he drove downtown to pick me up, since taking the bus at that hour was questionable. "Things could be worse. You could be installing toilets in the women's prison, as I did a few years back," he said. "I never want to go to prison after that experience."

I realized he was right, but I also knew he had gone to jail once. In 1938 he was arrested picketing the German Embassy in Washington, D.C., protesting the Nazi regime's detention of Jews. Unc worked hard, and he also stood up for his beliefs. His example made me determined to stand up for mine.

I vowed to be wiser when I found my next position. At the beginning of my senior year at Alhambra High, I became one of three campus representatives at a local, family-owned department store. Each was chosen from one of the area's three high schools. The representatives would wear the store's clothes to school and encourage other students to shop there. We'd be featured in the local paper, buy our clothes at a discount, and work after school and on Saturdays. Because I had retail experience and was considered a campus leader, I was hired. The job sounded ideal.

I reported to work every afternoon when school ended and each Saturday. The work seemed much easier than my previous job, but business was slow. The store was rarely crowded, and we often stood around rearranging the merchandise and chatting. I did acquire a great wardrobe that fall, using my employee discount. However, my bank account grew no larger, and I discovered that working left me little time to study or spend with friends. Because I worked Saturdays, I had to adjust my weekly cleaning schedule and spent many Friday evenings, when my friends were at the movies, cleaning house.

As Christmas approached, sales remained stagnant, and the store realized that having campus representatives did not boost buying. It let us go after Christmas.

My next foray into retail occurred shortly before I began college. By then, Unc and I had moved to West Los Angeles, and Rickie and her mother had moved to the La Brea Towers. Rickie told me that Ohrbach's department store on Wilshire Boulevard's Miracle Mile needed summer help. I applied and was hired because of my previous retail experience.

Unlike my previous positions, my job required me to stand in a "rounder" (circular booth) on the sales floor. I found myself surrounded by sunset orange, hot pink, fire coral, and lipstick-red girdles, or foundations as Aunt Shirley referred to them. I thought she would be proud. I would have enjoyed these colors more had I been in a garden.

When I accepted the minimum-wage job, I didn't realize that I'd spend my days helping overweight women try to fit into undergarments three sizes too small. "Honey, do you have this in a larger size?" they asked as they held up a colorful girdle while tossing the remaining garments in a heap.

"I'm sorry. These only come in size small and medium," I replied. Why would a small person need a girdle, I asked myself, realizing how ridiculous my situation was.

"Are you sure?" the women persisted.

I just smiled and nodded.

After work, Rickie and I spent time together, although not as much as before, because she had a new boyfriend. One evening he called after I'd had dinner at their apartment, and they began talking on the phone. After a half hour, I motioned that I had to leave. She indicated I should wait.

I stayed another fifteen minutes and said, "I've got to go home. Unc will worry."

Two days later while I stood in my rounder selling foundations, Rickie's mother strode into Ohrbach's. I smiled and waved to her. She marched up to me, straight-faced. "How dare you leave when Rickie was in the middle of a phone call," she screamed. "Don't you know she was talking to a boy? That was very rude."

My eyes misted over, and I fought back tears. "I didn't do anything wrong," I stammered. "I had to go home."

"But she was talking to a boy. He's someone special. You don't know anything about that, do you?" she continued. "You should not have left. You're just jealous because she has a boyfriend and you don't."

Even though what she said was not true, I didn't argue with her. I knew it wouldn't do any good, so I stood there and took her abuse for several minutes until my manager interrupted. "Libby, it's time for your break," she announced.

I nodded and hurried upstairs, embarrassed by the scene my friend's mother had caused and the tears streaming down my cheeks. After that, I was wary every time I went to work. Shortly after university classes began, I quit.

I did not work again until the summer following my freshman year. My friend Flossie from the dorm decided to remain in L.A. for the summer and we sought jobs together. Because I had a car and she didn't, we naively believed that employers would hire the two of us. After several job interviews in which we tried to be hired as a team, we realized that we had to go out on our own.

Fortunately, we each found jobs in a Culver City mall and could travel together. Flossie worked in a women's clothing store that was more upscale than my position at J.C. Penney, where once again I found myself in foundations.

Halfway through the summer, Flossie decided it was too difficult to live away from home *and* save money. She returned to her family in the Inland Empire. Her job became available, and I eagerly applied. She kindly gave me a glowing recommendation, and I was hired. Tired of being buried in foundations, I loved my work in this small, stylish clothing store only ten minutes from my apartment.

I enjoyed my colleagues, a coarse, crotchety manager with a Texas drawl named Sandy, whose tightly permed head of gray hair matched her conservative disposition, and a red-haired British woman, Marge, who lived with the memories of her World War II childhood in England. "I remember the air raids and the bombs landing nearby. Many times, I almost messed my pants, because I was so scared," she'd say. Marge disliked the French intensely and often repeated, "They just rolled over and let the Germans take charge of their country. That made France a great launching pad for the German air attacks on us."

Marge and Sandy told bawdy jokes, and much of the time I worked with them, I spent laughing. Toward summer's end, business declined, and once again I was out of work.

The following summer I sought a position in a boutique on the Santa Monica Mall. The Santa Monica Mall of the sixties stood on Third Street between Wilshire Boulevard and Broadway, where the present-day Promenade is located. It was an open-air mall with a J.C. Penney store at the Wilshire Boulevard boundary. Woolworth's and Newberry's were the other major chains anchoring the mall in addition to a small movie theater near Broadway. The remainder of the mall contained mom-and-pop businesses that sold clothing, shoes, jewelry, housewares, camera equipment, and sundries.

The boutique where I worked sat a few doors south of Santa Monica Boulevard and featured hand-crocheted women's dresses, sweaters, and skirts. The owners were French, but the other two employees were from Germany and Norway. The manager, Anna, a platinum-blond, buxom German woman who favored tank tops and sported a year-round tan, was married and told endless stories of her husband, Hans. "When I get mad at him, I say, 'Do you want a bust in the mouth?'" she'd joke. Looking at her ample breasts, I roared with laughter. "Can you imagine? He always says 'Yes,'" she'd laugh.

The Norwegian woman was quieter and an experienced retailer. She loved living on the beach in Santa Monica and hanging out at the local bars in the evening, drinking beer and playing darts. Her carefree existence differed greatly from my life.

Since I was "summer help," I arrived early and had to prepare to open each day. Anna would hand me a rag and some window cleaner and say, "Libby, please clean the fingerprints off the windows. After that, take the broom and sweep the entrance to the store. The sand blows in from the beach, and the vagrants leave trash all around. That's not the impression we want to make." Each morning, I performed these chores, often encountering one or two colorful characters who spent the night outside.

"Hi, there, honey. Do you need some help?" they'd ask. Others began odd conversations that encouraged me to complete my outdoor duties and head back inside as quickly as I could.

"There are some crazy people on the mall," I said.

"They're harmless," Anna replied.

Harmless or not, I took no chances and stayed inside whenever possible. Because of the store's location on the mall, its air circulation was poor. By afternoon, it became stuffy, making it difficult for me to breathe or think straight. Few stores in Santa Monica had air conditioning in the sixties, and I often found the store where I worked stifling.

"Do we have a fan?" I asked one day.

"No," Anna replied.

I positioned myself near the front door whenever possible, but by day's end, I'd have a headache and a stuffy nose. After a month of this, I made an appointment with my doctor.

"You're allergic to something in that store," he announced as he wrote prescriptions for nasal spray and antihistamines. "I advise you to find another job. You'll feel a lot better."

I did not want to quit, but I really felt the effects of that stagnant air. My brain felt stagnant, too. While I loved fashion, I yearned for more intellectual stimulation. I knew I would not find it among these colleagues.

A few weeks later I applied for a position as a part-time clerk typist in the chemistry department at UCLA. Although I really could not type, I was determined to learn and find a better paying, more challenging position. This one paid $1.98 per hour, which was a big improvement over my last job.

When they called to tell me I was hired, I gladly accepted. While happy that my days working retail would end, I feared that my new boss would discover my secret—I could not type—and I'd be unemployed once more.

21

Graduation Day

$\mathcal{M}$y favorite teacher turned to me as I gathered my books the last day of class. "Congratulations on being chosen commencement speaker. Are your parents coming to graduation tonight?" he asked.

I turned and said, "My parents are dead. But my uncle will be there along with my sister and brother-in-law."

Mr. Shipman looked shocked. "I'm sorry. I didn't know. I always wondered why your parents didn't attend open house."

In the sixties, school officials knew little about students' home lives. Every student was treated the same. I preferred it that way and expected no special treatment, although I desperately wanted to be like my classmates and have a mother and father, a nice home, and siblings. I rarely mentioned that I had been orphaned at fifteen and lived a very different life from the other kids.

The previous year, my life improved dramatically. Changing my appearance gave me the confidence to reach beyond my inner circle and experience a social life plus academic recognition.

Toward the end of that year, I also experienced my share of disappointments by not being elected to student council, not making cheerleader, and not being chosen campus representative at a Pasadena department store. These "failures" upset me so much that I was inconsolable and cried for days. Unc did not know what to say or do. He was still learning how to deal with a teenager.

My selection as the school's representative to California Girls' State gave me a boost. The week I spent at the University of California, Davis, campus was the highlight of my summer. I made friends with young women from throughout California, who were all good students and college bound. Many kept in touch after that week ended, and several became my classmates in college.

At Girls' State, we formed a miniature state government. Girls were randomly assigned to cities, named for well-known figures in California history, and each city elected officials to represent it in state government. I was assigned to Jordan and elected its mayor. During that week, we had the opportunity to hold one working session in the California State Assembly's chambers, since the Assembly was not in session. I was enthralled with the multitude of desks and the room's elaborate decor. Enacting mock legislation within these sacred chambers felt humbling.

The week culminated by meeting the governor, Edmund G. "Pat" Brown. When that day arrived, many of us were tired from all the activities and late bedtime chats. We were also overcome by Sacramento's heat as we waited in the hall of the state Capitol. I leaned against what I thought was a wood-paneled wall for support. Imagine my surprise, when the panel moved inward, and I tumbled into Governor Brown's office! Embarrassed, I mumbled a quick "Excuse me," and hastily retreated. An aide quickly closed the door, I composed myself, and waited as Governor Brown strode out the front door of the Capitol and greeted each of us personally with a handshake. I glowed, knowing that I had just met the governor of California, the man responsible for building our great system of state universities.

Back in Alhambra, life returned to normal, except that Pedro had gone home to Chile. I missed him terribly that first month, and my social life was minimal. I rarely dated and wondered why. Was I not pretty enough? Was I too smart? Did I not "put out" like some of the other girls I knew?

During my high school years, I occasionally met someone I liked, but one of two things happened. Either I became extremely possessive, which destroyed the relationship, or the boy I dated liked me more than I liked him. One or the other of us was too needy, although none of these relationships were serious, simply high school crushes. I just did not know how to deal with them. I handled disappointment poorly, took every failure personally, and viewed each breakup as a rejection. Now I understand I had serious abandonment issues, although that word was not used in the sixties.

I often spent evenings at home crying, sometimes over minor mishaps, and poor Unc did not know what to do with me. Sometimes he suggested a weekend ride, and we got in the car and just started driving up the coast, as we had when my mother and I first arrived in California. Other times he'd say, "Let's go for a hike in the mountains," since Alhambra was near the foothills of the San Gabriel Mountains.

I would go anywhere with Unc, but I really did not like hiking. I constantly worried that I'd encounter a snake, and I was deathly afraid of snakes.

When we arrived in the mountains, he said, "C'mon, Libby, let's take a walk. Isn't it beautiful up here?"

I worried incessantly about my looks, since most girls in the sixties tried to emulate the dictates of fashion magazines. Besides, I did not want to sweat, because that meant having to do my hair and makeup all over again.

Halfway up a short incline, I'd complain, "I'm tired, Unc. Can we go home now?" He urged me on until he had his fill of my whining. Then we'd retreat to a nearby restaurant because the mountain air always made me hungry.

Little did I realize that the fresh air and exercise would have helped me. It took me years to appreciate Unc's efforts, and today when I hike and explore out-of-the-way places, I often think of him. He would be happy he instilled this love of the outdoors in me.

Unc encouraged me academically, too, and kept reminding me of my goal: to go to UCLA. Beyond that, he was at a loss. He had never been a parent, and inheriting a grieving, depressed teenage girl had never been part of his plan. He tried his best.

I dutifully focused on my school work, college applications, and social life. The social and service clubs I'd joined in my junior year required attending meetings plus engaging in activities several hours a week. My classes were not difficult, as I'd chosen to forego my fourth year of mathematics and foreign language and take mostly social studies and English classes.

I found the college applications daunting and was surprised that I had to pay so much to submit them. Unc and I talked about the cost, and in the end I only applied to one school: UCLA.

In January of my senior year, Mr. Shipman approached me and asked, "Would you accept an award from the Daughters of the American Revolution [DAR]? They've chosen you as 'Best Citizen of the Year.' You mentioned that you had some objections to the DAR, and I don't want an embarrassing situation."

When I told Unc, he said, "I don't like that organization. They would not let Marian Anderson perform, but go ahead and do what you want."

I accepted the award and added it to my accolades, having been named Alhambra High's Citizen of the Month in September.

In March, the letter I had been awaiting since I was twelve years old arrived. It said, "We are pleased to offer you admission to the University of California, Los Angeles, commencing in Fall Quarter 1966."

I could not wait for Unc to get home from work. "Unc, I made it. Look at this letter."

Unc read the letter and gave me a big hug. "I knew you could do it," he said. "Let's celebrate."

We went to dinner at our favorite coffee shop and celebrated not only my admission to UCLA but the fact that I had been awarded a UCLA Alumni Scholarship to help pay for my education.

That spring life improved once more. I was invited to be a Prom Princess at Senior Prom and awarded two more scholarships. Now I was a California State Scholar and an Alhambra High School PTA Scholar. Unc was delighted. We needed all the help we could get with college expenses.

His work situation was tentative. New construction had slowed down in the spring of 1966, and finding regular work as a construction plumber became increasingly difficult. Yet he persisted.

While Unc took care of financial matters, I continued to enjoy all the extracurricular activities high school offered. We had been told since freshman year that the more activities we participated in, the better our chance of being accepted to the college of our choice. I had taken this advice seriously, joining academic, social, and service clubs; giving speeches; and becoming involved in annual productions. Now that I had been admitted to college, I did not need to add any more activities to my resume. But I enjoyed being involved and keeping busy.

Alhambra High had an excellent drama teacher, and I loved drama. While this domain belonged to the Performers, my ability to speak in public made me one of them. My good friends Julie and Rickie were much better Performers than

As student directors, Julie and I learned so much from Mrs. Wilson, who is seated between us.

I. They had beautiful voices and sang in the Glee Club. Julie and I decided to try out for the senior play, *One Foot in Heaven*. Neither of us was chosen for a role, but we were appointed student directors. We were delighted and spent the next two months working closely together under the direction of our drama teacher. The play was a huge success, and we still look back on that time with fond memories.

As graduation neared, the administration announced that seniors would try out to give the commencement addresses, rather than having the valedictorian and salutatorian give them. One girl and one boy from the senior class would be chosen.

I tried out and wrote my speech on the path we each choose in life, comparing it to a great hallway with many doors. These doors led to future choices: higher education, the military, the working world, or marriage. I urged my classmates to become involved and contribute to the world, no matter which door they chose. Then I spoke of Dr. Paul Carlson, an Alhambra High School graduate who became a physician. As a devout Christian, he had taken his family to the Congo to serve as a missionary doctor in 1961. Dr. Carlson developed a close, loving relationship with the Congolese people. When a communist rebellion arose, Dr. Carlson was accused of being a spy and detained. After negotiations for his release with the United States government broke down, he was executed by firing squad on November 24, 1964.

Unc did not like my speech at all. "Dr. Carlson was a CIA spy," he insisted. "I can't believe you're preaching conservative doggerel."

I held my ground, although I was nervous on the day I tried out. Eight other students were competing. I was delighted when I was chosen, along with my classmate Steve Harrison. We were to speak before an audience of 5,000 people in the football stadium of East Los Angeles College the evening of graduation. I spent the next few weeks practicing.

Graduation day came, and the seniors arrived at school to clean out their lockers, sign yearbooks, and say good-bye to teachers and lower classmen. Julie and I spent most of the day with friends, when I suddenly realized I had to go home and get ready. For someone who always took such care with her appearance, I rushed through my graduation preparation, anxious about my speech and not wanting to arrive late.

The ceremony would be followed by the school's traditional all-night party at a local country club. Graduates would board buses to get there to ensure that all arrived and returned to school safely.

I remember marching into East Los Angeles College stadium that night to the strains of Edward Elgar's "Pomp and Circumstance." Because I was a speaker, I sat up front near the school officials and other presenters. As I looked out into the stadium, I felt blinded by the lights at first. As my eyes adjusted, I saw that the bleachers were filled with families and friends of the 568 graduates. Somewhere out there sat Unc, Blanche, and Vinnie.

When my name was announced, I stepped up to the microphone, but my voice cracked as I began to address the audience. The microphone gave feedback, making it difficult to know how I was doing, but eventually I relaxed and gave my speech. At the end, I beseeched classmates to live by the words of the poet Charles Kingsley:

> *Be good...*
> *Do noble things, not dream them, all day long;*
> *And so make life, death, and that vast forever*
> *One grand sweet song!*

My idealism seemed a sharp contrast to the family that awaited me. Blanche and Vinnie stood in the parking lot beside his Cadillac El Dorado with its huge fins. His hair was slicked back into a D.A. (abbreviation for a hairstyle that looked like a duck's tail in the back), Italian style, and Blanche wore a tight sheath dress and high heels. Her platinum-blond hair was teased into a long flip.

Afterwards, Julie told me that several people asked, "Who was that couple with Libby? They looked like members of the Mafia."

I laughed with relief. I'd graduated high school, and Unc, Blanche, and Vinnie all were there. How I wished my mother had lived to enjoy that day!

PART III
Dreams Realized

In dreams begins responsibility.

—William Butler Yeats

22

New Horizons

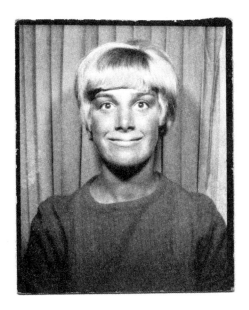

$\mathcal{U}$nc surprised me one morning in July when he said, "I think we should move to West Los Angeles, so that we'll be nearer to UCLA. I can rent a one-bedroom apartment not far from campus, since you'll live in the dorm. You can sleep on the pull-out sofa in the living room when you're home. That way we can save some money to pay for your dorm fees."

Ever since I'd lived in Alhambra, I'd heard that the Westside was *the* place to live in Los Angeles. "That sounds great!" I said. "I've always wanted to live on the Westside."

We discovered that rents were higher on the Westside than in Alhambra. After scouring the many communities surrounding UCLA—Westwood, Beverlywood, Palms, Mar Vista, and Culver City—we finally settled on a one-bedroom, second-floor apartment in a post–World War II, nondescript stucco building in Mar Vista. The building sat in a row of other identical utilitarian buildings and had no pizzazz. But our apartment was located in the back of the building, so it was light and airy, because its kitchen window and sliding glass living room door looked out on an alley. Cars came and went through the alley regularly to gain access to the carports behind the buildings that lined the block.

I wasn't thrilled about sleeping in the living room on a convertible sofa with my dresser along the wall, but considering our limited income, this was the best we could do. I knew I'd only stay there a few weeks and then move into the dorm at UCLA to start my new life.

One reason I chose UCLA came from reading an article in *Parade* magazine on a Sunday when I was twelve. The article featured UCLA as one of the first universities in the country to offer coed dorms. At the time, coed dorms placed their male and female occupants in different wings, but the idea that the two genders could dwell in the same building was quite novel.

I turned to Mommy, showed her the article, and said, "This is where I want to go to school."

Mommy glanced at the article, saw that the school was in California, and responded, "Libby, that's a long way from home, but you can always try." Little did she realize that the following year California would become our home.

On the day I moved into Sproul Hall, I felt that I'd realized my dream. "Unc, can you believe it?" I asked. "I'm starting school at UCLA and moving into a coed dorm."

As he helped me carry my things into my room, Unc asked, "Wouldn't it be great if you met someone from New Jersey here?"

The slim, young woman who was my roommate looked up and said, "I'm from New Jersey. Hi, my name is Jeanie."

"Hi, I'm Libby, and this is my uncle Richard. Where in Jersey are you from?" I asked.

"I'm from Newark. My father owned a bakery on Bergen Street," she replied. "But we moved to Las Vegas when I was a teenager."

"I can't believe it! I'm from Hillside, and my good friends' parents owned the Bergen Bake Shop. Maybe your father knew them? We moved to California when I was thirteen. Where did you live in Newark?"

Jeanie's radiant smile showed her warm personality. She was a beauty with light-brown hair and large brown eyes, and she welcomed me instantly.

Within the hour we discovered that the synagogue her family attended, Young Israel, was only a few miles from Sinai Synagogue, the one mine attended. We even frequented some of the same places on Weequahic Avenue.

Jeanie had moved to Las Vegas as a teenager, and like me, she was not pleased with the move. But the reason for her move differed from mine. Her parents had survived the Holocaust, and when her father discovered that the sister he thought was long dead was indeed alive, married, and living in Las Vegas, he wanted to live near her and make up for all the lost years.

After the move, her father went into business with his brother-in-law, and her mother, a gifted seamstress, created beautiful clothing for Jeanie to wear. Her mother possessed the ability to view a designer gown in a store, go home, create a pattern, choose fabric, and make something similar to the original. Jeanie's clothes were beautiful and never looked anything like the garments Aunt Bessie made for me.

"What happened to your eye?" Jeanie asked after Unc finished bringing in my belongings and said good-bye.

"I had a swimming accident," I replied. "I went to a farewell party in Alhambra last week, and we were playing water tag in the pool. I can't imagine why I chose to do the butterfly stroke while the game was on, but I did! I got socked in the eye so hard that I saw stars."

My arrival at Sproul Hall with a prominent black eye caused many double takes and a number of comments. I had a true shiner, which stood out against my fair skin and blond hair. Since I could not hide it, I decided to own it. At the time, Tareyton cigarettes ran television commercials and print ads stating, "Tareyton smokers would rather fight than switch." These ads featured good-looking models with prominent shiners. More than once, people came up to me and said, "I guess you'd rather fight."

"I'm a lover, not a fighter," I'd reply. In truth, I was a nonsmoker, who was mortified to head off to college with a black eye—until I realized how much attention I garnered.

Coincidentally, the date that took me to the swim party lived in the same dorm as I. When we arrived at school, he avoided me. A few other friends from Alhambra also lived in my dorm, and I was happy to see some but mortified by the one who was assigned the mailbox above mine. He was the classmate I ran into most frequently!

Since students moved into the dorms a few days before classes started, we explored the sprawling campus together. Jeanie and I made friends with other fifth-floor dwellers, including Marlene, Faye, Corky, Diane, Andy, Gail, and Susie. We developed a strong camaraderie and often spent time in each other's rooms, chatting, doing our nails, browsing through magazines, and choosing our classes.

In 1966, we enrolled in classes in person. To do this, we had to make a list of required classes, check when they were offered, and then participate in the quarterly rite of rising very early and trying to sign up for the classes needed. We called this practice "running for classes." Freshmen were warned to arrive as early as possible if they wanted to get any classes that quarter.

On the morning this rite took place, my friends and I rushed down the hill from the dorms onto campus around six o'clock to begin the process. We stood in huge crowds, each hoping to get into line and sign up for a class. Each of us had a different strategy, depending on her major. Since I had declared psychology as my major, I tried for a psych class first and got in. I filled out my schedule with French 4 and an introduction to cultural anthropology. Because this was my first quarter, I only enrolled in twelve units, which turned out to be a wise move. I lacked discipline and discovered that I did not know how to study. In the past, I had simply memorized the answers, but I soon learned that knowing the material was merely the first step to understanding what I needed to do.

On the first day of classes, I met this tall, skinny, dark-haired young man with horn-rimmed glasses talking to my friend Marlene outside Ackerman Student Union. Marlene was a petite beauty with black hair, striking green eyes, flawless ivory skin, and a curvaceous figure who lived in the dorm room next to mine.

Don Atwater was tall and thin and wore horn-rimmed glasses when we first met.

"Hi, Libby. How are you? I'd like you to meet Don Atwater," Marlene said.

"Hi," I responded.

"Hi," said Don, as he focused on Marlene.

"Why are you wearing a jacket with the number sixty-nine on it?" I asked.

Looking annoyed, Don answered, "It's a freshman letterman's jacket. I'm on the UCLA track team, and they put your graduation year on your jacket. I earned a letter last year, and I'll graduate in 1969."

"Oh, I wondered why so many guys are walking around campus with that number on their jackets. It seemed a bit odd," I said.

It was clear that Don Atwater wanted nothing to do with me, so I said good-bye to Marlene and headed back to the dorm. I thought he was cocky, and I had other male interests.

UCLA offered a freedom I'd never known. I was no longer tied to high school class schedules, home chores, and a social life limited to weekends. I no longer would spend Saturdays cleaning the apartment, a ritual begun when my mother became ill shortly after we moved to California. After doing that for several years, keeping my dorm room clean was easy.

Now I could plan my classes, study between, or choose from a number of activities, like going to the Rec Center, football games, parties, dates, visiting with friends, or walking to Westwood.

I went out on school nights with young men from nearby fraternities and the dorms. Some were gentlemen; others did not get a second chance. One freshman asked me to his fraternity party, and he seemed like a nice guy, so I went. After we'd been at the party for a while, and he'd downed several beers, he said, "I want to show you something in my room."

Naively, I agreed to go. Once in his room, he became a bit too friendly. "Watch it. I know judo," I lied.

Suddenly he grabbed my arm and flipped me. I lay flat on my back in his fraternity room, stunned by his sudden aggression.

"I was only kidding," I added. "That was mean. I'm leaving." And I headed for the door.

He tried to block my exit but swayed unsteadily on his feet. Just then the door opened and his roommate arrived. He looked at me and asked, "Would you like me to walk you back to the dorm?"

"Yes," I answered.

That experience taught me a lesson. Even though college offered end-less possibilities for fun, I had to choose my dates carefully. Fraternity parties with aggressive, beer-drinking guys were now off my list.

Sadly, the boyfriend I left behind in Alhambra, who was such a gentle-man, became a memory. We'd spent four wonderful months dating after we became friends while working on the senior play together and had developed a strong relationship when I moved to West Los Angeles to start school. But I looked forward to college and the bright future I hoped it would deliver. Once there, I never looked back or considered whether he could be part of it. I did not return his phone calls and was startled the day he arrived on campus riding his bicycle all the way from Alhambra. I then realized how he truly felt. I hurt him, and to this day I regret it.

My newfound social life almost overtook the reason I'd enrolled at UCLA. Perhaps my attitude developed because I did not like some of the classes I'd chosen. I quickly discovered that psychology classes consisted of studying rats in mazes and taking multiple-choice or multiple-guess tests. I never fared well with either of these. The introductory course bored me. I found cultural anthropology interesting and applied myself in that class. In many ways, I wish I'd chosen anthropology as my major, although science was not my strong suit.

French 4 challenged me, because the professor only spoke French in class, and I had not taken French since my junior year in high school. When she assigned Albert Camus's *L'Etranger* to read, I had to purchase the English version to read first. After reading it, I still did not understand what the book was about.

I also rebelled against the Friday morning French class that started at eight o'clock, unlike the other four days when class began at nine. After miss-ing a few Friday classes, *madame* took me aside and said, "If you don't come to class next Friday, I will fail you. You can pass the class if you show up and give a report in French." She assigned the subject, and I worked hard to research it, write a speech, and deliver it in class. I needed a good scare to make me realize that freedom came with responsibility.

Considering that I'd been awarded three scholarships to attend UCLA, I did not behave like a serious student that first quarter or the beginning of my second. At a university with more than 30,000, I could easily become lost. I no longer had to be involved in many extracurricular activities, and I did not want to stand out as a "brain," as I had in high school. The competition at UCLA soon showed me I was not as smart as I thought.

It was easy to become sidetracked while living on campus, and I was easily sidetracked. Shortly after classes began, and I'd sorted through the dating pool, I began seeing a quiet young fraternity man named Mark. He had been the backup center on the freshman basketball team that featured Lew Alcindor, the standout player recruited from Power Memorial Academy in New York. Mark did not make the varsity team in 1966, and he regretted that he would no longer be one of John Wooden's boys. He spent his days in class, his nights at the fraternity, playing intramural basketball, and some of his free time with me. Mark was a foot taller than I with dark blond wavy hair, cropped short, and big blue eyes. I developed a strong crush on him.

One fall Sunday he asked, "Would you like to go for a ride?"

"Sure," I replied and hopped on the back of his motorcycle.

"Hold on tight," he said, as he left campus and navigated the curves of Sunset Boulevard all the way to the Pacific Coast Highway.

I wondered where we were headed but was unable to communicate as we soared up the highway, the wind blowing in my face.

Mark steered his motorcycle all the way to Malibu Canyon Road and turned right. Then he continued for several miles until we arrived at a beautiful green area called Tapia Park.

I was happy to get off the motorcycle and sit in the park talking for a while. I was not a risk taker, and riding all the way from UCLA to the canyons of Malibu without protective clothing or a helmet was one of the biggest risks I took. I held on so tightly that I was stiff, and the uncomfortable seat made sitting difficult for days. I decided not to tell Unc about this adventure and declined future long rides.

That quarter I spent more time with my friends in the dorm and Mark than I worked on my classes. We attended football games and fraternity parties. I don't ever recall going out for a hamburger, an ice cream, or seeing a movie. I guess Mark's budget was as tight as mine. (Unc gave me a ten-dollar-a-week allowance my freshman year.)

He introduced me to drinks I'd never heard of, such as Purple Jesus (vodka, grape juice, and grapefruit juice). One night, after drinking one of these at his friend's apartment, I became dizzy and could not make it back to the dorm by the ten o'clock curfew. I wound up spending the night fully clothed on the floor of his friend's apartment with several other people who'd been struck by Purple Jesus.

When I stumbled back to my dorm room the next morning, Jeanie asked, "Where were you? I was so worried."

"I'm sorry," I answered. "I drank one of those crazy drinks, and I knew I would not make it back before curfew. Since I was not feeling too well, I decided it was better to stay at the party than get into trouble at the dorm."

"Please don't ever do that again," Jeanie asked. "You really scared me."

I did not learn my lesson that fall night. Several weeks later Mark's fraternity held its initiation party, a semiformal event at a lovely house some distance from campus. Dinner was not being served, so I wolfed down barbecued beef in the dorm before heading out in my woven winter-white wool dress and silver sandals with my hair and makeup done to perfection.

"Would you like a drink?" Mark asked when we arrived at the party.

"Yes," I answered, naively thinking it was fruit punch.

The pledges and their dates were in high spirits that night, having survived Hell Week. Mark and the other second-year members were also celebrating. I don't remember any food being served, but I was terribly thirsty after dancing and talking to other guests. By the time I was halfway through my second drink, I felt sick and rushed to find a bathroom. When I did, I discovered the door open and several other girls hunched around the toilet heaving. I joined them, and suddenly my winter-white dress wore a coating of barbecue sauce. I threw some water on my face, tried to calm my queasy stomach, and begged Mark to take me home. He did not sit too close to me on the long ride back to campus.

The next morning, when I showed up for a late breakfast in the dorm, my friend Jim, a first-year medical student, looked at me and said, "Libby, what happened to you? You look awful."

"I feel awful. I went to a fraternity initiation party last night and had too much to drink. I got sick all over my beautiful white dress."

"If drinking makes you feel like that, why do it?" he asked. "You've got so much going for you. It doesn't sound like Mark has a lot of respect for you if he tries to get you drunk."

"You're right," I answered sheepishly. Jim behaved like a big brother to me, and we often chatted at meals. He owned a car and occasionally gave me a ride into Westwood.

I would help him out when I could. The day he brought his ripped shirt and slacks to me and explained that he'd sat on his scalpel, I carefully stitched them back together. When I returned them, I said, "Be more careful next time."

He and the other medical students often asked to take me to class to practice inserting IVs, because the veins on my hands stood out. I always refused.

While I was having fun during my first quarter in college, Unc faced a new reality. Construction had slumped in Southern California, and he was forced to accept whatever jobs he could. He began working nights.

One morning in late November he called, sounding upset. "Hi, Libby. I had a big surprise last night."

"What happened?" I asked.

"I came home from work and discovered that someone broke into our apartment and took everything: money, my stereo, the TV, even the radio. Someone must have been watching me come and go and had an old key, because there was no sign of forced entry. From now on, I'll leave the light on when I go to work," Unc said.

"Oh, Unc, I'm so sorry," I said. "I know how much you love your music."

"It will be a quiet Christmas vacation for you," he added. "We can't afford to replace those things right now, and we didn't have insurance on our apartment. But I will insist that they change the locks."

I asked myself "Why is it that people who are struggling and have so little are the ones to get robbed?" Then I said, "It's not fair."

"You know that life's unfair," Unc answered.

I knew what he said was true and vowed to apply myself to my studies. I even asked if I should seek a part-time job, but Unc firmly assured me that school was my priority.

At UCLA, one priority besides going to class was attending basketball games. For two dollars apiece, I could sit in Pauley Pavilion and watch the Bruins play and win every game. With starting players like Lew Alcindor, Lucius Allen, Mike Warren, Lynn Shackleford, and Kenny Heitz, it was hard to lose. Often I went to games with Mark, but many nights my dorm friends and I went to games together.

As finals approached, Mark said, "I'm going to the game alone tonight and then back to the house to study. You should stay home and study."

A letterman's jacket and a tan
do wonders for a guy.

"Okay," I said.

When I told Jeanie about the conversation, she asked, "Are you going to let him tell you what to do? Let's go to the game together. After it's over, I have to study for my final tomorrow, but there's no reason you have to stay in."

On December 9, 1966, Jeanie and I went to the game together. We loved watching the Bruins play and win. Afterwards, we walked back to the dorm, and she went upstairs to study. I stayed in the lobby for a while, not ready to turn in so early on a Friday night. Besides, I was hungry, and I'd used up most of my ten-dollar allowance that week. I hoped to find something I could afford in a vending machine.

As I passed my mailbox, I recognized three guys leaning against the opposite wall: Vic, a football player; Rich, Mark's fraternity brother; and Don Atwater, whom Marlene had briefly dated. All three wore freshman letterman's jackets with the number '69 prominently stitched on them. Rich and Vic said "Hi," and Don stepped forward and said, "Hi, I'm Don Atwater. I'm on the track team with Rich."

"I know who you are," I replied. "We met the first day of classes. You went out with my friend Marlene."

Don looked puzzled and said, "Oh, yeah." It was clear he did not remember me.

Then he asked, "Would you like to go out for pizza?"

"Sure," I answered.

"My friend Will is going to come along," he added.

"I'd like one of my friends to come, too," I thought. I did not like the idea of getting into a car with two guys I barely knew.

Along came my friend Mary Lou, who happily agreed to join us.

Don took us out to his yellow Mustang, which I later learned was his high school graduation gift. (He earned half the money, and his parents contributed the remainder.) Off we headed down Wilshire Boulevard to La Barbera's, a nearby restaurant known for great Italian food.

Over pizza, we laughed and talked a lot. Don told us all about getting ready for the track season, as he was a member of the varsity track team with Rich. His friend Will played water polo. While eating, we told where each of us lived.

Don said, "I live in Mar Vista in a big white house with my parents."

"I live in an apartment in Mar Vista," I answered. "We're neighbors." It was true. He only lived a few blocks from me.

Mary Lou was a Pasadena girl, and Will hailed from one of the beach towns in the South Bay.

Don deposited Mary Lou and me back at our dorm before curfew, and I thought I'd never see him again.

I felt a bit guilty about my pizza date, because Mark had already asked me out for New Year's Eve and his fraternity's winter weekend in Yosemite in January. We were seeing each other exclusively.

I spent all of Saturday in my dorm room studying for the coming week's finals. On Sunday morning, the phone rang and a voice said, "Hi, sports fan."

"Hi," I answered, having no idea who was calling.

"I have a Chanukah gift for you," said the voice. "Come downstairs. I'm at the front desk."

I took the elevator to the main floor and was surprised to see Don Atwater standing there. "Happy Chanukah," he said and handed me a white tee shirt with UCLA Track Team written on it.

"Thank you," I responded. "That was very thoughtful and unexpected."

"Well you are a sports fan, and I'm on the track team. Now you'll have to come and see me run."

"That will be great," I answered, feeling even more uncomfortable. Don was so kind, but I was dating Mark.

"Since we live so close, maybe we can get together during winter break," Don added.

I gave him my phone number, but I had no intention of ever seeing him again. At that point, I was committed to Mark.

We wished each other luck, and I went back upstairs to study for finals. I had a lot of studying to catch up on, as the first ten weeks of college life had sped by. I hoped for a miracle but was realistic enough to know I'd get what I deserved.

When my grades arrived on individual postcards a few days after I returned to our barren apartment, I'd earned two Cs and a B, the lowest grades I'd ever received in my life. I knew I'd have to change if I wanted to remain at UCLA and keep my state scholarship.

23

Arrivals and Departures

I dreaded returning to our Mar Vista apartment for the holidays. My friends at school had all gone home, and I faced an empty apartment with no form of entertainment, thanks to our November burglary. Unc now worked days, and I would spend most of mine alone. Julie had taken a full-time job after high school, and Rickie and I lost touch.

I spent my first few mornings sleeping in, trying to make the day pass more quickly. One morning about eleven o'clock the doorbell rang. I looked through the peephole and saw Don Atwater standing there.

"Hi," I said through the closed door. "What a surprise! Why are you here?"

"I couldn't find your phone number, but I remembered that you said you lived on McLaughlin Avenue. I've been driving up and down the street checking mailboxes until I found your name. I thought maybe you'd like to go out for lunch."

"I'd like that a lot, but I'm still in my pajamas," I answered.

"Can I come in and wait?" he asked.

"Just a moment. I'm going to take my clothes into the bathroom and get ready. I'll open the front door, and you can wait in the living room."

I hurried into the bathroom, washed and dressed, and then spent a half hour on my hair and makeup. When I emerged, Don looked me over and said, "I was beginning to think it would be a dinner date by the time you came out."

That day he took me to Blum's in Beverly Hills for lunch, and he was impressed with what a good eater I was. I was impressed that he chose such a lovely restaurant, one I'd always wanted to try.

When he dropped me off that afternoon, Don asked, "Would you like to go to Disneyland on Friday?"

"Yes," I answered immediately. I loved Disneyland, and going there with Don would certainly be fun.

When he picked me up on Friday morning, I wore my red wool blazer and a plaid skirt with dark tights and flat-heeled shoes. I didn't realize that my outfit resembled that of Disneyland's guides until people approached and asked me for directions. Many were from the Purdue University football team, which was visiting Disneyland that week before preparing to play in the Rose Bowl. Don pointed out several of the star players, such as Bob Greasy. I secretly hoped they'd beat USC, since it had received the Rose Bowl bid, despite UCLA defeating its team in the annual cross-town rivalry.

Unc greeted Don with a handshake and a smile when we returned from our daylong outing. "I'm happy to meet you," he said. After Don left, Unc turned to me. "Libby, Don is a great guy. If only you cared about him the way you do about Muscle Man," his nickname for Mark.

Unc's words rang in my head, but I had a crush on Mark. I felt torn but continued to date Don during the holidays, because we had fun together. He was full of surprises, too. On Christmas Eve he showed up at our front door and said. "I brought you a gift," and handed me a small box. Inside was a beautiful gold compact filled with powder.

"Thank you, it's lovely, but you shouldn't have brought me a gift," I replied.

"I wanted to," Don answered. "I can't stay. My parents and I go to Mass on Christmas Eve. I just wanted you to know I was thinking about you."

I felt sad when he left and realized I liked him a lot. Beneath that brash exterior was a kind, thoughtful guy.

On Christmas morning, I asked Unc what our plans were for the day. "I just want to stay in and relax. It's been a long week, and now that I've replaced my record player, I'd like to listen to some music and read."

Even though we did not celebrate Christmas, I felt that we should do something special that day, such as go to a movie. It was a major holiday, but since I was Jewish and Unc was agnostic it did not matter to him.

"I'm going for a ride," I announced and took the keys to the used blue-and-white Dodge with gigantic fins that Unc purchased after our faithful, ten-year-old Plymouth Belvedere died. I drove toward campus, hoping to find someone or something to do, but there was no activity there. Finally, I circled back to Sunset Boulevard and drove around campus, not realizing how fast I was going. When I almost lost control on Dead Man's Curve, I gripped the wheel hard and slowed down. Tears fell and I could not stop them. I pulled over onto campus and just sat and cried. I missed my family so much. Other people were out celebrating, and I had almost killed myself driving. I felt so alone.

A few days before New Year's Eve, Don came over and said, "Let's go for a ride. My parents are entertaining friends this evening, and they'd like to meet you."

"All right," I said, although I was apprehensive about meeting his parents. What if they didn't like me?

We arrived at his house, a small, white post–World War II wood and stucco single-story with a huge yard. It was not the big white house he described nor I imagined. Don took me to the back door, and out stepped this petite woman with short, dark brown hair and sparkling blue eyes, dressed in a navy fitted skirt and white blouse. She extended her hand and said, "Hi, I'm Marie. Welcome to our home." Don looked so much like her, I thought, until his father joined his mother at the door. "This is Don's father, Don," Marie continued.

"Hello, Mr. and Mrs. Atwater. Thank you for inviting me over," I responded. We stayed for a short while and then headed back to my apartment to play cards.

On New Year's Eve, I kept my date with Mark. He asked if I could find a date for his friend, and Julie agreed to come if I picked her up in Alhambra. She'd spend the night with me and Unc in Mar Vista.

Mark and his friend picked us up in Mar Vista and drove us to a party near his home in Orange County. The hostess was pretty and very friendly, but when she began speaking, I realized I was at the wrong party. "I was first runner-up in the Miss Teenage America Contest," she announced, "but I lost to a black girl. Can you imagine?"

Other guests began laughing and pointing at her, saying "You lost to a n-----," a word that was forbidden in my household.

I knew the "black girl" she referred to. She was Jeanie and Marlene's sorority sister, Don's and my classmate, and a lovely person. "You should get to know her," I answered. "She's very nice, and she's also quite smart. She'll be successful."

The party grew more uncomfortable when our hostess and her friends then expressed their opinions about Jews. Julie and I held our tongues; we felt out of place among this Orange County crowd. After Mark drove us home, we both said, "Never again." Julie could not understand what I saw in Mark.

On New Year's Day, Don showed up to drive Julie back to Alhambra. When we arrived, Mrs. Frank greeted him with a welcoming hug. Julie's sister Chris, and her husband, Dennis, were visiting with their new baby, Tim. "Would you like to hold the baby?" Mrs. Frank asked Don. Before he could respond, Tim was in his arms.

I watched Don hold that adorable towheaded infant so gently and realized that for all of his bravado, he had a soft side. He was beginning to grow on me.

We went out one more time before I planned to return to the dorm. That evening before he left, I said, "I'm sorry, but I can't see you again."

"Why not?" Don asked. "Aren't we having fun together?"

"I'm having a great time with you, but I have a boyfriend. I'm supposed to go on his fraternity's winter weekend in Yosemite after school starts. I can't go away with him and keep dating you."

We discussed my declaration for several minutes, and I began to cry. I really liked Don and did not want to hurt his feelings, as I had my high school boyfriend. Suddenly, he leaned over, took me in his arms, and kissed me. I kissed him back and realized I had a dilemma. He was a great kisser!

Classes began the following week, and Don and I discovered we had both enrolled in political science, along with Marlene, Jeanie, and about 296 other students. We began sitting together in class.

The fraternity weekend arrived and Jeanie warned, "You know you're expected to sleep with your date."

"I know that," I answered. I naively misunderstood the word "sleep," thinking the weekend would be more like a girls' slumber party, where people slept in the same room. Even if we shared the same bed, I had no intention of becoming intimate. I knew all too well from Blanche what that resulted in.

I packed my warm clothes and flannel nightgown and boarded the bus with Mark, his fraternity brothers, and their dates late one Friday afternoon. I fell asleep on the bus and awoke to a fairyland. Beautiful ice-laden trees and snow-covered grounds surrounded us. When we stepped off the bus, I discovered it was freezing. Although I'd grown up in New Jersey, I had not been in snow in five years.

That weekend was a big disappointment. Mark and I definitely had different expectations, and neither of us knew how to express ourselves. We did not communicate well. We also lacked the money to ski and engage in the weekend's other activities. While the other guys and their dates played, we took a ride through the snow in an outdoor vehicle. The cold we experienced in Yosemite became a metaphor for our relationship. It had come to an end. Both of us remained quiet on the bus ride back to campus.

I did not date Mark again, but I still cared for him. He never called after that weekend, and I did not see him for a while until he arrived at the dorm to pick up his new girlfriend, someone I knew casually and liked. When I saw them together, I faced reality.

Although Don and I dated during winter quarter, he had other friends and interests. He loved to play cards, and some weekends chose to do that with a friend named Liz or some of the guys from the track team. I began to feel possessive and jealous.

I decided to go out with my girlfriends and occasionally dated guys from the dorm, but I soon realized I'd rather spend my free time with Don. I really liked him, and he treated me so much better than other boys I'd dated.

The two of us threw ourselves into our courses during winter quarter 1967, since he was a math major and had a heavy extracurricular schedule with track practice and ROTC (Reserve Officers Training Course).

I knew that the track team worked out on the football practice field adjacent to Pauley Pavilion, and I often stopped and stood by the fence on my way back to the dorm, hoping to see Don. I could see him from afar, focused on his workout running the 440-yard intermediate hurdles. He completely ignored me. Don's teammates, whom I'd met, would come over to the fence to chat until Coach Busch grabbed his megaphone and said, "Guys, get back to work." I enjoyed his teammates' attention and thought Don was stubborn. He acted true to form. He had a job to do, and he planned to do it—without interruptions.

He wore his ROTC uniform proudly and planned to join the Army as a second lieutenant after he graduated from UCLA. He'd already earned medals for marksmanship and served in the honor guard when Emperor Haile Selassie of Ethiopia visited the UCLA campus.

The Vietnam War was underway at that time, and I was not thrilled that he planned to join the United States Army. Don felt it was his duty to serve his country, and he'd rather serve as an officer than an enlisted man, especially since mandatory conscription was the law. He could either enlist or be drafted.

While Don focused on his studies and activities, I officially changed my major to English literature my second quarter. I loved to read, write poetry, and compose essays. I enrolled in only twelve units, determined to improve my first quarter's performance. I loved my English composition class and enjoyed political science, but I simply could not understand physics, even though it was designed for non-science majors to fulfill a breadth requirement. I read the material and tried to solve the homework assignments, but I could not get it—and I never asked for help.

Other things occurred that winter that made it harder for me to concentrate. Unc called one morning in January to deliver the news. "Blanche and Vinnie have split up," he announced. "She's taken off with her friend Lana, and no one knows where she is."

"Are they getting a divorce?" I asked.

"They said that Vinnie's first marriage ended in a Mexican divorce, so they were never really married. They just plan to live apart.

"I have more bad news. I can't find work in Southern California, but there are jobs out of state. I may have to take one if things don't improve."

I began to feel like my family was deserting me once more. Although I applied myself harder that term, I also tried to escape what was going on in my life by having as much fun as I could.

When Jeanie announced one Saturday shortly before midterms that Sigma Chi was holding a beer bust that afternoon, I said, "I'm coming." We walked to the Sigma Chi house, where the party was in full swing. Jeanie and I danced with several guys, and I even drank a beer. One of the guys at the party was on the track team with Don, and we had become friends. "Do you need a ride back to the dorm? I'll take you on my motorcycle," he offered.

I hopped on the back, although both of us had been drinking, and should not have been riding a motorcycle. Fortunately, we arrived safely back at the dorm in time for me to get ready for my date with Don that evening. When I came down to the lobby, Don gave me a hug and said, "You smell just like a brewery. What have you been drinking?"

"Jeanie and I went to a beer bust at the Sigma Chi house this afternoon," I answered. "Your friend John took me home on his motorcycle, and I got cleaned up for our date. I didn't know I smelled bad."

"Let's go get something to eat," Don said. After hamburgers and fries, he took me back to the dorm. "We need to talk," he said. "What are you doing here? You're supposed to be getting an education, and you received three scholarships to attend this university. Are you trying to throw it all away?"

"No," I answered, hurt by his tone. "I just wanted to have some fun, and it was such a pretty day."

"Libby, midterms are next week. You need to get serious and decide what you want to do. You should have stayed home and studied this afternoon."

I knew Don was right. No one had ever spoken to me like that. He was so serious and had such a sense of purpose. I followed the wind, drifting aimlessly. Were we mismatched? Or was he the person I needed to give my life some direction? I didn't know, but that night I went back to the dorm and thought about what he'd said. I also decided to give up beer, a drink I never really liked.

After taking Don's advice and studying, I passed my midterms, although my physics grade was low. On Valentine's Day, the day before my birthday, Don handed me a numbered key to a locker in Ackerman Student Union. "Take a look in that locker," he said.

I hurried to the locker and opened it. Out tumbled all of my favorite things: Mother's frosted animal cookies, red licorice, bubble gum, a note pad, pens, and a plethora of other useful items. No one had ever given me such a gift!

"Thanks," I said. "You are so thoughtful. Happy Valentine's Day!"

"Wait until tomorrow," he said. "I have a big surprise for you."

"I can't wait, but you've already given me a big surprise," I answered. I knew he and Jeanie had gone shopping the previous Saturday, and I wondered what they were up to.

The following day, when I turned nineteen, Don handed me a small, gift-wrapped box. It looked like a ring might be inside, and I was almost afraid to open it, but I did. A lovely cultured pearl and gold ring sat in the velvet-lined box. The pearl was set in an X-shaped piece of gold, and the ring's design suited me perfectly. It also fit. "Thank you," I said, as I hugged and kissed Don. "It's too much. You shouldn't have gone to so much trouble. I wondered what you and Jeanie were shopping for."

"You're worth it," he answered, pleased that his gift had made me happy.

That quarter Don and I studied for our political science final together at his parents' house. With his help, I acquired test-taking and study skills. He was more disciplined and organized than I. Don anticipated questions and challenged me to answer them. Before I met him, I relied on my photographic memory to earn good grades. I had no idea how to think or apply my knowledge, and I was Last-Minute Libby when it came to writing papers or studying for exams.

While we studied, Don's mother stood nearby, fortifying us with food every few hours. I thought she was determined to make me fat, but she was just being her gracious self.

Thanks to Don's strategy I earned some higher grades that quarter. In English, I was rewarded with the only A in my class. Physics was my nemesis, but I believed I could get by. When I received a D—the first and only D I ever got in my life—I broke down in tears and called Don. He arrived at the dorm to find me sitting in the downstairs lounge, smoking a cigarette and sobbing. Don looked shocked, because I never smoked and believed smoking had killed my parents. The cigarette in my hand showed him just how upset I was, and he tried to assure me that things would be all right. I cried harder. Others began staring at us. Later Don confided that he thought those people may have thought he'd gotten me "in trouble," the code used for pregnant.

Spring quarter held promise. I was seasoned enough to understand what I had to earn good grades, and Don was my cheerleader. Now that I had become an English major, my workload increased. Some classes assigned us to read one book a week plus a number of papers. I tried to balance those classes by taking at least one "Mick," short for Mickey Mouse, a term used to describe an easy class. Unfortunately, some classes known to be Micks were not. I managed to find them.

In my first year of college, I developed a habit of breaking down about the third or fourth week of each quarter. I'd lose my confidence, collapse in tears, and insist I did not belong at UCLA. The first quarter Jeanie and other friends listened to my fears and inspired me to continue. By spring, this task fell to Don. It was one he assumed for the remainder of my undergraduate years and beyond.

In addition to my worries about school, my family situation grew more complicated that spring. Blanche's friend Lana called to say they were working in Las Vegas and would be in touch. She refused to give me any contact information. She added that Vinnie had moved to Arizona and was living with a woman. He'd been in a motorcycle accident and survived, but he was in the hospital in a full body cast.

I received a letter from a cemetery in Philadelphia informing me that Zayde Berger died. As one of his grandchildren, I was being asked to contribute money toward the maintenance of his grave. At first I could not believe that I was being approached for money. I had none. So I sat and wrote a polite letter to the cemetery explaining my circumstances. I never heard from it again.

Towards the middle of the spring quarter, Unc called to say he'd found work—in Ypsilanti, Michigan. He left immediately, wrote often, and sent me money to pay the bills. He did not know how long he would have to stay in Michigan, but he knew he would not be home for the summer.

I began to look for summer work, hoping to help our financial situation. We agreed that I could not return to the dorm in the fall, because I could live more cheaply in an apartment, either with roommates or with Unc, when he returned.

I also sought a roommate from among my friends at school. Facing the summer alone frightened me.

24
Dream Girl of '67

$\mathcal{A}$t the beginning of fall quarter 1967, my phone rang. "Is this Libby?" the caller asked. "My name is Bob, and I'm a producer for a new television show called *Dream Girl of '67*. Your friend Marsha sent us your picture, and we'd like you to be on the show. We start production in October. Are you interested?"

"What kind of show is it?" I asked.

"It's a daytime show, much like *The Dating Game* [a show in which a woman chooses a date from among three competing men] and has the same producer. We invite young women to compete for the title of *Dream Girl of '67*."

"You're kidding, right? Marsha is playing a joke on me," I said.

"I'm serious," Bob answered. "We think you'd be perfect."

"Yes," I responded. "It sounds like fun."

I could not believe that call, but I figured I had nothing to lose by competing. My self-image was poor, despite my high school metamorphosis. I considered myself fat and compared myself to friends who had different body types and genes. Jeanie, my freshman roommate, could eat an entire cheesecake and not gain a pound. I did not have her metabolism.

During my first year at UCLA, I worked hard to lose weight. Walking to campus from the dorms provided great exercise, and I restricted my diet severely while I lived in the dorm. Unlike most freshmen who gain the Freshmen Fifteen, I lost weight that year. I only ate two meals a day, breakfast and dinner. I made lunch daily, from the food the dorm provided, and gave it away to Don. I would sit and watch him eat.

Sunday was the one day I'd treat myself. I'd eat ice cream for dessert because the dorm brought in huge tubs from a local shop. I did not have the healthiest eating habits, but starving myself brought results. By the summer of 1967, I was ten pounds lighter. Perhaps I could be a contender on *Dream Girl* after all. I still monitored my diet carefully, and since I did not have a lot of money, it was easy. I didn't keep much food at home.

I dreaded living alone that summer and sought someone to room with me. Flossie, a friend from the dorm, accepted. Right after finals ended, she moved in and we found summer jobs.

We carpooled to work and spent much of our free time together, since our boyfriends were track teammates at UCLA. In fact, I had introduced Flossie to Buzz, and they soon became a couple. She was striking, with black hair, big brown eyes, and the longest eyelashes I'd ever seen. No wonder Buzz asked for an introduction. Her outgoing personality made being with her fun.

But by the end of July it became clear that neither of us earned enough to make ends meet *and* save money for the next quarter. Before we got paid, we ran low on food, and one week we ran out. Our refrigerator contained only butter and jam. Fortunately, that night Mrs. Atwater invited us over for dinner, and we quickly accepted.

Flossie soon realized that she'd be better off living at home and called her parents, who were thrilled, because they did not care for her boyfriend.

After Flossie left, I slept with one eye open. I was only nineteen, and I'd been a fearful child. Still a child in many ways, I found living alone a huge challenge. After our apartment was burglarized the previous fall, it never felt comfortable to me. I'd watched too many TV shows where the intruder entered through a sliding door. Although I was on the second floor, I realized it was still possible to break in. It had happened once!

When Unc made his weekly call, I said, "I think we need a bigger apartment so that I can find a roommate. I'll be commuting to school in the fall, and I'm sure someone would rather live in an apartment than the dorm."

Unc agreed, especially since he had no idea when he might return to California. He had plenty of work in Michigan, and California still offered no new construction jobs. "Look for a place not too far from campus," he suggested.

While driving down the street, I spotted a two-bedroom, two-bath apartment in a newer building less than a block away. It seemed more secure than my present place and was definitely larger. The apartment was on the second floor and had no sliding doors, making me feel safer. Several young families lived in the building, and they were quite friendly.

I began advertising for roommates. The big problem with taking in a roommate was if Unc returned. I could not imagine too many coeds wanting to live with me and my uncle.

I packed up Unc's and my belongings in boxes and slowly began moving them from one apartment to the other after I got home from work. There was a two-week overlap in the rental start and end dates, allowing me to move the small items a few at a time. Mr. Atwater offered his truck for the kitchen set, dresser, and bed. But he could not lift the sleeper sofa or refrigerator, because he had a bad back, and he suggested I hire a mover for those two items.

Moving day came, but the mover did not show up. After repeated calls to the moving company, in which I was told they'd arrive later, I realized that they were not coming. My job was too small. At five o'clock I called Don. "Can you help me?" I asked. "The mover never showed, and I have to be out of this apartment tonight. I don't know what to do."

"I'll come by with my father as soon as he gets home from work," Don answered. "Just sit tight." He could hear my voice quivering and knew I was upset.

Mr. Atwater worked long hours in the summer. He was a landscaper and gardener who left the house at daybreak and often returned after dark. A kind, quiet man, he helped everyone. His customers trusted him and knew he would take good care of their homes when they were away. He never charged extra, but he readily pitched in whenever he saw the need. Unfortunately, because he

Don and his dad had a major challenge navigating my sofa and refrigerator down these stairs.

had injured his back years earlier, he wore a brace when he worked. I felt bad about asking him to lift anything heavy, especially since he'd have to unload his equipment-laden truck after a long day at work to rescue me.

As promised, Don and his dad showed up as soon as they could. About eight o'clock they tied up the sofa bed and slowly carried it down the open stairs. They could lift the sofa as high as the liftgate on Mr. Atwater's truck, which they did, securing the sofa to the truck bed with heavy rope. Next they took the refrigerator downstairs on a dolly. There was no room in the truck for it, and it was too heavy to lift.

Don and his dad talked, and then Don said, "We'll leave the refrigerator on the dolly and walk it down the alley behind the truck."

"That's crazy," I said. "It's dark, and my new apartment is two blocks away."

"Here, hold the flashlight and walk behind me," Don ordered. "My dad will drive the truck with the sofa on it."

We could see neighbors peering out their windows at this odd parade proceeding down the dark alley that evening. No one stopped us, and I moved into my new apartment that night, thanks to Don and his dad.

I continued to work at the women's boutique and was surprised when Mrs. Atwater rushed in one afternoon holding a letter. "Libby, Libby, look at this," she said. "It just came for Don, but I opened it. I know I shouldn't have, but I couldn't wait until he got home." The letter stated that Don had not passed the physical exam to continue with ROTC, because he'd had asthma as a child. He could not go into the United States Army as a second lieutenant, as planned.

Mrs. Atwater and I began jumping up and down. "Do you know what this means?" she asked.

"He won't have to go to Vietnam!" I exclaimed.

We both knew that second lieutenants had high mortality rates in the

Vietnam War. Mrs. Atwater hugged me and the two of us jumped up and down with joy.

Don was not pleased with the letter—or that his mother had opened it before he could. He wanted to serve as an officer. "They can still draft me," he said. "I just won't be an officer. This may not be such good news."

But a few weeks later, a second letter arrived releasing him from military duty. We all felt relieved.

Toward the end of the summer, I was laid off. Business had been slow, and I was grateful that the store kept me employed as long as it did.

That fall quarter I spent my days commuting to my classes at UCLA and studying. Sometimes Don and I drove together and shared parking costs.

In the evenings, I ate dinner at his house—nearly every night. This custom began innocently enough. One night Mrs. Atwater invited me over for dinner. She always made hearty, home-cooked meals that reminded me of my mother's cooking. I really enjoyed them, but most of all I loved being with their family. After dinner, Mrs. Atwater asked me to join them the next evening. I tried to decline, but she insisted. After a while dinners at the Atwaters' home became routine.

At first I felt embarrassed. My mother had taught me not to impose on others, but Don's parents were so generous, although they were not wealthy. They each worked hard: his mom managed an elementary school cafeteria and served for a catering company on weekends; his dad toiled in people's gardens in tony Beverly Hills and Beverlywood. "It doesn't make sense for you to cook for one, and we have plenty," Mrs. Atwater insisted. "Besides, I've always wanted a daughter, and I enjoy having you here."

In truth, I enjoyed being there. I felt so comfortable in their modest home, because they were a "real" family. I remembered dinners with my family as a child, and dinners at Don's house brought back warm memories. Life seemed normal, and I desperately wanted to be normal like everyone else.

I lived alone most of fall 1967 until just before Thanksgiving, when Unc returned from Michigan. He missed me so much and hugged me so tightly that I could barely breathe. I thought it ironic that the man who didn't really want me, but inherited me as a teenager when he was fifty-five years old, had finally accepted me as his child.

We soon returned to our old routines. Unc did the shopping and the cooking, I washed the dishes and cleaned the apartment, and together we did the laundry. However, unlike my high school classes, my courses at UCLA demanded a great deal more time. I adhered to a strict schedule each day, including weekends, in order to get everything done.

I thought back to the surprise call from the producer earlier in the fall. I no longer felt like a "Dream Girl," more like a "Drudge Girl." To make matters worse, the show *Dream Girl of '67* never materialized. A directors' strike shut down television production that fall. I kept receiving regular updates, but the show became more illusory. By the time the strike ended, it was nearly 1968.

Bob, the producer, called again. "I'm sorry, but the show never went into production. We think you'd be ideal for *The Dating Game*."

"Thanks so much for the call," I replied. "I've been dating someone for nearly a year, so I'll have to say 'no'."

"Call me if you break up," Bob said and gave me his number.

"Thanks," I responded, smiling.

That Christmas Don's parents invited Unc and me for Christmas dinner. Unlike our quiet Christmas of 1966, Christmas 1967 became very special. Despite their modest lifestyle, his parents prepared a delicious prime rib dinner, presented us with gifts, and made us feel very welcome in their home.

Don and I spent that New Year's Eve together at my friend Marsha's apartment. She had sent my picture to the television show, and she wanted us to celebrate the New Year with her and her husband.

As Don and I shared a New Year's kiss at midnight, I believed that 1968 would bring many surprises.

25

A Year of Surprises

The year 1968 would be filled with surprises—some pleasant, others shocking. While Don and I were cocooned at UCLA, the outside world overflowed with problems. In January the *Pueblo*, a United States Navy warship was seized by North Korea in the Sea of Japan and accused of being a spy ship. This seizure created a hostage situation that lasted all year.

The civil rights struggle remained at America's forefront. Progress had been made with the passage of the Voting Rights Act in 1965 and the appointment of Thurgood Marshall to the United States Supreme Court. But the riots that created upheaval in several major American cities along with violence against civil rights workers showed that much more had to be done.

The Vietnam War, which began during President Kennedy's term, now divided the country. After Lyndon Johnson was elected president of the United

States in 1964 and Congress approved the Gulf of Tonkin resolution, United States involvement in Vietnam escalated. By 1968, this war that raged half a world away continued to claim the lives of young Americans in alarming numbers. Those who fought bravely for their country and survived were treated poorly when they returned home alive. Families and friends grieved for those who did not. Some young Americans of draft age sought refuge in Canada to avoid serving.

Citizens staged demonstrations against the war and those in power, whose moniker became The Establishment. Students accepted the slogan, "Never trust anyone over thirty," literally, and demonstrations against the war and The Establishment spread to college campuses throughout the country.

Unc was against the war and convinced me it was wrong. I was not shy about expressing my opinions on this subject, which often led to lively discussions with Don and his parents, who were conservative, blue-collar workers.

The use of recreational drugs like marijuana and LSD increased during this period and became readily available.

While Don and I often felt it necessary to shut out the world at large so that we could complete the tasks at hand, we were aware of what was going on around us. But we both wanted to finish college and improve our lives, and we worried that we could jeopardize our futures if we became too involved.

By winter of 1968, I doubted Don and I would break up, although we certainly had our differences. Some loomed larger than others. I was Jewish; he was Catholic. I was an Aquarius, a free spirit, who loved to try new things and often flitted from one to another. He was a Virgo, orderly, regimented, and serious. He disliked change. My political beliefs leaned to the left, while his were more conservative. Yet we had fun together going to movies, concerts, and sporting events, eating in local restaurants, and going to the beach. By the end of my first year at UCLA we were dating each other exclusively, and by winter 1968 we'd been together more than a year.

My grades improved my second year at UCLA, and I retained my California State Scholarship, which I kept my entire four years. But my course work grew harder as I delved further into my major. I still became overwhelmed by the assignments, but now I had a cheerleader.

Don would look at me and say, "Of course you can do it. You just need to get organized and apply yourself. I'll help you." And he did, *every* quarter. He grew used to these outbursts and handled them well. His calm determination helped me make it through UCLA and the years that followed.

Unc returned to Michigan shortly after the 1967 holiday season. He could not find work in California and hated to leave me alone again, but he had no choice. I had not found a roommate, so once again I was on my own.

When winter quarter began in January 1968, I enrolled in a course called Twentieth-Century American Literature. The first day, I sat next to a pretty young woman with honey-blond hair and huge turquoise eyes. She was well dressed and wore engagement and wedding rings on her left hand. "Hi, I'm Dennie," she said. "And this is my friend Barbara."

"Hi, I'm Libby. Where are you from?" I asked.

"I grew up in Beverlywood, but I now live in Palms with my husband, Mike. He's a second-year student at UCLA Law School."

We chatted for a while until the professor entered and gave his first lecture. His knowledge of American literature was extensive, and his lectures were dynamic. I looked forward to his class but also feared it. I did not understand how to interpret literature, although I kept up with the extensive reading list and course work: ten books in ten weeks plus five papers. I began to feel overwhelmed.

I enjoyed sitting next to Dennie and Barbara nearly every day. Barbara had recently married a pharmacist, and she loved to talk about her luxurious lifestyle. When she and Dennie asked about my life, I said, "My father died when I was fourteen, and my mother died sixteen months later. I live with my uncle in an apartment in Mar Vista."

Barbara didn't believe me! She told Dennie, "No one can have that bad a life and seem so normal. She's a liar."

Dennie related that story to me one day when we were studying for midterms, and I asked where Barbara was. "We're not close friends," Dennie said. "We just sit near each other in class, but we don't have the same interests."

Fortunately Dennie and I did have the same interests. She helped me get through that American literature class, although she earned a higher grade. She understood the material! Although I only got an average grade in that class, I gained a lifelong friend in the process.

She and Mike and Don and I began going out together, although money was tight for all of us. Dennie and Mike were both full-time students, and their household budget was small. We often entertained each other at home, playing board games and having dessert.

My dear friend Julie married a widower that spring. Her husband had an adorable two-year-old son. I was delighted to be in her wedding, and we got together a few times after that, but then our lives headed in different directions. I really missed my good friend.

Jeanie now lived in the sorority with Marlene. Each of them had steady boyfriends, fraternity men, and our lives diverged, too. We saw each other on campus but not as often as when we lived in the dorm together, and I wished for our old camaraderie.

The following quarter I began to learn how to learn, a skill I had not acquired in high school, where my memorization skills got me through. While my memory helped at UCLA, it did not allow me to interpret and apply what I'd learned. I listened to other students in class explain symbolism in a text, and I felt so stupid. I wondered where they had learned how to analyze what they read and why I had not. Being an English major at such a prestigious university made me realize how little I knew. I grew determined to do better.

Don joined the UCLA track team once again that spring. He loved to run, and true to form, he chose to run a hard event: the 440 intermediate hurdles. No challenge frightened him, but halfway through the quarter, he suffered an injury—a pulled left hamstring. For the second year in a row, he spent many sessions with trainer Ducky Drake and much time in the whirlpool, but his hamstring did not heal.

"I'm going to quit the track team," he announced one afternoon. "My body is telling me something, and I can't compete against the world class runners that UCLA recruited. I was a walk-on, I lettered my freshman year and gave it a good try this year and last, but it's time to hang up my track shoes."

I felt bad for him but knew he had made up his mind. Once Don made a decision, it was done.

We still attended all the UCLA home track meets, and the annual UCLA/USC cross-town rivalry, cheering his former teammates on. I learned all about the different events, what was a good time, who had Olympic potential, etc. and had truly become the sports fan he thought I was back in December 1966.

Despite being busy with our own lives, we could not escape the political atmosphere in the United States that spring. President Johnson announced he would not seek re-election. Robert F. Kennedy, younger brother of the slain president, became a contender for the Democratic nomination.

We watched from a distance. Surrounded by these serious issues, we often had to shut out the world around us to reach our immediate goals.

Our relationship grew closer, and in March 1968, Don said, "You're the girl I want to spend my life with. I have to finish school first, but I'd like us to be more than boyfriend and girlfriend. Libby, will you marry me?"

"Yes, oh yes," I replied without hesitation. "I love you."

"And I love you. Let's get engaged and plan our wedding for next June, after I graduate. You can finish school after we're married."

"You know the joke about girls going to UCLA to get their 'MRS degrees'?" I asked. "I plan to do both: get my MRS and my BA. I know I can do it."

Because neither of us had much money, I offered Don my mother's rings. "We can reset the stones and create our own ring."

Don agreed and went home to tell his parents, although only his mother was home that afternoon. I waited outside while Don informed his mother. She came out and said, "I knew you were 'the one' the first time I met you. Congratulations and welcome to the family."

"Thank you, Mrs. Atwater," I responded.

"Now that you're engaged, I wish you'd call us 'Mom' and 'Dad,'" she replied.

It felt awkward at first. Don's parents were not my parents, but they were kind, welcoming people who hoped to make up for those losses. After a week or two the new monikers became more comfortable, just about the time we went to pick up my ring.

On April 4, 1968, the jeweler called to tell us it was ready. After classes, Don and I rushed into Westwood to the jewelry designer. Don placed the gold ring with my mother's diamond on my finger, and I thought it was the most beautiful ring I had ever seen. We were elated.

As we drove to his parents' house to celebrate, we turned on the car radio. The announcer described chaos in Memphis, Tennessee, and it took a few minutes for us to realize that Dr. Martin Luther King Jr. had been assassinated.

Much of the joy I felt dissolved as I heard the terrible news. We rushed into Don's parents' home to share the engagement ring and the news we'd just heard. I was close to tears.

His parents thought my ring was beautiful, but neither seemed as upset as I about the assassination.

"I'm so sad," I stated. "He stood up for what he believed in, and he was a nonviolent man. Someone should not be killed because he stands up for others. That's not how people solve their differences."

Mrs Atwater glared at me, and that afternoon I discovered we had more differences than I initially realized.

Don ushered me to the door and suggested we go out for a bite to eat. We got into his car and drove in silence. One of the happiest days of my life had become bittersweet.

Two months later the California primary election was held, and Robert Kennedy won. Moments later he was gunned down as he walked through the kitchen of the Ambassador Hotel in Los Angeles. The sadness that I felt with President Kennedy's and Dr. King's deaths returned, as I joined the nation to mourn a young leader cut down by an assassin's bullet. I asked myself when this madness would end. I had experienced too much death in my own life, and the deaths of these public figures brought back my own pain.

But the violence continued when the Democratic Party held its political convention in Chicago that August. Demonstrations erupted, and innocent people were arrested and beaten along with those who committed acts of violence. Dr. King's philosophy of passive resistance had vanished and been replaced with aggressiveness by demonstrators and law enforcement.

I wished that life would have fewer surprises and more harmony. But the discord continued, as the world around me continued to change.

26
Self-Sacrifice

*D*on was already sitting in the quad outside the UCLA administration building when I arrived for lunch. "I'm going to get fired," I wailed, holding up a sheaf of papers. "Look at this! These are all the typing mistakes I made this morning. I can't type, and they're going to find that out very quickly."

"Calm down," Don said. "They won't fire you because you made a few mistakes. Don't worry! You'll get better at typing. You just need to practice."

"I don't think so," I shot back. "Each letter I send has to be perfect."

Shortly after we became engaged, Don had been hired by the UCLA Graduate Admissions Office, which was just entering the computer age. With his mathematics background and analytical mind, he quickly proved his abilities and made friends among his coworkers. One perk was that he had access to campus job listings before they were posted publicly.

That summer I toiled in a boutique on the Santa Monica Mall for minimum wage. I needed a job that paid more to save for our wedding. Don alerted me when a clerk-typist's position was posted for the UCLA Chemistry Department's Graduate Office. "You should apply," he'd said. "The job pays $1.98 an hour."

"But I can't type," I protested.

"You can type," he responded. "You've been writing papers for the past three years. You'll just have to learn how to type faster."

I applied for the job, took a typing test, and was hired. My boss Phyllis and coworker Bonnie welcomed me and showed me my duties. Bonnie planned to leave at the end of the summer, and I would be transitioning to her position. But that first day, I was so nervous that I kept making mistakes as I tried to improve my speed on the IBM electric typewriter at my desk. Ever patient, Phyllis said, "Don't worry! It's your first day; you'll get the hang of it."

She introduced me to many of the graduate students and some of the professors. One, whose office was a few doors down the hall, Willard F. Libby, received the Nobel Prize for chemistry in 1960. He discovered radiocarbon (C-14) dating in 1949. His discovery gave archaeologists, geologists, geophysicists and other scientists the ability to date artifacts accurately and establish worldwide chronologies. He had worked with a colleague named Rainer Berger.

Because my name was Libby Berger, people joked. "You made your name up." Some professors in the department became confused, thinking that when Phyllis said, "I'll have Libby bring that up to your office," she was referring to the celebrated Nobel laureate. I only met Dr. Libby once, when I had to drop off an exam in his office. I was in awe of someone who had accomplished what he had.

As usual, Don was right about my abilities. After a few weeks of work, I began to type fast and well, and I remained at the Chemistry Graduate Office for two-and-a-half years. The money I earned helped pay for our wedding and beyond. Eventually I received a raise to $2.12 per hour.

That summer I took in a roommate once more, since Unc was still working out of state. Becky was the girlfriend of one of Don's track teammates, and the four of us went out together occasionally and got along well. She and I both worked during the day and divided the household chores.

I was rigid about housework, and because of my busy schedule, I planned for it, as I did my other activities. Becky was more relaxed. She'd do something when she felt like it or had the time. This became a sore point between us, and finally Becky announced, "If you don't relax a little, you're going to have a nervous breakdown by the time you're thirty!"

"This arrangement isn't working," I said, secretly knowing she was right. I was a perfectionist and quite inflexible. I thought that if things were perfect, nothing bad would happen. It took me years to understand that my neurotic behavior, which began after my mother's death, made me believe I could control the world around me. My life had been out of control for so long, and I desperately sought stability.

Becky moved out, leaving me on my own once more. Most of the time, I kept busy with school, work, and wedding planning. Although Don and I spent a great deal of time together, he still lived at home with his parents, and many times I felt lonely.

After we became engaged, Mrs. Atwater wanted to help plan our wedding. She often began her sentences with the phrase, "In my family, we do...," explaining how her family arranged a wedding. Her list included telling me who should be in the bridal party, holding the wedding in the Catholic Church, and what type of reception we should host.

"But I'm not Catholic," I protested. "What about my family?"

At that point, Unc and I made up my family. Blanche had been gone since January 1967, and we did not know her whereabouts.

Unc was agnostic and did not care where we got married, as long as I married Don. He adored him. But Unc also wanted me to be happy. "Libby, you decide," he said. "This is the first of many decisions you'll have to make when you marry Don. If it's really important to him and not to you, then give him this gift. Marriage is about compromise." Wise advice from a man who'd been married and divorced once and later had his heart broken by a woman he loved.

Unc gave good advice and
supported my decisions.

Don's mom urged me to convert. "Libby, Don's dad converted for me, and my cousins', Ann and Marge, husbands converted. Why don't you follow their examples? It would make things so much easier."

"Because that would be living a lie, wouldn't it? Pretending to believe something you don't is a sin to me," I responded.

"You're right," she answered and never raised the subject again.

I conceded and agreed to get married in the Catholic Church. Because I was not Catholic, we could not have a Mass, only a ceremony. Getting married in the church meant having to attend counseling sessions with Don's parish priest, Father M., a young Italian with a conservative outlook. Don warned me to say as little as possible.

I took his advice as a challenge. The session in which we discussed the church's stance on birth control became heated. "Artificial birth control is immoral," declared Father M.

"How can you talk to me about immorality, when the United States is killing innocent people in Vietnam?" I shot back.

Don kicked my leg.

"I don't think we agree on that subject, but I can assure you that I have good values. I don't lie, and I won't pretend to be someone I'm not. Those qualities are important," I added.

I did agree to raise our children Catholic, since I felt that children should have a strong base. Not being allowed to attend the Hebrew school of my choice had prevented me from having any religious education. I wanted my future children to have that opportunity.

Father M. agreed to perform our wedding ceremony, but it was clear he had reservations about whether our marriage would endure.

Wedding plans consumed most of our spare time after our engagement in April 1968. We hoped to marry in June 1969, shortly after Don received his bachelor's degree. When we tried to schedule a church date, all the Saturdays in June were taken. The soonest we could get married would be July 12, 1969.

Unc returned to California just before the holidays in 1968, and he stayed in California to help plan the wedding. Once we set the date, we found a reception hall, located in a Marina del Rey hotel restaurant overlooking the water. It would be ideal for the sit-down luncheon we'd planned for about one hundred guests.

Bad news intervened that spring, when Don's mom returned from the doctor and announced, "I have breast cancer again. I'm scheduled for a mastectomy in two days."

I felt so bad for her and saw the worried faces of Don and his dad. Mrs. Atwater had her first mastectomy four years earlier. Now she would have to go through the pain of a second surgery and face the uncertainty that her diagnosis brought.

"We'll postpone the wedding," I offered. "We can wait until you feel better. It's more important that you're well."

Mrs. Atwater would not hear of it. She was tough. Having survived a gunshot through her pelvis at age three, a lifetime filled with health issues, and her first mastectomy, she was not going to let this second surgery stand in the way of her son's wedding. "We'll have the wedding on the date scheduled. I'll be fine," she said.

"Please, let me help," I begged. Despite our disagreements, I had come to love Mrs. Atwater as a mother. She had been so kind to me the past few years. The thought of losing her broke my heart.

Mrs. Atwater underwent successful surgery, although it was radical and left her scarred and in pain for a long time. Stoically she followed her doctor's orders, did her arm exercises daily, and willed herself to heal.

Her mother, affectionately known to all as Grandma, arrived from Chicago to care for her. When I met Grandma, I realized where Don's mom's strength originated. The two Maries were alike in many ways. They both had the most beautiful blue eyes and strong-willed personalities. Neither was afraid to speak her mind, and each was determined to get her way.

This determination caused problems with our wedding plans. I had given in on many issues but began to feel bullied. I wondered if we ever would get married. The thought of marrying Don made me happy, and happiness had eluded me for years. Each obstacle that arose increased my fear that something bad would happen. I could not believe that good things would ever happen in my lifetime.

But they did.

As wedding discussions grew more heated, Unc said, "Libby, this is your wedding. You have a say in what occurs. I'll back you up, no matter what you decide."

About that time, Blanche surfaced after a two-year absence. "Hi, Lib. How are you?" she asked, as if we'd spoken yesterday.

"I'm fine," I said. "Where are you? We haven't heard from you in a long time."

"I got married a few months ago, but right now I'm in the hospital. I had to have a hysterectomy, so I'm not feeling very well. Will you come see me?" she asked.

"Of course," I said and took down the directions to the hospital, which was at least an hour's drive from us.

"What's your husband's name?" I asked.

"Melvin. Melvin Black," she responded.

I began to laugh! My sister's name was now Blanche Black.

"What's so funny?" she asked.

"Do you realize that your name means White Black?" I answered. "I'm getting married in two months. Will you be well enough to be my matron of honor?"

"I hope so," came her reply.

The next day I drove to the hospital in West Covina where she'd had her surgery. During the drive, I thought about Blanche's life. She'd had two children out of wedlock when she was a teenager and given both up for adoption. Now that she was twenty-five and married, she could no longer have children. Life had played a cruel joke on her.

After Blanche recovered, she and Melvin drove to West Los Angeles to meet Don and his parents. They both agreed to be in our wedding party.

We received more good news that spring. Aunt Florrie called and said, "I'd like to come to your wedding. I know you'll like my new husband, Sam."

Tears ran down my cheeks. My dear aunt, whom I hadn't seen in nearly nine years, planned to come all the way to California for me. "I'd love to see you and meet Uncle Sam," I said. "Blanche just remarried, and she'll be my matron of honor. I know she'll be so happy to see you."

Don's mother's family from Chicago all planned to attend, and we asked all of his first cousins to be in our wedding party. I looked forward to meeting them.

Jeanie would be a bridesmaid, too. Julie, now several months pregnant, declined. I asked her to host the guest book. She happily agreed. Although I had been her bridesmaid, she could not be mine. Dennie very much wanted to be in the bridal party, but after Mike finished law school and passed the bar, they were assigned to Fort Monmouth, New Jersey and had to report by July first.

Shortly after the members of the wedding party were settled, a new problem arose. We received a call from the restaurant manager of the hotel where the reception was scheduled. "Hello, I'm Mr. Swindell," said the caller. "I'm sorry, but we've sold the restaurant, and it will be closed for construction starting June first. You won't be able to hold your reception here."

Don and I asked if Swindell was his real name and questioned him relentlessly but kept receiving the same answer. The restaurant was closed; our contract was no longer valid. Unfortunately, that weekend I was scheduled to have four wisdom teeth removed, so Don had the unenviable job of finding a new reception hall.

Fortunately, he found one at a hotel near our first choice. The room was lovely, even though it did not have marina views. We signed the contract immediately and proceeded with our plans.

Two weeks before the wedding, Don called the hotel to confirm the final number of people attending the luncheon. "Mr. Atwater, we had to change the reception room," the banquet manager informed him. "We have a large convention that booked the room you were originally in."

"What type of convention?" asked Don.

"The John Birch Society. We expect five hundred people," the manager answered.

One more setback, I thought, after Don called with the news. Unc will not like this!

When Unc arrived home from work that evening, I said, "Guess what? The John Birch Society is holding its convention at the hotel where we booked the reception. There will be five hundred Birchers right next door."

The irony did not escape Unc, a former member of the Communist Party, whose Jewish niece was marrying a Catholic boy. Members of the wedding party came from a variety of backgrounds, none of them fitting the Birch Society profile.

"I'll call the hotel right now to see what other arrangements we can make," Unc declared.

Unfortunately, the hotel could not change our reception's location, but it did agree to pay for the champagne punch that would be served.

Auntie Deutsch, Grandma's sister, arrived from Chicago one week before the wedding, and the two women shared the sofa bed in Don's parents' den. One night Auntie Deutsch ran out the back door gagging.

"What's wrong?" Don's mom asked, worried about her mother and aunt.

"My sister ate too many strawberries and keeps breaking wind. I can't breathe!" Auntie replied. "Tell her to stop."

Don's mom could hear Grandma laughing inside the house. She knew she had no control over her mother and just shrugged.

The next day she enlisted the sisters' help making paper flowers to decorate Don's Mustang, while she took the relatives sightseeing. She showed them what to do and handed them several rolls of pink toilet paper. When she returned later that day, Grandma said, "Whoever thought I'd be sitting here making flowers out of shit paper?"

Mom laughed at Grandma's words, since she never heard her mother curse. However, she was delighted with the bags filled with paper flowers.

Mrs. Atwater planned to show relatives California—Disneyland, Malibu, Universal Studios—before the wedding. Although she was still recovering from her mastectomy, she insisted on cooking elaborate meals each evening and invited her family and mine. I worried that she was doing too much, and she began to look very tired.

The day before the wedding, she drove everyone to Universal Studios in North Hollywood. I declined, knowing I had many things to take care of before our big day. That evening we'd hold the rehearsal, followed by a dinner given at the catering company where Don's mom worked.

Most people know the adage, "It never rains in California in the summer." But the day before our wedding, it poured. A huge thunderstorm arose while the family drove from Universal Studios back to Mar Vista on the freeway. The rain grew so intense that Mrs. Atwater had to pull over to the side of the road. Aunt Florrie later told us how frightened she was.

Would this rain be a bad omen or simply one more obstacle in planning the event I thought might never happen? That night I broke down in tears, while Blanche tried to comfort me.

"I can't take it. Everything seems to be going wrong," I whined. "Don's family is overwhelming. There are so many of them, and I'm expected to do everything his mom and grandmother want."

I was thrilled to have my family at my wedding. From left, Melvin,
Blanche, Don, me, Uncle Richard, Aunt Florrie, Uncle Sam

"Calm down, Lib," Blanche said. "Let's have a cup of tea. It will be all
right. I promise you. It will be all right."

At that moment, I felt so grateful to have my big sister back in my life.
Her hugs and comforting words made such a difference.

The next morning dawned
clear and crisp. A light breeze blew,
and the smog that usually sat over
the Southern California sky had
been washed away. July 12, 1969,
was a beautiful day for a wedding.

A few hours later, we ar-
rived at the stately Gothic church,
filled with relatives and close
friends. The wedding party pre-
ceded Unc and me down the aisle,
where a nervous Don awaited.
I smiled and walked proudly by

Don's parents welcomed me
to the family.

Don and I share our joy.

Unc's side. The day I awaited had finally arrived.

Father M. did not seem as certain as I about our marriage. His homily talked about love but really focused on self-sacrifice. Throughout the hour-long ceremony, which had magically become a full Mass, he said those words a dozen times as he sprinkled us with holy water. As we knelt at the altar, I could not see our friends' faces. Afterwards, several told me they were amused by Father M.'s repetition, "Self-sacrifice, self-sacrifice."

I did not care. I knelt beside Don, my sister at my side, his cousin Joe at his, our families and friends behind us, knowing that my chance for happiness had finally arrived. The decade that had begun in freefall had taken a definite upswing.

Afterword

*M*y marriage to Don offered me the chance for happiness I had longed for since losing my family, but I soon realized that living "happily ever after" occurred only in fairy tales. Creating a life together required communication, teamwork, maturity, perseverance, and lots of love. We were both so young when we said, "I do," that we did not realize how much growing up we needed to do. Fortunately, we grew up together and made our marriage work. Father M. knew what he was saying when he preached self-sacrifice. It took us many years to realize what he meant.

After our wedding, Don began graduate school at UCLA and earned a master's degree in mathematical economics over a two-year period. I completed my bachelor's degree in English in the summer of 1970 and then began graduate school in education that fall. To support ourselves we both attended UCLA full time and worked part time. We earned little money and had no spare time, but those years were magical because we were together, our lives were simple, and we shared common goals.

After I completed my elementary teaching credential in June 1971, I was hired to teach English in the Beverly Hills Unified School District. Don was urged by his mentors to seek a Ph.D. in economics, and he did so at UCLA while continuing to work a series of part-time positions.

Don earned his Ph.D. in December 1974, three months before our first son, Darryl, was born. Three years later Darryl was joined by his brother, Ross.

Completing our degrees and having children took our lives in new directions. Some of our experiences during this period are chronicled in the sequel, a memoir in progress, with excerpts to follow.

But what happened to the other people that appeared in the preceding pages?

Sadly, Unc died at the age of sixty-three, leaving a hole in my heart. I'll always remember his wish for me: "One day I hope you will grow up to have sweet, beautiful children." His wish came true; if only he had lived long enough to share it.

Blanche continued to appear and disappear. She was absent for long periods during our childhood, and these absences continued into our adult lives. I don't know if she ever found her birth family or the two children she gave up for adoption. I last saw her in December 1979, and we last spoke on the telephone in 1993. I have made many attempts to contact her to no avail. I hope she is well.

Neil Goodman and I last saw each other in 1977, when he and his wife visited us in California. We lost touch after that visit.

My cousins Neal and Martin Berger returned to my life in 1982, thirty years after I had last seen them. Their mother, Aunt Rose, welcomed me back into the family.

Don's parents treated me like the daughter they'd always hoped to have. I had the privilege of being their daughter longer than I was the Bergers' little girl. Each died at age eighty: Don's father in 1995, and his mother in 1998.

Aunt Florrie was widowed a second time, and as she grew older she moved to an assisted living facility in Montana, near her granddaughter Judy. She lived into her nineties and died in 1993.

Cousin Sue, Aunt Florrie's daughter-in-law, remarried after the untimely death of her husband Tim. She also was widowed a second time, but today she remains strong and healthy at age ninety. We talk on the phone several times a year.

Davida developed Alzheimer's disease, and her husband, David, took excellent care of her until his death in 2011. She now lives in an assisted living facility in New York near her daughter.

Mimi and her husband Bud have been married more than fifty years and live in Chicago.

My cousin Stanley and his family have been absent from my life since the day I moved out of their home in January 1964. They declined an invitation to our wedding.

Julie, Jeanie, and Dennie are still close friends, although we don't see each other as often as we'd like. They will always be part of my life.

In 2004, I began searching for my birth family to learn more about my health background. I found them easily with the help of the Internet and was surprised to discover a large, close-knit Italian family who welcomed me with open arms. This discovery led to a new chapter in my life, one in which I gave Don Atwater something he never had before—a mother-in-law.

* * *

When I think back to July 1969, I remember the biggest event after our wedding was the first manned expedition to the moon. Apollo 11 blasted off carrying astronauts Neil Armstrong, Edwin "Buzz" Aldrin, and Michael Collins on July 16, while we were on our honeymoon. These pioneers ventured where no one had gone before. They aimed to fulfill President Kennedy's dream: to land a man on the moon before the end of the decade.

We returned home one day before the actual moon landing and watched this monumental event on July 20, 1969 with Don's parents, grandmother, and aunt. The astronauts' accomplishment reinforced my belief that anything is possible.

More than forty-three years have passed since I married Don, and we remain happily together, striving to reach new goals, and reminding each other that anything is indeed possible. Marrying him was the best decision I ever made.

Acknowledgments

My story would never have been written without the support of many others, especially Don Atwater, my cheerleader and greatest fan; my son, Ross, who read several chapters and urged me to keep writing; my son, Darryl, and daughter-in-law, Kendi, who encouraged me; and my dear friends Julie Frank Bustillos and her wonderful mother, the incomparable Lois Frank, who read portions and begged for more.

Special thanks go to my colleagues and fellow writers, especially Catherine Baker, Pamela Daugavietis, Pickens Halt, Susan T. Hessel, Debra Moore, and Dawn Thurston, who read the manuscript and offered valuable suggestions; Rae Jean Sielen, who diligently reviewed the formatted text; the late Anne Lowenkopf, a writing teacher with abundant enthusiasm for my ability; my fellow classmates, including Pickens Halt, who introduced me to the class and helped shape my tale; members of the APH 2004 Memoir Writing Group, including Diane Dassow, Judy Fischer, Lissa Ann Forbes, Robin Fowler, Mary Ryan Garcia, Sue Knight, Laurie North, Kathy Rosenwinkel, and Karen Ryan, with whom I began my story; the Thursday Writers' Group, consisting of Barbara Hopfinger, Maryon Lears, Bud Lesser, Muriel Schloss, Martina Winn, and Carolyn Zucker, who transformed me from a teacher to a writer; mentor John M. Wilson; and editors Libby Motika and Bill Bruns, who gave me my first break in journalism.

Cousin Martin Berger offered missing details from my abbreviated childhood, and his wife Pat gave valuable feedback.

I would also like to thank an unnamed editor I met in 2003, who challenged me with her comment that I was a good "technical writer." I've always enjoyed a good challenge, and I think I've proven her wrong. You, dear reader, are the judge.

About the Author

photo by Pamela James

Libby J. Atwater began telling people's stories more than two decades ago and opened her writing and editorial services business, *Choose Your Words,* in 1994. She wrote for businesses, nonprofit organizations, educational institutions, magazines, and community newspapers. In 1997 she began writing memoirs and family histories, and five years later she began to teach others how to write their life stories. In 2004 she decided it was time to tell her own story. Tales from her life have been published in several anthologies. *What Lies Within* is her first memoir, and its sequel is in progress.

Excerpts from sequel

1987: The Other Side of Paradise

"Please let me call the doctor," I pleaded with Don, my thirty-nine-year-old husband, as he sat up in bed, pale and sweating. He nodded.

In a couple of minutes, I spoke with the hotel's doctor. She suspected a heart attack and dispatched an ambulance from Waimea—twenty miles away.

I didn't know then that our planned ten-day Hawaiian trip would last three extra weeks. Nor did I suspect that the events of that day would change our lives dramatically.

That morning Don awakened feeling ill. His neck, back, and shoulders ached. Muscle strain? Tennis? Too many suitcases? When he broke out in a cold sweat and felt nauseated a few minutes later, I knew it was more serious.

While we waited for the ambulance to arrive, two hotel managers enrolled our nine- and twelve-year-old sons in the hotel's day camp. I grabbed Don's shirt and shoes so that he'd have something to wear back to the hotel. It never occurred to me that he would not return that day.

2004: A Worthwhile Search

My hands shook as I touched the telephone keypad, carefully inserting the ten digits that would connect me with someone I had been waiting my entire life to meet—my birth mother. Only one day earlier, on September 27, 2004, the ninety-eighth anniversary of my adoptive mother's birth, I had sent out six e-mails before lunch. The message read:

> I am a personal historian seeking information on Angela Scaglione, who lived in Irvington or Newark, New Jersey, in the late 1940s. I found your name through the Google search engine and thought you might help me with this project. If you have any information that might help my search, please reply via email or telephone me at the number listed below. Thank you.
> Libby Atwater

Within an hour I received a reply from a man named Jerry Scaglione. It read:

I know this person. What kind of information are you looking for? For whom and why? Thanks. Jerry Scaglione

I wrote back immediately.

Thank you for responding to my query. The reason I am seeking this information is for my own personal history. I was born in Irvington General Hospital on February 15, 1948, and my birth mother is listed as Angela Scaglione. I was given up for adoption shortly after my birth, and I have always wondered about my birth mother. My adoptive parents (Harry and Ruth Berger of Hillside, New Jersey) died in 1962 and 1963, when I was a teenager. I was afraid to seek my birth mother and family for many years, unsure of what I would find. However, I would really like to know my history for a number of reasons. I have had some health problems that may have biological links, and I have two grown sons who share my heredity. It would also be very nice to meet my birth family, if, and only if, they feel the same way. I hope the information I have provided will not shock or upset you. I would really appreciate your help.

The reply came back within minutes.

Yes, it is a little shocking, and I am investigating this with a few family members. I will get back to you ASAP. Take care, Jerry

After this reply, I became nervous—afraid I would not hear from Jerry again, and I volunteered some additional information that I had been given about my birth. I heard nothing for the remainder of the day.

The next morning I opened my e-mail immediately. The note from Jerry read as follows:

You are definitely a member of our family. The circumstances of your birth are a little different from what you were told—except for the Italian part. I am your first cousin. My father, your uncle, will talk to his sister today and ask her if she'd like to meet you. Please send me a phone number and the times you can be reached, and I'll call you later. Whether or not she wants to talk to you, you have a right to know.

I was so excited, I felt I could fly, and no one was around to share my news. My husband was in business meetings all day, and my sons and daughter-in-law were at work. I couldn't leave the house, afraid I'd miss Jerry's call, but eventually it came—at 5:30 p.m. "You have a mother, a brother, and a sister who all want to meet you. Unfortunately, your father died in August 2003, but the rest of your family is alive and very happy that you found them. Here are their phone numbers."

And now I was dialing the phone. I listened as it began to ring—once, twice, a third time—and then a woman picked up. "Hello," she said."

"Is this Angela?" I asked. "I'm Libby, your daughter."

"How are you?" she replied. "I always wondered what happened to you. It's been more than fifty-six years. What took you so long?"

* * *